Sexual Assault in the U.S. Military

Sexual Assault in the U.S. Military

The Battle within America's Armed Forces

ROSEMARIE SKAINE

Praeger Security International

An Imprint of ABC-CLIO, LLC
Santa Barbara, California • Denver, Colorado

Library of Congress Cataloging-in-Publication Data

Skaine, Rosemarie.
Sexual assault in the U.S. military : the battle within America's Armed Forces / Rosemarie Skaine.
pages cm. — (Praeger security international)
Includes bibliographical references and index.
ISBN 978-1-4408-3378-6 (hard copy : alk. paper) — ISBN 978-1-4408-3379-3 (ebook)
1. Rape in the military—United States. 2. Rape in the military—Law and legislation—United States. 3. United States—Armed Forces—Women—Crimes against. 4. United States—Armed Forces—Women—Violence against. 5. Sexual minorities—United States—Crimes against. 6. Sexual minorities—United States—Violence against. 7. Military offenses—United States. I. Title.
UB783.S63 2016
355.1'334—dc23 2015027358

ISBN: 978-1-4408-3378-6
EISBN: 978-1-4408-3379-3

20 19 18 17 16 1 2 3 4 5

This book is also available on the World Wide Web as an eBook.
Visit www.abc-clio.com for details.

Praeger
An Imprint of ABC-CLIO, LLC

ABC-CLIO, LLC
130 Cremona Drive, P.O. Box 1911
Santa Barbara, California 93116-1911

This book is printed on acid-free paper ∞

Manufactured in the United States of America

To all who serve

Contents

Tables and Figure

TABLES

FIGURE

Preface

When the U.S. military reported in 2013 that 26,000 sexual assaults had occurred in the military in 2012, public concern ignited about why there were so many assaults. The 2013 Department of Defense (DoD) *Annual Report on Sexual Assault in the Military, Fiscal Year 2012* stated that the 26,000 sexual assaults was a 40 percent increase over the prior two years. Of these 26,000 assaults, 3,374 were reported, 2,558 cases were pursued by victims, 302 went to trial, 238 were convicted, and 64 were acquitted.[1] The reporting and prosecution record raised additional concerns as to why the numbers were so low. Questions were raised about the manner in which the cases were handled and the legal provisions under which they were prosecuted.

With widespread attention being given to the problem of sexual assault, the American society is demanding that the government take action to reduce and eliminate it in the military. To determine what part each has played in the 26,000 sexual assaults and the prosecution record, factors such as gender, gender bias, and sexual preference and elements like unit readiness and cohesiveness are examined. Attention is focused on the military chain of command because it is the method by which the military governs itself and processes its justice system, including sexual assault cases. Cases have traditionally been decided within the chain of command and did not make use of civilian courts.

Historically, the military processed all cases according to military law. The stated purpose of military law is to promote justice, assist in maintaining good order and discipline in the armed forces, promote efficiency and effectiveness in the military establishment, and thereby strengthen the national security of the United States.[2]

The military justice system dates back to revolutionary times. On June 30, 1775, the Second Continental Congress established 69 Articles of War to govern the conduct of the Continental Army. Effective upon its ratification in 1789, Article I, Section 8 of the U.S. Constitution provided that Congress has the power to regulate the land and naval forces. On April 10, 1806, the U.S. Congress enacted 101 Articles of War (which applied to both the army and the navy). These articles were not significantly revised until over a century later. The military justice system continued to operate under the Articles of War until May 31, 1951, when the Uniform Code of Military Justice (UCMJ) went into effect.[3] The word "Uniform" in the code's title refers to the congressional intent to make military justice uniform or consistent among the armed services.[4]

Sexual assault does not just affect women. It affects men and women in all branches of the military. The number of assaults on men outnumbers those on women, but because men comprise 85 percent of the military personnel and women 15 percent, the percentage for women is higher. In 2012, overall, 6.1 percent of women and 1.2 percent of men indicated they experienced unwanted sexual contact.[5] For the same year, there were a total of 3,374 cases reported: the Army reported 2,149 incidences; the Navy, 1,057; Marine Corps, 808; and Air Force, 1,047.[6]

Sexual assault impacts the gay and lesbian military personnel. Measuring the severity of the problem for homosexual service members is more difficult, because only 13 percent of men reported sexual assault, and sometimes, when they do report it, the gay person is viewed as the perpetrator rather than the victim. The *Baltimore Sun* found that reports show that men are less likely to identify a suspect, to refer charges to court-martial, or to discharge the perpetrator than in cases involving a female victim. In addition, the 2011 repeal of "Don't Ask, Don't Tell," which lifted the ban on gays and lesbians serving openly chilled reporting by male victims, gay and straight alike.[7]

On May 23, 2014, when he was addressing the newly commissioned officers at the U.S. Naval Academy, President Barack Obama said, "Those who commit sexual assault are not only committing a crime, they threaten the trust and discipline that makes our military strong."[8]

Congress held hearings on sexual assault in the military, after a decade's silence, in the Senate Armed Services Committee. Debate focused on language in the FY2014 Defense Department Authorization bill. A major issue was Senator Kirsten Gillibrand's (D-NY) amendment that would grant military prosecutors, rather than commanders, the power to decide which sexual assault crimes to try. The Personnel Subcommittee approved the provision, but Armed Services Chair Carl Levin (D-MI) replaced it with the stipulation that required a senior military officer to review any decisions not to prosecute a case instead.[9]

On March 6, 2014, the Senate fell five votes short of proceeding to a vote on the bill sponsored by Senator Gillibrand to move sexual assault cases outside the military chain of command, but, by a 97–0 vote, did support reforms to the military justice system included in a bill sponsored by Senator Claire McCaskill (D-MO). McCaskill's bill includes the elimination of the "good soldier" defense and allows the victim to have input on whether the case is tried in military or civilian court.[10]

Sexual Assault in the U.S. Military recognizes sexual assault has been a significant problem for the military and the United States and examines it within the context of the rapidly changing military and American Society.

Chapter 1, Sexual Assault in the Military and Society, examines sexual assault from the perspective of the military and civilian society. The military and civilian society have similarities and differences in the causes of sexual assault, the way it is defined, and the way cases are processed. In the military, some forms of sexual harassment are viewed as a form of sexual assault, whereas in civil society, sexual harassment may or may not be defined as assault.

The chapter provides the framework for understanding prevalence leading up to the current day by including a longitudinal view of the number of incidents by years.

Chapter 2, Sexual Assault Scandals in the Military, provides historical perspective. The typical member of the military, historically, was a male with above-average physical qualities who was heterosexual and the American society accepted these qualifications for those who enlisted or were drafted into the military. Women were excluded as were homosexuals. Today, that has all changed. Today, the military includes women and homosexuals as essential to the effectiveness of the U.S. military. This chapter demonstrates that historically all groups are attacked: women, men, gay, lesbians, and nonmilitary personnel.

The 35th Annual Tailhook Association Symposium held in September 1991 was a major scandal for the U.S. Navy. Tailhook '91, as it came to be known, had multiple incidences of sexual assault and harassment. Assault and harassment have occurred at military academies and university military programs including the U.S. Naval Academy at Annapolis in 1989; U.S. Air Force Academy in 1990 and 2003; Texas A&M University in 1991; U.S. Military Academy, West Point, in 1994; and Aberdeen Proving Ground in Maryland in 1996.

Chapter 3, Policies and Laws, delineates the policies and laws applicable to sexual assault. It examines the chain-of-command/reporting structure and demonstrates the loopholes that hinder good order and conduct such as impediments to reporting.

The UCMJ defines two types of sexual assault: sexual contact offenses and sexual penetration offenses. "Sexual contact offense" is defined as intentional sexual contact characterized by use of force, threats, intimidation, or abuse of authority or when the victim does not or cannot consent. Sexual penetration offenses include rape, aggravated sexual contact, abusive sexual contact, forcible sodomy (forced oral or anal sex), or attempts to commit these acts.[11]

The National Defense Authorization Act 2014 passed requiring sweeping changes to the UCMJ, particularly in cases of rape and sexual assault.[12] It significantly changes the Manual for Courts-Martial.

Chapter 4, Jurisdiction and Courts, includes laws that prohibit sexual assault, sexual assault legal cases, prosecution of sexual assault cases, and decisions that demonstrate the problems with the chain-of-command structure.

Chapter 5, Women, details sexual assaults involving women. Special attention is given to effects on women and men's response to the crime. Incidence and gender roles are examined.

Chapter 6, Men, focuses on sexual assaults on men within the context of the traditional roles of men in the military and traditional sexual behavior of military men. It discusses sexual assault incidents involving men and the response of military men to sexual assault.

Chapter 7, Sexual Assaults on Gay, Lesbian, Bisexual, and Transgendered Service Members, examines the issues surrounding sexual assaults on gay and lesbians. Historically gays and lesbians were forbidden to serve, or to serve openly during the "Don't Ask, Don't Tell" era. The chapter discusses the effects of the repeal of that law. Sexual assault incidents involving gay, lesbians, bisexual, and transgendered are discussed taking into consideration their response to sexual assault, the response of heterosexual males, and the effect on male reporting (see Appendixes B and G)

Chapter 8, The Impact of Sexual Assault on the Military, addresses the impact of sexual assault on the military that clearly reveals a national security challenge including its effect on the military's strength, readiness, and morale.

Chapter 9, Approaches That Reduce or Eliminate Sexual Assault in the Military, focuses on the need to change the military culture. It includes ways to prevent sexual assault and suggests remedies for the method of investigating and prosecuting sexual assault cases. Pending legislation is included.

Sexual assault in the military has been given intense attention since the report of 26,000 cases in 2012. Some progress has been made, but more changes and actions are likely to be implemented soon.

Acknowledgments

I extend thanks to Steve Catalano, Praeger/ABC-CLIO, my editor and mentor.

I am grateful to James C. Skaine, Emeritus Professor, Communication Studies, University of Northern Iowa, for his research and editing skills.

Special thanks to interviewees who, with their special skills and military expertise, increased the knowledge base: CAPT Lory Manning, USN (Ret.); MAJ Lillian Pfluke, USA (Ret.); and RADM D. M. "Mac" Williams Jr., USN (Ret.), former NIS Commander. For past interviews and counsel, special thanks to BGen. Wilma Vaught, USAF (Ret.), President of the Board of Directors of the Women in Military Service for America Memorial Foundation, Inc.

Appreciation for guidance from CAPT Jeffrey C. Casler, OJAG, Front Office, USN.

I am grateful to Suba Ramya, Project Manager, Lumina Datamatics Ltd. for her thoroughness in production.

I thank family members, Richard L. and Nancy L. Craft Kuehner, and William V. and Carolyn E. Guenther Kuehner, for their unwavering support.

I thank my friend, Cass Paley, of yesteryear for the invincible summer.

Abbreviations

OFFICIAL RANKS AND BRANCHES

ADM	Admiral, U.S. Navy
Amn	Airman, U.S. Air Force
ANC	U.S. Army Nurse Corps
BG	Brigadier General, U.S. Army
B Gen	Brigadier General, U.S. Marine Corps
BGen.	Brigadier General, U.S. Air Force
CAPT	Captain, U.S. Navy
Capt	Captain, U.S. Marine Corps
Capt.	Captain, U.S. Air Force
CDR	Commander, U.S. Navy
CNO	Chief of Naval Operations
COL	Colonel, U.S. Army
Col	Colonel, U.S. Marine Corps
Col.	Colonel, U.S. Air Force.
Cpl	Corporal, U.S. Marine Corps
CPT	Captain, U.S. Army
1LT	First Lieutenant, U.S. Army
1st Lt.	First Lieutenant, U.S. Air Force
GEN	General, U.S. Army

Gen	General, U.S. Marine Corps
Gen.	General, U.S. Air Force
Gy Sgt	Gunnery Sergeant, U.S. Marine Corps
IG	Inspector General
JAG	Judge Advocate General
JAGC	Judge Advocate General Corps
LCDR	Lieutenant Commander, U.S. Navy
LCpl	Lance Corporal, U.S. Marine Corps
LGen.	Lieutenant General, U.S. Air Force
LT	Lieutenant, U.S. Navy
LTC	Lieutenant Colonel, U.S. Army
Lt Col	Lieutenant Colonel, U.S. Marine Corps
Lt. Col	Lieutenant Colonel, U.S. Air Force
LTG	Lieutenant General, U.S. Army
Lt Gen	Lieutenant General, U.S. Marine Corps
MAJ	Major, U.S. Army
Maj.	Major, U.S. Air Force
Maj Gen	Major General, U.S. Marine Corps
MG	Major General, U.S. Army
MGen.	Major General, U.S. Air Force
NROTC	Naval Reserve Officer Training Corps
OJAG	Office of the Judge Advocate General
Pvt	Private, U.S. Marine Corps
RADM	Rear Admiral, U.S. Navy
Ret.	Retired
RMC	Chief Radioman, U.S. Navy
SECDEF	Secretary of Defense
SECNAV	Secretary of the Navy
SECNAVINST	Secretary of the Navy Instruction
2nd Lt.	Second Lieutenant, U.S. Air Force
SFC	Sergeant First Class, U.S. Army
SGM	Sergeant Major, U.S. Army
SGMA	Sergeant Major of the Army, U.S. Army
SGT	Sergeant, U.S. Army
Sgt	Sergeant, U.S. Marine Corps

Sgt Maj	Sergeant Major, U.S. Marine Corps
SSgt	Staff Sergeant, U.S. Air Force
SOF	Special Operations Forces
SPAR	Coast Guard Women's Reserve (from Coast Guard motto: *Semper Paratus*—Always Ready)
SPC	Specialist, U.S. Army
TSgt	Technical Sergeant, U.S. Air Force
USA	U.S. Army
USAF	U.S. Air Force
USAR	U.S. Army Reserve
USMC	U.S. Marine Corps
USMCR	U.S. Marine Corps Reserve
USN	U.S. Navy
USNR	U.S. Navy Reserve
VADM	Vice Admiral, U.S. Navy
WAC	Women's Army Corps
WAFS	Women in the Air Force
WASP	Women Air Force Service Pilots
WAVES	Women Accepted for Voluntary Emergency Service
WM	Women Marines

CHAPTER 1

Sexual Assault in the Military and Society

MILITARY CULTURE

The issues of military sexual assault should be evaluated within the specialized, military society and, the larger component, civilian society. As American society changed, it brought changes to the military, George Vukotich noted.[1] Perhaps sociological theorists say it best. All people in a society need the quality of mind that helps them understand what is going on in the world, and what is happening in themselves in relation to their biography and history within society. Sociologist C. Wright Mills calls this understanding "the sociological imagination."[2] "The sociological imagination is important because all players need to understand their own experience and gauge their own fate by locating themselves within a particular period of history. They can thus know their chances in this particular life situation by becoming aware of those of all individuals in their circumstances."[3] Peter Berger reasons we are located in society in space and time, but sometimes players lack the quality of mind to gauge their own fate.

Such was the case in Tailhook '91. The standards of involved observers did not enable them to judge the behavior they observed as sexual harassment. The leadership permitted the activities to continue demonstrating a "marked absence of moral courage and personal integrity." The majority interviewed responded, "What's the big deal?" Rear Admiral (RADM) George W. Davis VI, the Navy Inspector General (NIG), concluded, "The atmosphere condoned, if not encouraged, the gang mentality that eventually led to the sexual assaults."[4]

The sociological imagination is basic to considering some particular characteristics of a changing military culture including the changing role of women. Vukotich illustrates that past operational military male dominance was accompanied by a culture, language, and behavior that often were negatively directed toward a number of diverse ethnic groups, gays, and women. When society changed, it provided impetus for changes to the military. Women are now fully integrated into all roles including combat.[5]

The change means men and women work in the same time and space 24/7 and sometimes in remote areas. The military culture has changed, bringing conflict with what it was in the past. Vukotich believes that sometimes progress in one area such as integration has caused issues in another. Sexual assault of women is a likely resulting issue.

A COMPARISON: CIVILIAN AND MILITARY CULTURES

When we consider the fact that the military consists of individuals from the larger society, it makes sense to examine sexual assault in civilian life, specifically colleges and universities. The U.S. Commission on Civil Rights heard testimony that people 18 to 24 years old are at maximum risk for sexual assault, and any situation like the military or college that has high concentration of young people will have higher rates than the general population.[6]

RAND Corporation's report for the Department of Defense (DoD) is another indication that the military believes an examination of universities is advantageous. RAND found that over the past 20 years, public concern about sexual assault, with a focus on university campuses and within the military, has increased considerably.[7] Reports of sex offenses increased significantly at the top 25 U.S. universities from 2011 to 2013. The number of reported sex offenses increased from an average of 12.5 in 2011 to 20.1 in 2013, according to an *America Tonight* analysis of new campus crime statistics.[8] The 2014 federal investigation of 64 colleges and universities over concerns about how they responded to sexual assault cases on campus is one indicator that sexual assault is a public concern. Specifically, the Office for Civil Rights of the U.S. Department of Education began revealing all colleges under review after a White House task force investigation on campus rape. The Department of Education, facing pressure from activists and members of Congress, pressed for greater transparency from the colleges because colleges typically did not discuss or disclose their federal investigations unless asked.[9]

Captain (CAPT) Lory Manning, U.S. Navy (Ret.), sees some of the sexual assault in the military as similar to what goes on in college campuses. She explains,

> When you have young people, both men and women, who are suddenly totally free with at least some money in their pockets and some of them drink too much, both men and women [sexual assault is a possible outcome]. Some of them are just

trying on everything they can try on. So, some of it is just a question of the age group of some of the people who end up being victims. Particularly among those who have been accused of sexual assault. We often hear about people saying, "She, or he depending on the victim, shouldn't have done this or shouldn't have done that." But the same thing applies to the people who are the accused. They shouldn't have been drinking; they shouldn't have been behaving the way they were. And their peers around them, whether we were talking about the predators or the people who have not grown up enough to know how to behave, know who they are, and we do not have a culture that allows people who know who they are, to come forward and say, "That sergeant, that lieutenant, are sexual predators." Or say to a friend, "You know you got to get the drinking under control."[10]

Since the DoD Sexual Assault Prevention and Response (SAPR) program was implemented, the number of service members accounted for in reports of sexual assault has increased by 131 percent.[11] Table 1.1 shows the overall increase in reporting and the increase in the number of service members accounted for in sexual assault reports from 2004 to 2012. In 2013, the DoD *Annual Report on Sexual Assault in the Military for the Fiscal Year 2013* found a 50 percent increase in reports; 5,061 in FY13 compared to 3,374 in FY12. Since 2006, the average annual increase in reports of sexual assault has been about 5 percent.[12] In 2014, DoD reported more precisely, "From fiscal year 2012 to fiscal year 2013, there was an unprecedented 53% increase in victim reports of sexual assault. In fiscal year 2014, the high level of reporting seen in fiscal year 2013 was sustained with 6,131 reports of sexual assault . . . This figure represents an increase of 11% over fiscal year 2013 numbers. . . . Overall, surveys of sexual assault victims suggest that those who reported their sexual assault were satisfied with their decision."[13]

In 2014, RAND conducted an independent assessment of sexual assault, sexual harassment, and gender discrimination in the military. DoD last conducted this type of assessment in 2012 through the Workplace and Gender Relations Survey of Active Duty Personnel. The RAND Military Workplace Study found that about 20,000 active-duty service members were sexually assaulted out of 1,317,561 active-duty service members or approximately 1.0 percent of active-duty men and 4.9 percent of active-duty women.[14]

RAND estimated that 1.5 percent of the military service member population experienced at least one sexual assault in 2014 (Table 1.2) and that the total number of service members in RAND's sample who experienced a sexual assault was between 18,000 and 22,500. The estimated rate by gender of sexual assault varied considerably: fewer than 1 in 100 men but approximately 1 in 20 women. Smaller but significant differences by branch of service existed, with men and women members of the air force were at lower risk than members of the other branches. However, a significantly higher proportion of women in the Marines and Navy

Table 1.1.

Number of Reports of Sexual Assaults to DoD and Number of Service Member Victims Accounted for in Sexual Assault Reports, CY04–FY12.

No. of reports	1,700	2,374	2,947	2,688	2,908	3,230	3,158	3,192	3,374
No. of victims in reports	1,275[1]	1,774[2]	2,289[3]	2,223[4]	2,395	2,670	2,617	2,723	2,949
Year	CY04	CY05	CY06	FY07	FY08	FY09	FY10	FY11	FY12

1. CY04 was prior to the implementation of restricted reporting. The 1,275 reports for the year are unrestricted reports by service member victims only.
2. The 1,774 reports of sexual assault in CY05 contain both unrestricted and restricted reports by service member victims; however, restricted reporting was initiated in June 2005. Therefore, CY05 has only half a year of restricted reports.
3. CY06 and FY07 share one-quarter's worth of data (October through December 2006) because of the change from CY to FY reporting. For reporting analysis purposes, both CY06 and FY07 contain 12 months' worth of sexual assault reports.
4. The remaining victims in reports of sexual assault to DoD are non–service members (e.g., civilians and foreign nationals) who reported being sexually assaulted by a service member.

Source: Department of Defense, *Annual Report on Sexual Assault in the Military, Fiscal Year 2012*, vol.1 (Washington, DC: Department of Defense, Sexual Assault Prevention and Response, 2013), 24: Figure 8, http://www.sapr.mil/index.php/annual-reports; Department of Defense, *Annual Report on Sexual Assault in the Military, Fiscal Year 2013*, 45.

Table 1.2.

Estimated Prevalence of Active-Duty Service Members Who Experienced Any Type of Sexual Assault in the Past Year, by Gender and Service Branch.

Service	Total %	Men %	Women %
Total	1.54	0.95	4.87
Army	1.46	0.95	4.69
Navy	2.36	1.48	6.48
Air Force	0.78	0.29	2.90
Marines	1.63	1.13	7.86

Source: Andrew R. Morral and Kristie L. Gore, *Sexual Assault and Sexual Harassment in the U.S. Military: Top-Line Results from the RAND Military Workplace Study* (Santa Monica, CA: RAND Corporation, National Defense Research Institute, 2015), 10, Table 1. Used by permission of RAND Corporation through the Copyright Clearance Center, Inc.

experienced sexual assault than women in other services. In investigating the nature of assaults, 43 percent of assaults against women and 35 percent of assaults against men were classified as penetrative (rape).[15]

Pentagon press secretary George Little stated that it does not matter if military rates are similar to the rest of society. Little said, "We must hold ourselves to a higher standard, and that's what the American people demand."[16] A military acquaintance echoes Little: "How we differ from the civilian population is that we are subsidized by the American people. So consequently, all of our flaws seem to come out more readily than say the thousands and thousands of rape kits that have never been processed and that have set on the shelves for years and for decades."

However, because the existence of college and university students parallels military service members in a variety of ways, comparisons can offer insights into sexual assault in the military. Living in close quarters, sharing common space, and age and age-related activities within an institution are similar. But differences also exist, according to West Point graduate Major (MAJ) Lillian Pfluke, U.S. Army (Ret.):

> The military is a unique environment and so, that means it has a few special considerations that you need to have, but, on the whole, you are seeing the same problems in American colleges as you are seeing in some of these military cases where you have young people engaging in behaviors that are not appropriate, with alcohol involved, and people regretting the things they've done in different situations. You have the same kind of things going on in the military that you have in colleges. In the military, you have this command structure where you have superior officers and NCOs [Non-Commissioned Officers] and subordinate soldiers that you don't have in other situations.

The most important issue [in sexual assault] is: we have this very separate society with its own chain of command, its own judges, its own lawyers, its own ethics, its own whole value system that is sheltered from the rest of society and, certainly, especially when you are in a deployed situation or an overseas situation where the military controls everything about you, where you live, what you eat, etc. So that puts the whole dynamic of what to do when the chain of command is involved and how to get the chain of command uninvolved or more responsive to things that happen.[17]

The U.S. Commission on Civil Rights explains the differences in the two environments in that service members live in an insular environment where they are required to live and work with others not of their own choosing. Group cohesion and loyalty are expected, which makes transferring out of the unit, because of sexual assault, difficult. Transfers may be denied and a criminal penalty for leaving without permission (AWOL) or insubordination is a possible result.[18] Pfluke adds that the military is a separate society with a command structure in-your-face.

An important difference is in definition. A military acquaintance of mine explained "perception" this way:

Sexual assault, most people go "you are talking rape." No, for the Department of Defense, because of the way the *Uniform Code of Military Justice* defines sexual assault. It ranges anywhere from improper touching, feeling somebody up in a sexual way, all the way to forcible rape or sodomy. So there is a range of inappropriate sexual conduct that covers sexual assault for the military, whereas for the civilian world, when they say sexual assault, most often, they are talking rape. So there is a difference.

The military's definition of "sexual assault" is broad in scope and differs from most civilian perceptions. Within the DoD, the term "sexual assault" does not refer to one specific crime. Instead, it includes a wide range of sex crimes that represent a broad spectrum of offenses from rape to nonconsensual sodomy to wrongful sexual contact as well as attempts to commit these offenses. As a result, the definition of "sexual assault" in the military is broader than the crime of rape. A DoD directive based in Article 120 of the Uniform Code of Military Justice (UCMJ) defines "sexual assault" as:

Intentional sexual contact characterized by use of force, threats, intimidation, or abuse of authority or when the victim does not or cannot consent. Sexual assault includes rape, forcible sodomy (oral or anal sex), and other unwanted sexual contact that is aggravated, abusive, or wrongful (including unwanted and inappropriate sexual contact), or attempts to commit these acts.

The directive also defines "consent":

Words or overt acts indicating a freely given agreement to the sexual conduct at issue by a competent person. An expression of lack of consent through words or conduct means there is no consent. Lack of verbal or physical resistance or submission resulting from the accused's use of force, threat of force, or placing another person in fear does not constitute consent. A current or previous dating relationship or the manner of dress of the person involved with the accused in the sexual conduct at issue shall not constitute consent. There is no consent where the person is sleeping or incapacitated, such as due to age, alcohol or drugs, or mental incapacity.[19]

In addition, the UCMJ further defines "sexual assault" according to military law. The sexual crimes within the SAPR policy are included in Article 120, Rape and Sexual Assault generally, and, Article 125, Sodomy. Article 120 includes the crimes of rape, sexual assault, aggravated sexual contact, and abusive sexual contact. Attempts to commit these crimes are covered under Article 80 and are also included under SAPR policy.[20]

In civilian society, the Department of Justice defines "sexual assault" as "any type of sexual contact or behavior that occurs without the explicit consent of the recipient. Falling under the definition of sexual assault are sexual activities as forced sexual intercourse, forcible sodomy, child molestation, incest, fondling, and attempted rape."[21]

States define "sexual assault" based on the national definition. Most states approach sexual assault as an umbrella term for other crimes, for example, as in rape and unwanted sexual contact. Some differentiate between crimes involving penetration and crimes involving coerced or involuntary touching. Penetration is then considered an aggravated or first-degree sexual assault, and the touching crimes, a lower level sexual assault.[22]

Another difference is that, in the civilian community, when someone files a complaint in the jurisdiction, the way the investigations are done, the prosecuting attorney can make some decisions on the merits of the case on whether or not they are going to go to trial. There are similar provisions as far as the *UCMJ* is concerned. It is hard to know when you start talking about prosecution rates, you start talking about investigations, you are talking totally different systems. You have to be sure that you are comparing. [The] military's is a matter of public record. For the Department, investigations, courts martials are a matter of public record. Not so in the civilian community. You have to dig long and hard to get anybody's statistics on arrests, investigations, and prosecutions. Often times, when you are talking about [that] the military doesn't do a very good job of this, how do we know? How do we know that the military is doing worse than the civilian community? Because there is very little data that indicates how they are doing. It is difficult because [the military is] moving in the direction of full-disclosure. That is not so in the civilian world and for every jurisdiction, every state, the laws are different.

Manning finds the comparison of the military and college campuses "bizarre," adding,

It is an interesting comparison, too. It never occurred to me, but, as I have been reading some of the stuff going on in colleges, it is not the local city police that are investigating these things, it is the college, and that is very like the military. I was staggered when I figured out that, when they're talking in the D.C. area about a rape at Georgetown or American University, it's the people at Georgetown, their own private security force, their own deans and things that are making the decisions, it's not the D.C. police. So it is analogous, the military problem and the college campus problem. It is analogous when that civilian police are not taking care of things on the college campuses either. They are inbred just like the military is. Everybody wants to avoid scandal and not scare the new students off and not scare the parents in sending their kids to that particular school. So they can learn a lot from each other.[23]

In education, victims have to go first within the system to complain before they can go outside the system. Manning responds,

Yes. And that's why. Let's say if I worked for the department of the treasury and something happened, why should I have to go through the department of the treasury before I can call the cops? It's amazing. Especially when it's a felony. If we are talking about cheating on a test, that is academic to me and that should not be a criminal offense, but once you get into the sexual assault category, we're talking crime. A similar thing is going on on college campuses as in the military with the institution wanting not to have the police come.[24]

Institutions seek to protect themselves.

The general public sometimes does not understand military programs designed to address discrimination and violence. For example, the sexual harassment program falls under the equal opportunity, the sexual assault program under SAPRO (SAPR Office), and the Family Advocacy Program (FAP) oversees domestic violence and child abuse. Any of those programs may on the outside look the same, but they are very different programs and serving different populations as far as the military is concerned.

Another aspect of military life that the general public does not always understand is domestic violence. Domestic violence does not fall under the DoD's SAPRO, but under the FAP. The goals of the FAP are very different from the goals of sexual assault program. Under the FAP, the goal is to repair the family, if it is possible. But, if a crime has been committed, FAP takes action. If the perpetrator is married or a domestic partner, which is beyond the scope of DoD SAPRO, the crime falls under FAP. Child sexual abuse also falls under the FAP. The reason for much of that is: people who even take the child sexual abuse complaint are social workers; they are care providers. People who take SAPRO complaints of sexual assault are sexual assault response coordinators (SARCs) or victims' advocates; a medical professional can also take a complaint. The SARC is an administrator. The victim's advocate is there to advocate for the victim, but is not a service provider.

The U.S. Army's FAP, for example, focuses on the prevention, education, prompt reporting, investigation, intervention, and treatment of spouse and child abuse. Victim advocacy is one of the available programs. Services offered to soldiers and families are to enhance relationship skills and improve their quality of life. This purpose is realized through a variety of groups, seminars, workshops, and counseling and intervention services.[25]

Justice

Justice, then, when pursued, may depend on which jurisdiction a victim's complaint falls. Every jurisdiction should compel the military's inclusion in order to see the complete extent and parameters of sexual assault. Jurisdiction should not limit the military's study of the problem.

A case in point is Senator Kirsten Gillibrand's (D-NY) report that the extent of sex-related violence in the military communities is "vastly underreported" and that victims continue to struggle for justice. Incomplete material from DoD revealed that the spouses of service members and civilian women who live or work near military facilities are especially vulnerable to being sexually assaulted. They "remain in the shadows ... because neither is counted in Defense Department prevalence surveys which total over half, or 53%, of the cases analyzed. This is over double the rate of civilian survivors that are listed in the DoD SAPRO Report (Sexual Assault Prevention and Response Annual Report for FY 2013)," Gillibrand reported. The inclusion of civilian survivors in a total count of estimated sexual assaults could potentially raise the number of civilian survivors to 5,000–6,000. This is in addition to the 20,000 service member survivors. Further Gillibrand reasons,

> Applying the higher rate from these four bases, 53%, demonstrates that the inclusion of civilian survivors in a total count of estimated sexual assaults could more than double the number of currently-estimated survivors of sexual assault by a service member (an increase of 22,000) to a total of approximately 42,000. This estimate represents a significant increase in sexual assault survivors who are part of the overall military community, yet remain in the shadows.[26]

In February 2014, the Associated Press (AP) conducted an investigation into the U.S. military's handling of sexual assault cases in Japan, which revealed a pattern of random and inconsistent judgments. To find out whether the same situation existed at major U.S. bases, Gillibrand requested the details of sexual assault cases investigated and adjudicated from 2009 to 2014 at the army's Fort Hood in Texas, Naval Station Norfolk in Virginia, the Marine Corps' Camp Pendleton in California, and Wright-Patterson Air Force Base in Ohio. The DoD provided data for 2013 only. AP had obtained over 1,000 reports of sex crimes involving U.S. military personnel based in Japan between 2005 and early 2013.[27] In DoD's response to Gillibrand, out of 107 civilian women, 32 percent of reported assaults (33 alleged assaults by service members) were uncounted in the DoD's sexual assault prevalence surveys. In addition, out of 107 civilian military spouses. Twenty one percent (22 alleged assaults by service members) of reports were by civilian military spouses, uncounted in the DoD's sexual assault prevalence surveys.

Gillibrand found of 107 sexual assault cases, some punishments were too lenient and the word of the alleged perpetrator was more likely to be believed than that of the victim. Less than a quarter of the cases went to trial and 11 resulted in conviction for a sex crime. Female civilians were the victims in more than half the cases (see Table 1.3).

Table 1.3.

Case Disposition of Sexual Assaults at Major Bases of Spouses of Service Members and Civilian Women Who Live or Work Near Military Facilities in 2013.

Category	Army	Navy	Air Force	USMC	Total
Unrestricted reports	37	15	5	50	107
Allowed to resign/be discharged in lieu of court-martial	2	0	1	0	3
Proceeded to trial	6	2	1	15	24
Convicted of sexual assault	2	2	0	7	11
Convicted of a non-sexual assault crime (often adultery or violation of an order)	1	0	0	5	6
Acquitted	3	0	1	3	7

Source: Kirsten Gillibrand, *Snapshot Review of Sexual Assault Report Files at the Four Largest U.S. Military Bases in 2013* (Washington, DC: Office of U.S. Senator, May 2015), 9, http://www.gillibrand.senate.gov/imo/media/doc/Gillibrand_Sexual%20Assault%20Report.pdf.

Nearly 73 percent of military spouses declined to pursue charges. One case of the 22 sexual assault incidents the military command proceeded to trial, and in that case the husband was acquitted. Gillibrand found a lack of faith in military justice and a hostile climate for survivors. Almost half of survivors who took first step toward justice by filing unrestricted report later declined to move forward. Of that half, many voluntarily submitted to an intrusive sexual assault evidence collection kit, showing a strong commitment to pursuing justice. The fear of retaliation could be a major concern. Research shows the rate of false accusation in sexual assault cases is similar to other crimes (2 percent to 8 percent). The attrition rate of unrestricted reports also directly undercuts DoD claims of building confidence of service members in the military justice system.[28]

Other findings reflect how the perpetrators fared. Lesser punishments could signify an absence of justice, which in turn leaves assailants free to strike again. Of the 20 percent of the 107 cases that went to trial, about 10 percent were convicted of a sexual crime, 6 percent of a non-sexual assault crime, and 3 percent were allowed to resign or be discharged in lieu of court-martial. In one case, sufficient evidence existed and the case was referred to court-martial. The convening authority approved a discharge in place of a trial.

If the two parties have a previous sexual history, the alleged assailant is more likely to be believed. When the accused reported that the sex was consensual, or denied it happened, the command took action just 10 times out of 34. In these cases, there were zero convictions of sexual assault. Significantly, 27 of 34, or about 79 percent of these cases, did not go to trial.

Finally, Gillibrand concludes that low and inconsistent case numbers and incomplete data are cause for concern. For example, the Naval Station Norfolk provided a strikingly low number of cases in proportion to the number of service members stationed there. The actual number of air force sexual assault reports is unclear, as the number of cases provided is inconsistent with numbers reported previously in the media. And, many of the Fort Hood case files are incomplete and do not contain the most basic case narratives.

Senator Gillibrand's findings are consistent with the previous reporting of mishandled sexual assault cases at military bases in Japan. She concludes,

> This suggests a large scale systemic failure and a culture that protects the accused and ostracizes the survivor at the expense of the public and the servicemembers' safety. The lack of an effective military justice system, with the commander making untrained evidentiary decisions, not only threatens the men and women serving in uniform, but also, this data clearly shows, threatens the civilian population. This further demonstrates the need for an independent, trained military

prosecutor, unbiased by the chain of chain of command, making evidentiary decisions about felony-level crime.[29]

A COMMON GOAL

Military service members and civilian members of society have much in common. The military service members and college students, in particular, have a similar age range; they live in similar campus-style communities; and they have similar experience with sexual assault. Comparing the military with colleges provides insight into the problem of sexual assault and can provide answers to how it can be reduced, if not eliminated.

CHAPTER 2

Sexual Assault Scandals in the Military

Typical sexual assault in the military involves a perpetrator and a victim, but, all too often, the assault involves multiple perpetrators and victims. Although incidences of sexual assault involving multiple perpetrators and victims had occurred before 1991, none is as well known or had the repercussions that U.S. Navy's Tailhook '91, as it became known, had. It was one of the sexual assault scandals that occurred at military events and on military bases in the 1990s. Tailhook '91 had behavior that was not discouraged until one female staff member complained. The aftermath of the event had far-reaching consequences.

TAILHOOK '91

The sexual assaults at the 35th Annual Tailhook Association Symposium from September 8 to 12, 1991, were numerous and were typical for this event. Tailhook '91 is representative of the problems women were facing as they served their country and, more specifically, that resulted from reporting sexual assault and harassment. A positive outcome was that Tailhook '91 was definitely a catalyst for change. I was researching Tailhook '91 at the time it occurred and wrote the following assessment in my book *Women at War*:

> Women officers were among the targets of attack by Navy and Marine carrier airmen at the Tailhook Association Convention in 1991. Tailhook '91 had a tremendous impact on the military. Lt. Paula Couglin, female Navy helicopter pilot, formally complained that she had been physically and indecently assaulted by a group of naval officers at the 1991 Tailhook symposium at the Las Vegas Hilton. Indirectly, her courage was a factor in causing the Navy leadership to move.

Not only did all services reexamine policy on sexual harassment, they also along with Congress reexamined combat exclusion law. Tailhook raised broader concerns about the process of changing how the military culture views the role of women in the armed forces. Specifically, the issue of sexual harassment and discrimination in the military was the focus of the House Armed Services Committee report, sometimes referred to as the Aspin Byron Report.[1]

LT Paula Coughlin's Complaint

In September 1991, a U.S. Navy helicopter pilot, Lieutenant (LT) Paula Coughlin, complained to Rear Admiral (RADM) John Snyder, Commander, Naval Air Test Center, that she had been physically and indecently assaulted on September 7, 1991, by a group of naval officers at the 1991 Tailhook Symposium at the Las Vegas Hilton.[2] Unsatisfied with RADM Snyder's lack of response she wrote to Vice Admiral (VADM) Richard M. Dunleavy, the Assistant Chief of Naval Operations (Air Warfare), who immediately notified his superior, Admiral (ADM) Jerome Johnson, the Vice Chief of Naval Operations (VCNO). Johnson immediately requested the Commander of the Naval Investigative Service (NIS), RADM Duvall M. "Mac" Williams, to open an investigation.[3] The investigation was initiated on October 11, 1991. Snyder was later relieved of his command for dealing inappropriately with Coughlin's complaint.[4] A jury awarded Coughlin $6.7 million, which the judge reduced to $5.2 million and the Tailhook Association paid her $400,000 to settle her case against it.[5]

The following is a brief account of LT Coughlin's assault based on what I wrote in my first book *Power and Gender*. As LT Coughlin approached the third floor hallway of the Las Vegas Hilton, she found rough and rowdy behaviors. When she attempted to pass a man on the right side, he bumped into her with his right hip. Coughlin excused herself. One man yelled, "Admiral's Aide!"[6] He lifted her off the ground and ahead a step. As he assaulted her, she asked, "What the f— do you think you are doing?" She bit one assailant and kicked the other; she later explained, "I felt as though the group was trying to rape me. I was terrified and had no idea what was going to happen next." She attempted to escape into an administrative suite, but men blocked her entrance. She noticed one man turned to walk away. "I reached out and tapped him on the right hip, pleading with the man to just let me get in front of him. The man stopped, turned . . . and pivoted to a position directly in front of me. With this action, the man raised both his hands and put one on each of my breasts." She eventually broke free into an administrative suite. As she sat in the darkness she was, "attempting to understand what had happened to me . . . I was appalled not only by the brutality of the incident, but the fact that the group did that to me knowing I was both a fellow officer and an admiral's aide."

The Role of the Flag Panel

The Flag Panel attracted more attendees than any other symposium function and did not require registration. The panel consisted of eight navy admirals and one Marine Corps general.[7] Questions relating to the possibility of women flying combat aircraft brought strong reactions.[8] Some witnesses felt that the "mood" of the attendees changed for the worse because of the exchanges about women in combat, but the Department of Defense Inspector General (DoDIG) did not find sufficient evidence to conclude that male officers later turned their frustrations over this policy matter into violent acts against women on the third floor.

The Gauntlet

When women attempted to walk down the third floor hall outside the corporate and navy/marine-sponsored suites, a changing number of males lined a narrow portion where the women were "encircled and sexually molested to varying degrees, from being patted on the buttocks to having other portions of their anatomy groped and grabbed." The Naval Inspector General's (NIG) report details that NIS reported assaults on female naval officers and several civilian female attendees by the gauntlet. Of the 26 female victims NIS identified, more than half were naval officers.[9]

The Investigations

Coughlin's complaint was the beginning of a long and rigorous inquiry that culminated in three investigations of which the navy conducted two. The NIG released his report on April 29, 1992. The NIS Commander released his report on April 15, 1992, and followed it with a supplemental report on May 13, 1992. The DoDIG released its first report, *Tailhook 91, Part 1—Review of the Navy Investigations*, on September 21, 1992. Subsequently, on October 22, 1992, the navy released a little-known document titled *Response to Report of Investigation: Tailhook Part 1, Review of the Navy Investigations*. DoDIG released its second report, *Tailhook 91, Part 2: Events at the 35th Annual Tailhook Symposium*, dated February 1993. The Las Vegas Police Department also investigated and the air force and army conducted special inquiries to determine the participation of their personnel.[10]

The Navy Inspector General

The main findings of the NIG were reported to the chain of command. The standards of the observers at Tailhook '91 did not enable them to judge the behavior they observed as assault or sexual harassment. Interviews of junior officers (JOs) reflect that a number of JOs attended solely for the social events and neither registered nor attended any professional events. NIG concluded that the serving of beer (97 half kegs or 1,503 gallons or 16,000 twelve-ounce glasses) and lack of uniforms detracted from the professional aspects of the symposium.

The leadership permitted the activities to continue, demonstrating a "marked absence of moral courage and personal majority of those interviewed responded, 'What's the big deal?' " NIG concluded, "The atmosphere condoned, if not encouraged, the gang mentality that eventually led to the sexual assaults. In spite of the alcohol consumption, participants were aware of their actions." Further, the conduct created an atmosphere demeaning to women, which needed to be addressed by the Chief of Naval Operations (CNO) and the Commandant of the Marine Corps (CMC) throughout the naval services, without overlooking those individuals who should be held accountable for misconduct. NIG recognized how little empathy, understanding, and support existed within the Navy and Marine Corps for the "zero tolerance" policy.[11]

Naval Investigative Services

The NIS's investigations of assault and misconduct were also reported to the chain of command. In its mammoth investigation, NIS interrogated 2,193 people (92 of whom were interviewed or interrogated multiple times) and expended nearly $1.2 million.[12] Despite the investigation's staggering size, Derek J. Vander Schaaf, Deputy Inspector General of DoD, in a February 1993 memorandum for the Secretary of Defense, wrote, "Misconduct at the 1991 Tailhook Symposium was more widespread than previously reported by the Navy."[13] DoDIG stated the NIS investigation focused almost exclusively on indecent assaults. The NIS investigation found that a total of 26 women, 14 of them naval officers, had been assaulted. An NIS interim report dated February 1992 listed 18 naval officers who were considered suspects or subjects, but its final report of investigation, issued in mid-April 1992, identified only three indecent assault suspects.[14] RADM "Mac" Williams, NIS Commander, says he was shocked at DoDIG's conclusion because NIS did uncover and forward additional misconduct to the NIG. Even though NIS's jurisdiction was to investigate felony criminal charges, NIS's final report of investigation referred 10 cases, 3 of which involved serious indecent assault suspects.[15] Williams says, "Of the 26 women who allegedly were assaulted, nine of them declined to look at any of the 450 photographs we had taken to attempt to identify their assailants."[16]

Naval Investigative Services Supplemental

The 55-page NIS supplemental report, dated May 13, 1992, created political controversy because one witness placed SECNAV (Secretary of the Navy) Garrett in the vicinity of a hospitality suite at Tailhook '91.[17] The report contained a page that stated the secretary came by one suite, once. It was no secret the secretary was at Tailhook '91, but he maintained he had not witnessed any wrongdoing.[18] NIG Davis acknowledged Garrett was at Tailhook '91. On February 7, 1994, in the court martial trial of Miller, Tritt and Samples, Judge Vest was able to place senior officers in a distinct place at Tailhook '91. Vest heard witnesses corroborate what senior officers observed.[19] Garrett acknowledged witnessing "female leg shaving" activities,[20] which aids in linking ADM Frank B. Kelso II, Chief of Naval Operations, witnessing improper conduct such as leg shaving; this demonstrates Kelso had personal knowledge of misconduct.[21] It was unclear whether witnessing a striptease act violates a current navy rule of conduct for an officer even though his judgment in doing so might be severely criticized.[22]

DoDIG *Tailhook 91, Part 1—Review of the Navy Investigations*

DoDIG issued its first report, *Tailhook, Part 1*, in September 1992. In *Tailhook, Part 1*, no mention is made of the earlier favorable review of NIS's investigation.[23] DoD's Deputy IG Derek J. Vander Schaaf's report identified 140 navy and marine officers, 83 women, and 7 men victims. When these cases were referred for disciplinary action, the prosecution did not result in a single conviction. Admiral's masts addressed 28 cases with fines, reprimands, or nonpunitive actions.[24] PBS reported 14 admirals and about 300 aviators had their careers terminated or damaged.[25] The first report, issued separately because the management issues were distinct from those pertaining to conduct at Tailhook '91, "addresses the actions of senior Navy officials, the Naval Investigative Service (NIS) and the Naval Inspector General (NIG) in conducting earlier probes into Tailhook 91."[26] In response to *Tailhook, Part 1*, the *Response to Tailhook 91 Part 1* was released October 22, 1992. Three admirals and other civilian and military leaders raise questions about the credibility of parts of the DoDIG's first report.

The second report, *Tailhook 91 Part 2: Events at the 35th Annual Tailhook Symposium*, was released in February 1993. *Part 2* included events that took place at Tailhook '91, including assaults, participants in the gauntlet, improper conduct, and the actions and inactions of the senior navy officials who were in attendance.[27] While it looks as though the government got tough, the seriousness of the issue justifies the actions.

Immediate Aftermath

After the public outcry, the Senate Armed Services Committee in the summer 1992 declined to approve any of the 4,500 promotions pending for navy and marine corps officers until the Pentagon official cleared more nominees of involvement in the scandal.[28] Aviators were disciplined according to the offenses committed. The Navy Consolidated Disposition Authority (CDA) at the Norfolk Naval Base, Norfolk, Virginia, handled the navy's adjudication of the cases involving criminal activity and other violations of the Uniformed Code of Military Justice (UCMJ) during the 1991 Tailhook convention.[29] Fines were imposed and nonpunitive letters of caution and counseling or punitive letters of admonition and reprimand and censure were issued. No officer was court-martialed, but the impact of the letters on careers is hardly inconsequential. These letters could have been the predecessor of more serious action later. To protect the rights of the accused, the navy stated it allowed and encouraged legal representation during hearings. The appellate court, however, in the case of *Samples v. Vest*, on January 11, 1994, concluded that the accused were not always represented.[30]

In the fall of 1994, the court-martial convening authority, LT Krulak, dismissed the charges against Marine Captain Gregory J. Bonam, the alleged assailant of LT Paula Coughlin, due to lack of evidence, even though LT Coughlin was a witness at the pretrial hearing.[31] On February 7, 1994, Coughlin submitted her resignation from the navy.[32] She said her resignation was the result of abuse she suffered at the gauntlet and continuing psychological abuse. Later in 1994, LT Coughlin made an out-of-court settlement with the Tailhook Association and won $6.7 million in a suit against the Las Vegas Hilton.

Navy Judge CAPT William T. Vest Jr. in *U.S. v. Miller, U.S. v. Tritt*, and *U.S. v. Samples*, on February 7, 1994, issued a pretrial ruling that placed responsibility for Tailhook with CNO, Admiral Frank B. Kelso II.[33] Pressure mounted on Kelso and he retired two months ahead of his original plans,[34] despite the apparent support both politically and in the military. President Clinton recommended that Kelso be retired at the rank of four-star admiral. On April 19, 1994, after a spirited debate, the U.S. Senate, on a surprisingly close 54–43 vote, approved President Clinton's recommendation.[35] Vest dismissed charges against Commanders Thomas R. Miller and Gregory Tritt, and LT David Samples, saying that Kelso's appointment for handling Tailhook discipline was inappropriate.[36]

The Navy's Efforts against Sexual Harassment

The navy's accomplishments for women and for prohibiting sexual harassment continued after Tailhook.[37] In February 1992, the CNO issued to the entire navy several unclassified messages regarding the zero tolerance policy.[38] On October 13, 1992, the three-month-old Standing Committee on Military and Civilian Women in the Department of the Navy recommended that, among other items, the navy establish two "tiger teams," one to track formal complaints and one to translate the department's definition for personnel at all levels.[39] In January 1993, the navy issued its definition of sexual harassment and a glossary of terms to help illustrate the range of behaviors that constitute sexual harassment.[40] In December 1992, on the recommendation of the Secretary of the Navy's Standing Committee on Women, a toll-free sexual harassment advice and counseling telephone line was established.[41] A total of 979 telephone calls were received between December 1992 and August 1993. The gender gap of callers narrowed significantly; 462 were female and 517 were male. Approximately half of the calls sought policy guidance.

The navy aimed its efforts at all naval and marine personnel. It released a handbook, *Resolving Conflict: Following the Light of Personal Behavior*, which was more specific than its policy examples.[42] The strength of the handbook was in encouraging personnel to resolve conflict in the workplace at the lowest possible level. The navy continued to train its leadership. In 1994, it issued the *Commander's Handbook: A Tool Kit for Prevention of Sexual Harassment*.[43]

The navy's 1992 annual survey addressed sexual harassment issues.[44] Results indicated that over 99 percent of enlisted and officer survey respondents said they had received sexual harassment training in the last 12 months. In 1991, only 78 percent of the enlisted and 72 percent of the officers said they had received training in the last 12 months. Seventy percent of the female enlistees and 82.3 percent of the female officers agreed or strongly agreed that, if they had a complaint, it would get a fair hearing compared to 38 and 24 percent, respectively, in 1991. About 76 percent of female enlistees and 93 percent of female officers agreed or strongly agreed that sexual harassment was not tolerated in their command, compared to 57 percent of the females in the 1988–89 DoD survey. About 90 percent of female enlistees and 93 percent of female officers said they understood the complaint procedures. Over 96 percent of all respondents felt they understood the definition of and regulations for sexual harassment. Sixty-five percent of enlistees and 60 percent of all officers said training helped them better understand the behaviors and attitudes the navy expects.

Implications

The DoDIG reports are a scathing attack on the investigations and the "collective management failures." Surprisingly, DoDIG took a velvet-glove approach to Kelso. In fact, the DoDIG report did not include Kelso in its term "collective management." In fall 1993, SECNAV John H. Dalton recommended Kelso be removed from his post for failure of leadership, but Kelso was strongly supported by Defense Secretary Les Aspin.[45] Kelso, whatever he was or was not and whatever he did do or did not do, had the support of both the Bush and the Clinton administrations. That is the role of power in the final outcome for Admiral Kelso. Rightly or wrongly, Kelso did not topple.

Collective management seemed to refer to the military leaders Davis, Gordon, and Williams and to civilian leaders (political appointees) Secretary Garrett and Undersecretary Howard, because, at the time, the senior uniformed officials, CNO Kelso and Commandant of the Marine Corps Mundy, were not criticized. In the civilian leadership, Secretary Garrett's career halted, but the careers of Undersecretary Howard and Assistant Secretary Pope continued. Acting Navy Secretary Sean O'Keefe believed all who met in the group that investigated Tailhook '91 had some responsibility for what happened. Those individuals whose careers were altered contended DoDIG, verbally and in writing, confirmed that their investigations were timely, thorough, professional, and extraordinary.[46] All attended weekly meetings and did respond to questions the DoDIG's investigators asked.[47] Williams says that DoDIG's earlier evaluation of the NIS investigation was that it was thorough, timely, and professional. Then complaints came. Then DoDIG looked at it again. The conclusion the second time was "It was horrible."[48]

At a news conference in September 1992, Acting Navy Secretary Sean O'Keefe inaccurately stated that Gordon and Williams were retiring as a matter of "conscience." Four weeks after the news conference, O'Keefe issued a memorandum that exonerated Williams, Gordon, and Davis of wrongdoing.[49] Although Gordon was scheduled to retire at that time, he did not do so because of Tailhook. In February 1995, Senator Sam Nunn (D-GA) confirmed that, "I have been informed by the Navy that the then-Judge Advocate general, Rear Admiral John E. Gordon, did not resign in response to the Tailhook report."[50]

All believed they had done what they had been tasked to do and could not go outside that tasking. Undersecretary Howard and NIG were tasked by the SECNAV. Howard felt it was not his job to direct the investigation, but to represent the Secretary of the Navy in dealing with two organizations, NIG and NIS, that were, by design, isolated from outside influence, his included.[51] Davis understood his tasking, but he could not go beyond his task. He was not allowed to broaden the investigation. Howard did not permit broadening the investigation; therefore, NIG was forced to conduct a smaller investigation. Howard advised Davis to let NIS take the lead. Davis told Howard that he (Howard) should task NIS specifically with investigating the misconduct issues, because that was not an area NIS normally investigated. The tasking was never done and Howard told DoDIG he does not remember such a conversation with

NIG.[52] The navy, like other branches of the military, operates with a definite chain of command; tasking NIS fell to the VCNO.[53]

If there was a "collective" management failure, why did the careers of some top management personnel continue? Time (two years after DoDIG *Part 1*) would show that there were more individuals in the collective management than the three military officers and two civilian officials criticized by DoDIG. Kelso was ultimately viewed by many in the U.S. Senate and by Judge Vest to be part of the collective failure. It could be said that the collective failure lay with navy management, but the failure runs much deeper. Of the approximately 2,100 people interviewed by NIS, Williams reminds us, females were also interviewed and, like males, were not of much help.[54] DoDIG met with similar results in its attempts to identify assailants. Few victims made absolute identifications.[55] Poor lighting, confusion, shock, and the fact that males all looked alike—because they were young, physically fit, Caucasian; had short, military style haircuts; and dressed in T-shirts and shorts—were among the reasons given.

Navy's *Response to Report of Investigation: Tailhook, Part 1—Review of the Navy Investigations* was followed by *DoDIG Tailhook 91, Part 2 Events at the 35th Annual Tailhook Symposium*, which focused on the events that took place, including assaults, participants in the gauntlet, improper conduct, and the actions and alleged inactions of the senior navy officials who were in attendance. Up to Section X of the report, DoDIG concerns its investigation with what happened and devotes little attention to why.[56] Of the 117 referrals DoDIG provided the navy for alleged misconduct (indecent assault, indecent exposure, conduct unbecoming for an officer, or failure to act in a proper leadership capacity), only 30 were also included in the navy and NIG referrals.[57] DoDIG said it found 90 victims of indecent assault, 83 women and 7 men (23 of these were officers), and a significant number of indecent exposure incidents (23 of which were by officers) and other types of sexual misconduct and improprieties by Navy and Marine Corps officers. DoDIG alleged 51 individuals made false statements to the DoDIG during the investigation.

DoDIG found that the predominant response of attendees was closing ranks and obfuscation.[58] RADM Ted Gordon, Judge Advocate General (JAG) believed it was overstated to say the predominant response of attendees was closing ranks or engaging in a conspiracy. The aviators were not protecting each other as much as they were protecting themselves. "Once an officer admitted seeing misconduct, he or she would be held accountable for not reporting it earlier and careers would be in jeopardy. I believe individuals 'couldn't remember' to protect themselves."[59]

What was the fate of the accused aviators? How did they fare? The Navy Consolidated Disposition Authority (CDA) at the Norfolk Naval Base, Norfolk, Virginia, coordinated the navy's adjudication of the cases involving criminal activity and other violations of the UCMJ during Tailhook '91.[60] In 1993, the Navy CDA reviewed all case files of alleged assault assailants. In more than half the cases, the files were not brought forward because the charge was inappropriate or evidence was lacking, for example, photograph or corroborating statement of a witness.[61] The Marine Corps reviewed over a dozen cases within its jurisdiction.

The Pilots of Final Flights

In the one-year period following Tailhook '91, over 30 officers who attended Tailhook Symposium died.[62] Most of the 30 officers died defending our country. The DoDIG points out that these factors do not justify the activities, but they help illuminate attendees' attitudes.

Analysis and Conclusions

By September 1991, we as a society had not had our public debate that elevated the issue of sexual harassment to a collective consciousness, such as we had in the 1991 Anita Hill/Clarence Thomas hearings.[63] A closet attitude was still dominant. The issue had not yet progressed far enough for the victims to find fewer contradictions and more support.

The gauntlet and accompanying behavior are not very pretty. Admiral Williams says it is painful to him when he reads my account of the gauntlet. Admiral Gordon says, "This was not our country's finest hour."[64] Further, the drama moved to the TV screen with an ABC movie in production.[65] The story also unfolds in vivid detail in Jean Zimmerman's book published by Doubleday, *Tailspin: Women at War in the Wake of Tailhook*. Zimmerman tells not only of female assault victims. Given significant access to navy vessels and their crew by the U.S. Navy, she also tells about its core, the men.[66] The misconduct went far beyond the "treatment of women" issues for which the navy had policies. The sexual traditions of the gauntlet deviated too far from the standards of behavior the nation expects of the military officers.[67] When an early report stated the hallway itself was described as smelling of spilled beer, vomit, and urine,[68] someone said to me, "Look for yourself, Tailhook is about a 'Mass of Humanity and Wretched Excess.' " The DoDIG puts all of this theory another way when it found great disparity between espoused navy policies and actual conduct.[69] If the navy had looked into its "cultural problem," it would have found a "cultural prohibition." Some in the navy did not keep pace with a changing society as well as it had kept pace with the changing technology of warfare. Kenneth Hagan, a naval historian and author of *This People's Navy*, believes the meaning of Tailhook '91 cuts deeper than the outrageous convention behavior, "because Navy aviators have gained influence far beyond their numbers in the service. Naval aviation is thought by many to run the Navy," conclude Cary et al.[70]

The navy was aware, however, that sexual harassment not only has significant economic costs but also has effects that are even more harmful—lowered productivity, diminished readiness, and impaired public trust. "While not easily quantified, these costs are real and seriously affect DON's ability to accomplish its mission."[71] It is important that the entire navy not be stigmatized by Tailhook '91. President Clinton said that he wanted "appropriate action taken," but DoDIG *Parts 1 and 2* should not be taken as a general indictment of the navy.[72] President Clinton emphasized that "the quality of our men and women in uniform today is higher than it has ever been and that the tragedy of Tailhook must be put behind us."[73] DoDIG stated in the forward to its report that it recognized the negative effect Tailhook '91 has had on the morale of many members of the navy.[74] Further, it believed Tailhook was not a reflection on the entire Navy and Marine Corps aviators who continually perform their duties in an exemplary fashion.

It is important to place Tailhook '91 in perspective. I was reminded by a naval person, "Don't forget our mission—to protect and defend our constitution." We have reason to honor the protection and defense the navy gives our country. Some topics of the professional symposiums of Tailhook '91 dealt with Operation Desert Shield, air-to-air combat, use of weapons, reconnaissance, surveillance, and intelligence support in war.[75] There was standing room only for an Iraq POW debriefing where the knowledge of how other association attendees survived sustained them.

Judgment of any offense, including sexual harassment, should be viewed within the totality of circumstances. We are mindful that, to understand the milieu, we must understand our history, our biography. We find the DoDIG report agrees when it says, "It is important to understand that the events at Tailhook '91 did not occur in a historical vacuum."[76] Mills may find the navy's attitude toward the problem of sexual harassment normal, that is, the navy personnel may have not had the quality of mind to help them understand what was going on in the world.[77] The conclusion was inevitable: personnel could not free themselves from harassment. A victim, Coughlin, used her own power and took her complaint through the structure. Although some responded with "what's the big deal," finally, the navy hierarchy did deal with the issue.

"The world of people, their institutions, their history and their passions" make people what is important rather than things.[78] Meeting navy personnel and visiting with and interviewing leaders who are very much affected by what happened make it mandatory to write from the theoretical perspective of people are what is important. Secretary Garrett resigned. Why? Why did what happened to other top officers happen? Although the law holds the institution liable, consider, if you will, the passions of top officers who feel that their careers were unjustly and unfairly affected. It may call for a broader definition of victim. Do honorable and/or humanistic leaders sometimes become the victims because of the law and/or political concession?

Gordon contends that the political dilemma present in Tailhook '91 needs to be explored. The moral dilemmas, he says, are being studied rather than solely the horror.[79] For me, his words pose a research implication.

> All of us in the military are tasked with the general duty to prevent sexual harassment, but the Judge Advocate General has the specific duty to ensure fairness and maintaining the integrity of the military justice system. I feel that I did my duty as best I could. Indeed, I believe that had Secretary Garrett not submitted to political pressure, the DoDIG not entered the picture, justice would have been served. I set out in the beginning of this process with one goal, and that was to ensure that command influence would not prevent the Navy from dealing with disciplinary cases. I succeeded beyond that which the political administration was willing to support.
>
> What I am trying to describe is that the U.S. Constitution and the Bill of Rights were written for this very situation, where political objectives strain fairness and what our country is all about. Whenever there is a conflict between constitutional rights and the need to get to the bottom of a crime, our law says the constitution is supreme. Everyone seems willing to accept this premise when serious crimes such as murder have been committed, but when social objectives are at stake, there are those who would throw away these values in a heartbeat to satisfy a political dilemma. I would not.[80]

Life is a continuum of rights and wrongs on all sides of an issue. At the center of the issue of sexual harassment are the rights of all parties in a complaint. The rights of "collective management" were compromised, if not ignored. The aviators who committed assaults and acts of misconduct and/or did not report the wrongs violated the rights of others. The rights of the assault victims were violated by both their perpetrators and the navy command. To break the aviators' wall of silence, the aviators' rights were violated. The very rights the institution sought to protect, it did not grant within. Yet, the valor of LT Coughlin caused the navy leadership to move. All services reexamined their policies to become better institutions. Eliminating sexual harassment is compatible with the services' mission of readiness. Preventing and acting against sexual violence and sexual harassment are the responsibility of all people within an institution and society.

Post Tailhook '91

Although Tailhook '91 dominated societal consciousness, The RAND Corporation pointed out that studies at the turn of the century existed, focusing specifically on military samples that reported a range from 2 to 51 percent among women and, in those that included men, up to 7 percent of the men studied had been sexually assaulted. By comparison, studies of college students revealed that 21 to 42 percent of women had experienced sexual assault.[81] The larger events that took place at Army Aberdeen Proving Grounds and the Air Force Academy along with high-profile cases indicate the problem of sexual assault was not yet resolved.

ABERDEEN PROVING GROUNDS, 1996

In 1996, over 50 female recruits at the Army Aberdeen Proving Ground brought complaints of sexual assault against 11 drill sergeants and 1 officer. Offenders received sentences ranging from prison time to dishonorable discharges. Although this event gave impetus to the establishment of the army's 1997 Senior Review Panel on Sexual Harassment, it produced no direct recommendations that addressed combating sexual assault directly.[82] Offender Sergeant Delmar Simpson received the most severe punishment and was convicted of multiple counts of rape and sodomy and sentenced to 25 years in prison.[83] Overall sentences ranged from prison time to dishonorable discharges.[84]

Reported cases of sexual assault involving army personnel, including reservists, increased 19 percent between 1999 and 2002, and an additional 5 percent between 2002 and 2003. The army continued to fall behind the other three services.[85]

AIR FORCE ACADEMY, 2003

Because it was alleged that the Air Force Academy had not taken appropriate action in response to reports of sexual assault against women cadets, the U.S. Senate Governmental Affairs Committee requested that the DoDIG investigate.[86] During the 10-year period preceding 2003 from January 1, 1993, through December 31, 2002, 142 allegations of sexual assault or an average of more than 14 allegations per year were made. The DoDIG May 2003 survey of academy cadets found that 80.8 percent of women who said they had been victims of sexual assault at the academy did not report the incident. Of the women cadets (classes 2003–2006), 18.8 percent reported they had been victims of at least one instance of sexual assault or attempted sexual assault. This number includes 7.4 percent who said they were victims of at least one rape or attempted rape. One in five responding male cadets did not believe that women belonged at the academy, which indicates that attitude has changed little in the past 10 years.[87] Assault offenders were both cadets who were not senior to the victim (84 or 48.6%) and cadets who were senior (65 or 37.6%).[88] Although Tailhook '91 had received substantial attention, the issue of sexual assault was somewhat dormant until the 2000 Air Force

Inspector General investigation of sexual assault at the Air Force Academy, prompting additional investigations. These inquiries were followed by the establishment of the DoD Sexual Assault Task Force (to investigate sexual assault allegations among deployed service members), the Task Force on Sexual Harassment and Violence at the Military Academies, and the creation in 2005 of the Sexual Assault Prevention and Response Office within DoD. In addition, in 2007, Article 20 of the UCMJ pertaining to rape was revised.[89] Kingsley R. Browne concluded that the reviews by the General Counsel's group and the Inspectors General of the Air Force and Defense Department identified some procedural shortcomings but they did not corroborate the central thrust of the scandal: "that the Academy was a hotbed of rape and sexual assault and that its leadership cared little for the plight of the victims."[90]

DoD Response

The DoD responded after each scandal, but when the media reported that several military women who served in deployed locations were sexually assaulted, its response intensified acknowledging the need for increased action. In February 2004, reports of sexual assault of military members in Iraq and Kuwait prompted a review on how the DoD cares for victims of sexual assault. The task force identified inconsistent sexual assault programs throughout the DoD and recommended establishing a single office responsible for sexual assault issues. The DoD then created the Joint Task Force on Sexual Assault Prevention and Response (JTF-SAPR). The task force concentrated on victim care, prevention training, and system accountability. In 2005, the JTF-SAPR became permanent under the name Sexual Assault Prevention and Response Office (SAPRO), which serves as the "single point of responsibility for sexual assault policy matters."[91]

In addition to DoD's action, through the 2005 National Defense Authorization Act, Congress directed the Secretary of Defense and the military services to develop policies and procedures to prevent and respond to sexual assault of military members. According to Megan N. Schmid, in response, the DoD issued two important documents: first, a directive containing the policy for sexual assault prevention and response; and second, an instruction providing guidance for the policy's implementation. It also required that the DoD provide an annual report to Congress on military sexual assaults that occurred during the preceding year and on action taken in substantiated cases.[92]

Series of Scandals, Twenty-First Century

In the wake of Aberdeen, two high-profile sexual assault cases occurred. Senior enlisted army soldier Sergeant Major of the Army

(SGM) Gene McKinney was accused by 22-year-old decorated soldier followed by five additional women accusers. He was acquitted of sexual misconduct, but found guilty of obstructing justice. Punishment consisted of a letter of reprimand and a reduction in rank to Master Sergeant. The second high-profile case was the 1999 filing of a sexual harassment charge by General Claudia Kennedy against General Larry Smith who was nominated for deputy army inspector general. A letter of reprimand led to the end of his career.[93]

Although scandals did not continue in the twenty-first century on as large a scale as Tailhook '91 or the Air Force Academy in 2003, Kingsley R. Browne noted the existence of a "A Medley of Little Scandals" that continued to plague the military in the twenty-first century.[94] The *Washington Times* listed incidents of sexual harassment as well as assaults and rape such as, in 2006, former Naval Academy star quarterback Midshipman Lamar Owens was accused of raping another midshipman, but was found guilty of conduct unbecoming an officer.[95] In 2004, reports surfaced that hundreds of female soldiers were assaulted while deployed in Iraq and Afghanistan.[96] In 2012, a large scandal in the air force involved 33 basic training instructors at Lackland Air Force base who were investigated for allegations of sexual misconduct involving at least 63 students.[97]

Although RAND Corporation concludes that prevalence rates vary considerably, taken in conjunction with these scandals, I conclude that current incidence statistics indicate sexual assault in the military continues to be a problem as it was historically (see Table 1.1). In 2012, the number of estimated unwanted sexual contact and sexual assault incidents increased by 36 percent, from 19,300 assaults in 2011 to 26,000. However, Senator Kirsten Gillibrand (D-NY) points out that the Pentagon estimates that the majority of victims (89 percent) do not report sex crimes. According to the Justice Department, in the civilian justice system, about 65 percent of sexual assaults go unreported.[98] In 2013, the total number of reports (5,061) represented an increase of 50 percent over FY2012 numbers (3,374). The average annual increase has been approximately 5 percent since the first full year of restricted reporting in 2006.[99] Restricted reporting permits the victim to receive confidential care. Unrestricted reporting results in a referral to a military criminal investigation organization.[100]

NEGATIVE AND DISCRIMINATORY CLIMATE

U.S. Military Academy, West Point

In 1976, the U.S. military academies admitted women for the first time. MAJ Lillian Pfluke, U.S. Army (Ret.), was a member of the first class of women at the U.S. Military Academy at West Point. Male prejudice against women at the academies proved to be a major obstacle.[101] Pfluke said:

> Overt, blatant harassment . . . was okay. Everybody did it. It was okay to do it. Many people were very, very resistant to the idea of women being there at all. And so we were ostracized, not only by our own students and our own classmates, but also by the faculty and also by the staff. Certainly, every once in a while, someone would do a random act of kindness, but, most of the time, you were reminded every single day that you weren't welcome there.[102]

THE CULTURE OF MILITARY ASSAULT SCANDALS

Sex scandals in the military would not occur if the culture did not permit it. The culture at the time of Tailhook '91 not only permitted it, but also encouraged it. The Tailhook conventions were paid for by the navy and were big drawing cards for navy aviators. What occurred at Tailhook '91 was not an aberration; it was the norm. The only reason that this one was different is that someone objected. Tailhook '91 would not have been remarkable or newsworthy if Paula Coughlin has not complained. Behavior goes on if no one complains. The culture stays in place if no one complains. If the culture changes and changes in the right way, sex scandals, like Tailhook '91, will not happen again.

CHAPTER 3

Policies and Laws

POLICIES

The policies of the U.S. Military are determined by the U.S. Congress and then implemented by the military through the Department of Defense (DoD). The authority of Congress was established first by the Second Continental Congress when on June 30, 1775, it established 69 Articles of War to govern the conduct of the Continental Army. Effective upon its ratification in 1789, Article I, Section 8 of the U.S. Constitution provided that Congress has the power to regulate the land and naval forces. On April 10, 1806, the U.S. Congress enacted 101 Articles of War (which applied to both the army and the navy). In 1947, the policies were made to apply to all of the services uniformly. The Uniform Code of Military Justice (UCMJ) was approved by Congress in 1949 and implemented in 1951.[1] (See Appendix 6.) The UCMJ has been revised and updated over the years.

The UCMJ is controversial today because, when it was instituted, it reflected the military world of World War II. The world today is vastly different. CAPT Lory Manning, U.S. Navy (Ret.), believes the system is broken because the UCMJ was based on the communication world that existed during World War II. Ships in the midst of the ocean had no way to communicate with those on the shore. Military units on mission in isolated terrain had no way to communicate with those even a few miles away. In that environment, the commanders had no one to fall back on when offenses occurred in their units and so they had to be the judge and jury for those offenses. At the same time, the unit's mission had to take its place as most important to accomplish. Manning says,

> The Uniform Code of Military Justice is based on a law passed by Congress in 1947 right after World War II and it was written with the World War II experience in mind. And it gives military commanders the sort of discretion they would need under World War II battlefield conditions: when a), you were probably remote,

like on some island in the middle of the Pacific or out in the middle of a battlefield somewhere in Europe or Italy or Northern Africa, when communication systems were light years away from what we have now. Now, even if you are on a ship in the middle of the Antarctic, you can pick up a phone and call somebody. But it gives the commander who might be under attack the discretion to put the mission before justice. Under some World War II situations, that was a very necessary thing, but it is just not the case anymore. Most people don't even understand that I am talking about commanders. That was written in there trusting the discretion of the CO to know when he is in battlefield conditions and then and only then, to have to make the tough decision about mission versus the war effort. Now, even in Iraq or Afghanistan, that this is not the case anymore, that the commander needs that kind of discretion. The commander ought to be told that justice comes first. And if you think mission comes first, you ought to have a good talk with your own boss, with your lawyer, and find a way to work around it. I am saying that the whole system needs to be re-thought in light of 21st Century conditions, particularly the use of telecommunication.[2]

The laws and policies of the military come down from the president and the secretary of defense to the unit commanders through the chain of command (Figure 3.1).[3]

The president of the United States, as commander-in-chief, is at the top of the chain and maintains civilian control over the military. The unit commander is at the lowest level of the chain. It is the unit commander who is charged with keeping the unit ready for the mission and to administer justice when confronted with on-base situations.

SEXUAL ASSAULT PREVENTION RESPONSE PROGRAM

The DoD established the Sexual Assault Prevention Response (SAPR) program in 2005 to promote prevention, encourage increased reporting, and improve victims' response capabilities.[4] The Sexual Assault Prevention Response Office (SAPRO) is responsible for the policies of this program and oversight that assesses effectiveness. Criminal investigative matters and legal processes relevant to sexual assault are assigned to the DoD Inspector General and the Judge Advocates General of the departments.[5] Primarily, sexual assault response coordinators (SARCs) implement the programs at military installations, including coordinating response to and reporting of incidents.[6]

DEPARTMENT OF DEFENSE AND SERVICES' POLICIES

In general, the DoD "is committed to being a national leader in preventing and responding to sexual assault."[7] To comply with military mission and law, DoD and each service have policies in place. In addition, the DoD

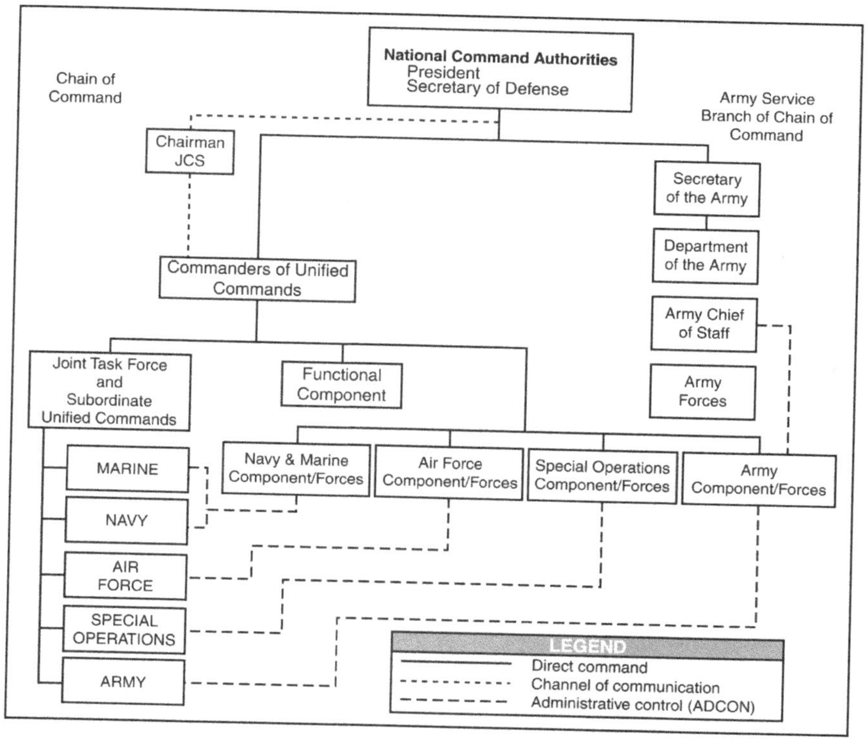

Figure 3.1.

Chain of Command (U.S. Army War College. "Chain of Command." The Battle Book IV: A Guide for Spouses in Leadership Roles. 2009: Ch. 2).

SAPR strategic plan states that establishing department policy is "essential to refining a professional culture and command climate/environment." It is key "to operationalizing, synchronizing, and ensuring consistent SAPR Program execution across the Department."

DoD Policy

The DoD's policy goal is to attain "a culture free of sexual assault through an environment of prevention, training, response capability, victim support, reporting procedures, and appropriate accountability that enhances the safety and well being of all persons." Further the SAPR program is to focus on the victim, doing what is necessary and appropriate to support his or her recovery; if the victim is a service member, to support recovery to be fully mission capable and engaged. Care is to be gender responsive, culturally competent, and recovery oriented.[8]

To develop policy to prevent and respond to sexual assault incidents, DoD took several steps, for example, establishing a standardized department-wide definition and procedures for confidentially reporting. "Sexual assault" is defined as

> Intentional sexual contact, characterized by the use of force, threats, intimidation, abuse of authority, or when the victim does not or cannot consent, [It] includes rape, forcible sodomy (oral or anal sex), and other unwanted sexual contact that is aggravated, abusive, or wrongful (to include unwanted and inappropriate sexual contact), or attempts to commit these acts.[9]

Victims have two reporting options, unrestricted (preferred by DoD) or restricted. Unrestricted reporting involves informing the chain of command who may initiate an investigation by the appropriate military criminal investigative organization. Restricted reporting allows a victim to confidentially disclose to select individuals and receive care without initiating a criminal investigation. A restricted report usually may be made only to SARCs, victim advocates, or medical personnel.[10]

The SAPR program materials are to be standardized at all appropriate levels and focus on awareness, prevention, and response. All commanders must establish and support sexual assault awareness and prevention programs and law enforcement and criminal justice procedures that make it possible for persons to be held accountable for their actions.[11]

Sexual assault cases are to be treated as emergency cases with the availability of, at all locations, immediate, trained sexual assault response capability. Victims are to be protected from coercion, retaliation, and reprisal. They are to be protected, be given dignity and respect, and receive timely access to medical treatment, including emergency care.[12]

Noteworthy are selected policies that aid treatment of sexual assault, for example, discipline and conduct, chain of command/reporting structure, and impediments to reporting.

The Services' Policies

In 2011, the Government Accountability Office (GAO) reported that the services had developed and implemented their own guidance on sexual assault investigations and, in some instances, took different approaches to investigations. Upon GAO's recommendation for consistent policy, DoD developed and implemented policy guidance on conducting investigations.[13] Key policy is similar throughout the services. Sexual assault will be eliminated through commander-focused, implemented, and trained response capability. Prevention depends on risk reduction, education and awareness training, victim support, confidential reporting procedures, and offender accountability to enhance the safety and well-being of everyone. Policy pledges to ensure victims are treated seriously according to policy with dignity, fairness, and respect; and to create a culture without fear so that victims are encouraged to report incidents. Specific service position statements follow:

Air Force

Air force policy states in part:

> The United States Air Force will not tolerate sexual assault. Sexual assault is criminal conduct. It falls short of the standards America expects of its men and women in uniform. It violates Air Force Core Values. . . . Inherent in the core values are: Integrity First, Service before Self; Excellence in All We Do. To have integrity is also to have respect: self-respect, mutual respect, and respect for the Air Force as an institution.
>
> It is Air Force policy to:
>
> 1.4.1. Eliminate sexual assault within the Department of the Air Force by fostering a culture of prevention, providing education and training, response capability, victim support, reporting procedures, and accountability that enhances the safety and well-being of all its members.[14]

Army

Army policy states in part:

> Sexual assault is a criminal offense that has no place in the Army. It degrades mission readiness by devastating the Army's ability to work effectively as a team. Every soldier who is aware of sexual assault should immediately (within 24 hours) report incidents. Sexual assault is incompatible with Army values and is punishable under the UCMJ and other Federal and local civilian laws.[15]

Marines

Marine sexual assault policy states in part:

> Sexual assault is a crime that is completely incompatible with our core values of honor, courage, and commitment. It is an affront to the basic American principles we so bravely defend. Sexual assault goes against everything we claim to be as Marines.[16]

Navy

The navy's policy states in part:

> Sexual assault is a criminal act incompatible with the Department of Navy (DON) core values, high standards of professionalism, and personal discipline. Military

personnel alleged to have committed a sexual assault offense may be subject to trial and, if found guilty, punishment by court martial ... [or] administrative separation. ... Commanders shall take appropriate action under U.S. laws and regulations.[17]

Coast Guard

Coast Guard policy states in part:

The ultimate purpose of [the SAPR] ... program, is to build a culture of prevention, sensitive response and accountability in keeping with the Coast Guard's values of honor, respect, and devotion to duty.[18]

Zero Tolerance

Zero tolerance directives and policies have been in existence over 20 years,[19] and, according to Manning, "Of such 'zero tolerance' policies one of the main questions that we are looking at right now, and we don't know the answer to, is, this is something the services, with the Congress looking over them, have been working seriously on for five to ten years now. They have been saying 'zero tolerance' for five to ten years now. They've done a lot of things with changes to the law, with educating people in command, everybody in the military and what's hot right now is to figure out how much any of this has worked. Is what they are doing effective? Are the numbers going down? We don't know. Are people more willing to come forward and report? More people are reporting it, but we don't know if that is because it is happening more or because more people are beginning to feel more comfortable coming forward and thinking that maybe they will get justice. So, one question is what we have done so far effective? Don't know. It may be, it may not be. Or, it may be somewhat effective. It's an ongoing thing. It's very hard to evaluate, because sexual assault, not just in the military, but on college campuses or anywhere, is one of the most underreported crimes that there is. I think at least of the felonies, the least likely to be reported whether in a civilian or military situation. So nobody knows how often it used to happen. We do surveys and things and are gathering data, but there is nothing to measure it against."[20] The concern that zero tolerance has not worked or has not been applied is ongoing.

LAWS PROHIBIT SEXUAL ASSAULT

The military definition of "sexual assault" is inclusive.

The UCMJ defines two types of sexual assault: sexual contact offenses and sexual penetration offenses. Sexual contact offense is defined as intentional sexual contact characterized by use of force, threats, intimidation, or abuse of authority or when the victim does not or cannot consent. Sexual penetration offenses include rape, aggravated sexual contact, abusive sexual contact, forcible sodomy (forced oral or anal sex), or attempts to commit these acts.[21]

Sexual assault is not one specific crime, but rather a wide range of sex crimes that represent a broad spectrum of offenses from rape to nonconsensual sodomy to wrongful sexual contact as well as attempts to commit these offenses. The definition is derived from a DoD directive based in Article 120 of the UCMJ.[22]

UNIFORM CODE OF MILITARY JUSTICE

UCMJ Revisions, 2014

Recent revisions to the UCMJ pertaining to sexual assault are mandated by the National Defense Authorization Act for FY2014.[23] According to David Vergun of the *Army News Service*, the changes are sweeping, particularly in cases of rape and sexual assault. The *Army News Service* reported that LTC John L. Kiel Jr., the policy branch chief at the army's Criminal Law Division in the Office of the Judge Advocate General, stated that the changes are the most that have been made to the *Manual for Courts-Martial* since a full committee studied it decades ago. Articles 32, 60, 120, and 125 were the main provisions of the UCMJ that were rewritten.[24] On June 13, 2014, President Barack Obama signed the amendments into law and subsequently they are placed at the end of the *Manual*.[25]

U.S. senator Claire McCaskill (D-MO) stated on her Web page, "Commanders have been stripped of the ability to overturn convictions, and will be held accountable under rigorous new standards." These standards are summarized in Table 3.1.

Article 32 Revisions

Article 32 hearings seek to determine if enough evidence exists to justify a general court-martial, the most serious type of court-martial used for felony level offenses such as rape and murder.[26] According to Vergun, this revision requires judge advocates to serve as investigating officers. Congress decided that trained lawyers, the judge advocates, often are in the best position to make determinations to go forward with general courts-martial.

LTC Kiel stated that an additional impact to courts-martial practice is the new requirement for a special victims counsel to provide support and advice to the alleged victim. For example, this counsel must inform the victim he or she may attend any forthcoming hearings such as pretrial

Table 3.1.

Summary of Congress-Approved and President-Approved Series of UCMJ Sweeping Reforms as Part of Annual Defense Bill, 2013.

- Commanders have been stripped of the ability to overturn convictions, and will be held accountable under rigorous new standards.
- Victims who report a sexual assault will get their own independent lawyer to protect their rights and fight for their interests—a reform that has no parallel in the civilian justice system.
- Civilian review is now required if a commander decides against a prosecution in a sexual assault case when a prosecutor wants to go to trial.
- Dishonorable discharge is now a required minimum sentence for anyone convicted of a sexual assault.
- It is now a crime for any service member to retaliate against a victim who reports a sexual assault.
- The pre-trial "Article 32" process, which came under scrutiny following a case at the Naval Academy, has been reformed to better protect victims.
- The statute of limitations in these cases has now been eliminated, a particularly important development in a sustained battle against sexual assaults.

Source: U.S. senator Claire McCaskill (D-MO), "Curbing Sexual Assault in the U.S. Military," *Combating Sexual Violence*, http://www.mccaskill.senate.gov/violence.

confinement, parole board, and clemency. The victim also will be notified in advance of trial dates and be informed of any delays. Additionally, the counsels "may represent the alleged victims during trial, ensuring their rights are not violated, as under the Rape Shield Rule, for example. The Rape Shield Rule, or Military Rule of Evidence 412, prevents admission of evidence concerning sexual predisposition and behavior of an alleged victim of sexual assault."[27] For example, alleged rape and sexual assault victims are no longer subject to extensive interrogation at the Article 32 hearing about the alleged victim's motivations, medical history, and apparel, as occurred at the case involving football players at the U.S. Naval Academy in June 2013.[28]

Article 60 Revisions

Article 60 revisions prohibit the convening authority from adjusting any findings of guilt for felony offenses where the sentence is longer than six months or contains a discharge. The convening authority cannot change findings for any sex crime, irrespective of sentencing time.

Additionally, military character of the accused should have no bearing on whether or not the accused has committed a sexual assault or other type of felony.[29]

Also, if the convening authority disagrees with the staff judge advocate that the case should go to a general court-martial, the case has to go to the secretary of the service concerned to decide whether to go forward. In rape or sexual assault in which the staff judge advocate and the convening authority agree not to go forward because of a lack of evidence, that case has to go up to the next highest general court-martial convening authority for an independent review.

Articles 120 and 125 Revisions

Articles 120 and 125 now include mandatory minimum punishments: dishonorable discharge for enlisted service members and dismissal for officers, according to Kiel. Article 120 applies to rape and sexual assault upon adults or children and other sex crimes, and Article 125 addresses forcible sodomy. In addition, the accused now must appear before a general court-martial with no opportunity to be tried at a summary (for minor misconduct) or special court-martial (for intermediate offenses). It is now mandated that all sexual assault and rape cases be tried only by general court-martial. The five-year statute of limitations on rape and sexual assault on adults and children under Article 120 cases no longer exists.

And finally, in keeping with previous Supreme Court precedent, Congress repealed the offense of consensual sodomy under Article 125 and barred anyone convicted of rape, sexual assault, incest, or forcible sodomy under state or federal law from enlisting or being commissioned into military service.[30]

Left as Is: Chain of Command Power

Whether the chain of command should remain involved in the handling of sexual assault cases is a most controversial issue. From my research, I get the impression that a lot of the commanders wanted to keep the power within the chain of command. Manning, explains why: "Number 1, because they have been told that is where it belongs. They can't conceive [otherwise]. Number 2, it's easier for them to keep doing things the old way."[31]

Article 120, Rape and Sexual Assault Generally

Rape

Rape is defined as occurring when using unlawful force against another person that causes or is likely to cause death or grievous bodily harm; threatening or placing another person in fear that any person will be subjected to death, grievous bodily harm, or kidnapping; first rendering another person unconscious; or using force or threat of force, or without the knowledge or consent of that person, to administer a drug, intoxicant, or other similar substance and thereby substantially impairing the ability of that other person to appraise or control conduct.[32]

Aggravated Sexual Contact and Abusive Sexual Contact

Sexual assault is further defined with the terms "aggravated sexual contact" and "abusive sexual contact."

> Aggravated sexual contact applies when a person commits or causes sexual contact upon or by another person, if to do so would violate the subsection on rape had the sexual contact been a sexual act, is guilty of aggravated sexual contact. Abusive sexual contact occurs when a person commits or causes sexual contact upon or by another person, if to do so would violate the subsection on sexual assault had the sexual contact been a sexual act, is guilty of abusive sexual contact.[33]

Sexual Act and Sexual Contact

Article 120 delineates the differences between the terms "sexual act" and "sexual contact," "bodily harm" and "grievous bodily harm," and "force" and "unlawful force." The term "sexual act" means contact between the penis and vulva or anus or mouth, and contact involving the penis occurs upon penetration, however slight; or the penetration, however slight, of the vulva or anus or mouth of another by any part of the body by any object with the intent to abuse, humiliate, harass, or degrade any person or to arouse or gratify the sexual desire of any person.

The term "sexual contact" means touching, or causing another person to touch; threatening or placing another person in fear; touch, either directly or through the clothing, the genitalia, anus, groin, breast, inner thigh, or buttocks with an intent to abuse, humiliate, or degrade any person; or any touching, or causing another person to touch directly or through the clothing, any body part of any person, if done with an intent to arouse or gratify the sexual desire of any person. Touching may be accomplished by any part of the body.[34]

Bodily Harm and Grievous Bodily Harm

The terms "bodily harm" and "grievous bodily harm" are differentiated. "Bodily harm" is any offensive touching of another, however slight, including any nonconsensual sexual act or nonconsensual sexual contact. The term "grievous bodily harm" means serious bodily injury, including fractured or dislocated bones, deep cuts, torn members of the body, serious damage to internal organs, and other severe bodily injuries. Not included are minor injuries such as a black eye or a bloody nose.[35]

Force and Unlawful Force and Threatening Conduct

Force differs from unlawful force in that the term "force" involves using a weapon or overpowering physical strength that would restrain, or injure a person; or inflict physical harm sufficient to coerce or compel submission by the victim whereas unlawful force is done without legal justification or excuse.[36]

The term "threatening" or "placing another person in fear" means communicating or acting in such a way to cause a reasonable fear that noncompliance will result in the victim or another person being subjected to the wrongful action contemplated by the communication or action.[37]

Article 125, Sodomy

The text of military law regarding sodomy first defines the act and then states punishment for committing the act. It states:

> Any person subject to this chapter who engages in unnatural carnal copulation with another person of the same or opposite sex or with an animal is guilty of sodomy. Penetration, however slight, is sufficient to complete the offense. Any person found guilty of sodomy shall be punished as a court-martial may direct.[38]

Elements that further stipulate the crime of sodomy include: That the act was done with a child under the age of 12, or with a child who had attained the age of 12 but was under the age of 16; and that it was done by force and without the consent of the other person.

Article 80, Attempts

Attempts include acts done with specific intent to commit an offense that amounts to more than mere preparation and tending, even though failing, to effect its commission, is an attempt to commit that offense. Offenders are subject to a court-martial and may be convicted of an attempt to commit an offense although it appears on the trial that the offense was consummated.[39]

SEXUAL HARASSMENT

The Pentagon released a report on May 15, 2014, that showed there were nearly 1,400 reported incidents of sexual harassment in 2013. Of the 1,366 cases reported, 59 percent were substantiated. Military-wide reported harassment cases were significantly lower than the number of reported sexual assaults. A significant finding of a 2012 survey revealed that of the sexual assaults that took place that year, nearly 30 percent of women and 19 percent of men reported that their offenders had sexually harassed them before and/or after the incident took place. The 2013 report stated, "This finding is reflected in similar DoD surveys and implies a direct connection between sexual harassment and sexual assault, both of which are unacceptable."[40]

Just as sexual assault covers a broad range of prohibited behaviors, sexual harassment is viewed differently than in civilian society, which acknowledges that it can include the crimes rape and assault. In fact, sexual harassment was not included in the two-volume DoD report of 2012 because incidents of sexual harassment fall under the purview of the Office of the Secretary of Defense, Office of Diversity Management and Equal Opportunity.[41] Sexual harassment is a form of sex discrimination that violates Title VII of the Civil Rights Act of 1964. The Equal Employment Opportunity Commission enforces these cases.[42] DoD policy defines "sexual harassment" as:

> a form of sex discrimination that involves unwelcome sexual advances, requests for sexual favors, and other verbal or physical conduct of a sexual nature when submission to or rejection of such conduct is made either explicitly or implicitly a term or condition of a person's job, pay or career; or submission to or rejection of such conduct by a person is used as a basis for career or employment decisions affecting that person; or such conduct interferes with an individual's performance or creates an intimidating, hostile or offensive environment.[43]

RAND's 2014 report of estimated prevalence of active-duty service members who experienced sexual harassment is summarized in Table 3.2, which represents the totals of the two types of harassment, *quid pro quo* and hostile environment, in Tables 3.3 and 3.4, respectively.

Of the two types of sexual harassment, *quid pro quo* and hostile environment, *quid pro quo* sexual harassment refers to conditions placed on a person's career or terms of employment in return for sexual favors. Threats of adverse actions are made if the victim does not submit or promises of favorable actions made if the person does submit. Army regulation provides as an example, "a Soldier who is not recommended for promotion and who believes that his or her squad leader recommended another Soldier in his or her squad for promotion on the basis of provided or promised sexual favors, not upon merit or ability."[44] This example also demonstrates that *quid pro quo* may affect a third person, or a bystander. Allegations of sexual favoritism or general discrimination may occur when a person feels unfairly deprived of recognition, advancement, or career opportunities because of favoritism shown to another soldier or civilian employee on the basis of a sexual relationship.[45]

Table 3.2.

Estimated Prevalence of Active-Duty Service Members Who Experienced Sexual Harassment in 2014, by Gender and Service Branch.

Service	Total %	Men %	Women %
Total	8.85	6.61	21.57
Army	9.80	7.67	23.07
Navy	11.78	8.37	27.82
Air Force	4.99	3.29	12.43
Marines	7.69	6.11	27.30

Source: Andrew R. Morral and Kristie L. Gore, *Sexual Assault and Sexual Harassment in the U.S. Military: Top-Line Results from the RAND Military Workplace Study*, RAND Corporation, National Defense Research Institute, 2014: 15, Table E7. Used by permission of RAND Corporation through the Copyright Clearance Center, Inc.

Quid pro quo harassment unlike hostile work environment is rare. RAND discovered that about 1 in 60 women and 1 in 300 men experienced *quid pro quo* in 2014. Air force members were at lower risk for both types of harassment. And even though the number experiencing *quid pro quo* is less, it may represent a serious crime. The majority of individuals who experienced *quid pro quo* were also sexually harassed under *sexually hostile work environment*.[46]

Table 3.3.

Estimated Prevalence of Active-Duty Service Members Who Experienced Quid Pro Quo Sexual Harassment in 2014, by Gender and Service Branch.

Service	Total %	Men %	Women %
Total	0.54	0.35	1.66
Army	0.65	0.41	2.12
Navy	0.80	0.50	2.22
Air Force	0.14	0.06	0.50
Marines	0.50	0.37	2.12

Source: Andrew R. Morral and Kristie L. Gore, *Sexual Assault and Sexual Harassment in the U.S. Military: Top-Line Results from the RAND Military Workplace Study*, RAND Corporation, National Defense Research Institute, 2014: 14, Table 6. Used by permission of RAND Corporation through the Copyright Clearance Center, Inc.

Table 3.4.

Estimated Prevalence of Active-Duty Service Members Who Experienced Hostile Environment Sexual Harassment in 2014, by Gender and Service Branch.

Service	Total %	Men %	Women %
Total	8.80	6.58	21.41
Army	9.75	7.65	22.87
Navy	11.73	8.34	27.71
Air Force	4.96	3.26	12.32
Marines	7.68	6.11	27.19

Source: Andrew R. Morral and Kristie L. Gore, *Sexual Assault and Sexual Harassment in the U.S. Military: Top-Line Results from the RAND Military Workplace Study*, RAND Corporation, National Defense Research Institute, 2014: 13, Table 5. Used by permission of RAND Corporation through the Copyright Clearance Center, Inc.

Hostile Environment sexual harassment subjects a person to offensive, unwanted, and unsolicited comments and behavior of a sexual nature that interferes with that person's work performance or creates an intimidating, hostile, or offensive working environment. Examples include the use of derogatory gender-biased terms, comments about body parts, suggestive pictures, explicit jokes, and unwanted touching.[47]

POLICY, LAWS, AND SEXUAL ASSAULT

The policies and laws that address sexual assault are changing in the effort to reduce or eliminate sexual assault in the military. The changes in the 2014 Defense Authorization Act are extensive and, if enforced, may be effective in achieving that goal.

CHAPTER 4

Jurisdiction and Courts

> Not all military personnel offenses are tried in military courts . . . nor should they be.
>
> —RADM Duvall M. "Mac" Williams, USN (Ret.), former NIS Commander[1]

JURISDICTION

Sexual assaults involving military personnel have been traditionally tried in courts-martial. This is no longer the case. The case may be resolved in military court, but it may be tried in civilian court or within the military's Family Advocacy Program (FAP).

Traditional Military Court Jurisdiction

Until the 1950s, offenses involving military personnel were tried in military courts. Even dependents of military personnel stationed in foreign countries were tried in military courts.[2] The Supreme Court generally held that it lacked jurisdiction to review decisions of military courts. The motivation for this "hands-off" attitude rested on strong historical precedent. Chief Justice Earl Warren said, "The tradition of our country, from the time of the Revolution until now, has supported the military establishment's broad power to deal with its own personnel." This long-standing policy, reaffirmed with the comments of Chief Justice Earl Warren, lay largely unchallenged before *O'Callahan v. Parker*.[3]

Trial in Civilian Court

O'Callahan v. Parker[4] determined that the proper jurisdiction for trying some crimes by military personnel is the civilian court, not the military. The case involved Army Sergeant O'Callahan who was:

> stationed in July 1956, at Fort Shafter, Oahu, in the Territory of Hawaii. On the night of July 20, while on an evening pass, petitioner and a friend left the post dressed in civilian clothes and went into Honolulu. After a few beers in the bar of a hotel, petitioner entered the residential part of the hotel where he broke into the room of a young girl and assaulted and attempted to rape her. While fleeing from her room onto Waikiki Beach, he was apprehended by a hotel security officer who delivered him to the Honolulu city police for questioning. After determining that he was a member of the Armed Forces, the city police delivered petitioner to the military police. After extensive interrogation, petitioner confessed and was placed in military confinement.
>
> [O'Callahan] was charged with attempted rape, house-breaking, and assault with intent to rape, in violation of Articles 80, 130, and 134 of the Uniform Code of Military Justice. He was tried by court-martial, convicted on all counts, and given a sentence of 10 years' imprisonment at hard labor, forfeiture of all pay and allowances, and dishonorable discharge. His conviction was affirmed by the Army Board of Review and, subsequently, by the United States Court of Military Appeals.
>
> Under confinement at the United States Penitentiary at Lewisburg, Pennsylvania, petitioner filed a petition for writ of habeas corpus in the United States District Court for the Middle District of Pennsylvania, alleging, inter alia, that the court-martial was without jurisdiction to try him for nonmilitary offenses committed off-post while on an evening pass. The District Court denied relief without considering the issue on the merits, and the Court of Appeals for the Third Circuit affirmed. This Court granted certiorari limited to the question:
>
> "Does a court-martial, held under the Articles of War, Tit. 10, U.S. C. § 801 et seq., have jurisdiction to try a member of the Armed Forces who is charged with commission of a crime cognizable in a civilian court and having no military significance, alleged to have been committed off-post and while on leave, thus depriving him of his constitutional rights to indictment by a grand jury and trial by a petit jury in a civilian court?"
>
> [The Supreme Court] accordingly decided that since petitioner's crimes were not service connected, he could not be tried by court-martial but rather was entitled to trial by the civilian courts.[5]

Military Courts and Military Dependents

The issue of dependents of military personnel stationed in foreign countries was decided in *Reid v. Covert* in 1956.[6] Clarice Covert was tried and convicted for the murder of her husband, a sergeant in the U.S. Air Force. At the time of the murder, Covert was residing at an airbase in England as a military dependent; she was not a member of the armed forces. She was tried and convicted by court-martial in the United States that was authorized under Article 2(11) of the Uniform Code of Military Justice.

Mrs. Covert alleged that her conviction by military authorities had violated her constitutional rights under the Fifth and Sixth Amendments. The district court, holding that "a civilian is entitled to a civilian trial," granted her petition. The government appealed to the U.S. Supreme Court.

In its initial decision of the case (351 U.S. 487), the Court held that Mrs. Covert's military trial was constitutional: the right to a trial by jury did not apply to American citizens tried in foreign lands. The Court held that Congress could provide for trial by any means it saw fit so long as such means were reasonable and consistent with due process. Justice Felix Frankfurter issued a lengthy reservation, and Chief Justice Earl Warren (with Justices Hugo L. Black and William O. Douglas) issued a strong dissent.

The Court agreed to a rehearing. The question the Supreme Court had to answer was: Do American citizens abroad retain the rights granted to them by the Bill of Rights thus rendering Article 2(11) of the UCMJ unconstitutional?

The Court answered, "Yes." In a 6–2 opinion written by Justice Hugo L. Black and joined by Chief Justice Earl Warren and Justices William O. Douglas and William J. Brennan Jr. with Felix Frankfurter and John Harlan concurring, the Court held that American citizens outside of the territorial jurisdiction of the United States retain the protections guaranteed by the U.S. Constitution. Accordingly, the decision of the lower court granting Mrs. Covert's habeas petition was affirmed. Black wrote:

> [W]e reject the idea that when the United States acts against citizens abroad it can do so free of the Bill of Rights. The United States is entirely a creature of the Constitution. Its power and authority have no other source. It can only act in accordance with all the limitations imposed by the Constitution. When the Government reaches out to punish a citizen who is abroad, the shield which the Bill of Rights and other parts of the Constitution provide to protect his life and liberty should not be stripped away just because he happens to be in another land.

Consequently, the plurality asserted that neither a treaty nor the Necessary and Proper Clause could confer upon Congress the sweeping power to try civilians by military court-martial[7]. The Supreme Court ruled that Article 2(11) of the UCMJ, providing for the trial by court-martial of "all persons . . . accompanying the armed forces" of the United States in foreign countries, cannot constitutionally be applied, in capital cases, to the trial of civilian dependents accompanying members of the armed forces overseas in time of peace The decision was 6 votes for Covert, 2 vote(s) against.[8]

Family Advocacy Program[9]

When a military service member is involved in actions that are domestic in nature, the situation is handled through the FAP. Each branch of the military has a FAP that is similar if not identical in what they do. In the army's program, its mission is:

> The US Army Family Advocacy Program is dedicated to the prevention, education, prompt reporting, investigation, intervention and treatment of spouse and child abuse. The program provides a variety of services to soldiers and families to enhance their relationship skills and improve their quality of life. This mission is accomplished through a variety of groups, seminars, workshops and counseling and intervention services.[10]

The FAP offers programs that include: (1) exceptional family member program, (2) new parent support program, (3) transitional compensation program, and (4) victim advocacy program. The victim advocacy program provides

> comprehensive assistance and support to victims of domestic abuse and sexual assault, including crisis intervention, safety planning, assistance in securing medical treatment for injuries, information on legal rights and proceedings, and referral to military and civilian shelters and other resources available to victims. Victim Advocacy services are available 24 hours a day/7 days a week to Soldiers and Family members.[11]

Domestic abuse is a major concern of the FAP services. "Domestic abuse" is defined as:

> an offense under the United States Code, the Uniform Code of Military Justice, or State law involving the use, attempted use, or threatened use of force or violence against a person of the opposite sex, or the violation of a lawful order issued for the protection of a person of the opposite sex, who is: (1) A current or former spouse; (2) A person with whom the abuser shares a child in common; or (3) A current or former intimate partner with whom the abuser shares or has shared a common domicile.[12]

The victim of domestic abuse has options for reporting. All branches of the military provide similar options; the navy's options are:

> Victims of domestic abuse are often afraid to get help. They may fear that reporting the abuse will only make things worse, or they may feel ashamed for tolerating the abuse for so long. Victims may fear losing the financial support provided by their abuser, including housing or medical benefits. Some victims may feel trapped because they fear ruining their spouse's military career or feel pressure to keep the relationship intact for the sake of the children.

The Navy is committed to addressing and ending domestic abuse and offers victims two different reporting options for seeking help. With either option, victims have access to victim advocacy services, counseling and medical care.

Restricted Reporting

Victims who prefer confidential assistance that does not include notification of law enforcement or military command may contact a FAP supervisor/clinician, victim advocate or a healthcare provider to request a restricted report.

A restricted report allows victims to evaluate their relationship choices while maintaining control over what and how much information to share with others. Because victim safety is a priority, victims at imminent risk of serious harm cannot use the restricted report option. A restricted report is also not available in cases where child abuse has occurred.

A victim of domestic abuse who makes a restricted report may receive victim advocacy services without law enforcement notification or command involvement. Victim advocacy services (VAS) include help developing a safety plan to prevent further abuse, referral to counseling, medical care, information about Military Protective Orders and information about military and local civilian community resources.

Unrestricted Reporting

Victims may contact the FAP, military police or chain of command to make an unrestricted report if they want an investigation of an abuse incident and command involvement.

The command can offer the victim added support and protection. An unrestricted report also gives the command the discretion to take administrative action against the offender.

For victims who choose to make an unrestricted report, a FAP advocate will also assist victims in making a report to law enforcement, provide information on legal rights and offer assistance in applying for Transitional Compensation, if applicable.

The choices in an abusive relationship are never easy. But, knowing that there are options for seeking help is the first step in ending abuse and having a safer and happier life.[13]

Courts-Martial

The UCMJ gives courts-martial jurisdiction over service members 16 as well as several other categories of individuals to the commanding officer. Jurisdiction of a court-martial does not depend on where the offense was committed; it depends solely on the status of the accused.[14]

The UCMJ authorizes three types of courts-martial: (1) summary court-martial, (2) special court-martial, and (3) general court-martial. Depending on the severity of the alleged offense, the accused's commanding officer enjoys great discretion with respect to the type of court-martial to convene. Generally, each of the courts-martial provides fundamental constitutional and procedural rights to the accused, including, but not limited to, the right to a personal representative or counsel, the opportunity to confront evidence and witnesses, and the right to have a decision reviewed by a lawyer or a court of appeals. The Military Rules of

Evidence apply to all classifications of courts-martial. An accused must be proven guilty beyond a reasonable doubt.[15]

Summary Court-Martial

The summary court-martial can adjudicate minor offenses allegedly committed by enlisted service members. It can adjudge maximum punishments of 30 days' confinement, hard labor without confinement for 45 days, restriction to specified limits for 45 days, forfeiture of two-thirds' pay for one month, and reduction to the lowest pay grade. In the case of enlisted members above pay grade E-4, the summary court-martial may not adjudge confinement or hard labor without confinement and can only reduce the accused to the next lower pay grade. Summary courts-martial are composed of one commissioned officer who need not be a lawyer. The accused must consent to the proceedings and normally is not entitled to a lawyer. If an accused refuses to consent to a trial by summary court-martial, a trial may be ordered by special or general court-martial as may be appropriate, at the discretion of the convening authority. A summary court-martial may try only enlisted personnel for noncapital offenses. The punishment that may be imposed depends on the grade of the accused. In the case of enlisted members above the fourth pay grade, a summary court-martial may impose any punishment not forbidden by the law except death, dismissal, dishonorable or bad conduct discharge, confinement for more than one month, hard labor without confinement for more than 45 days, restriction to specified limits for more than two months, or forfeiture of more than two-thirds of one month's pay. In the case of all other enlisted members, the court-martial may also impose confinement for not more than one month and may reduce the accused to the lowest pay grade, E-1.

The accused has the absolute right to refuse trial by summary court-martial. The accused does not have the right to representation by an attorney. The accused does have the right to cross-examine witnesses, to call witnesses and produce evidence, and to testify or remain silent.[16]

Special Court-Martial

The special court-martial can try any service member for any noncapital offense or, under presidential regulation, capital offenses. Special courts-martial generally try offenses that are considered misdemeanors. A special court-martial can be composed of a military judge alone, not less than three members, or a military judge and not less than three members. Contrary to civilian criminal trials, the agreement of only two-thirds of the members of a court-martial is needed to find the accused guilty. Otherwise, the accused is acquitted. There are no "hung juries" in courts-martial. Regardless of the offenses tried, the maximum punishment allowed at a special court-martial is confinement for one year, hard labor without confinement for up to three months, forfeiture of two-thirds' pay per month for up to one year, reduction in pay grade, and a bad conduct discharge. The accused is entitled to an appointed military attorney or a military counsel of his or her selection, or he or she can hire a civilian counsel at no expense to the government.[17]

General Court-Martial

A general court-martial is the highest trial level in military law and is usually used for the most serious offenses. It is composed of a military judge sitting alone, or not less than five members and a military judge. It can adjudge, within the limits prescribed for each offense, a wide range of punishments to include confinement; reprimand; forfeitures of up to all pay and allowances; reduction to the lowest enlisted pay grade; punitive discharge (bad conduct discharge, dishonorable discharge, or dismissal); restriction; fines; and, for certain offenses, death. The accused is entitled to an appointed military attorney or a military counsel of his or her selection, or the accused can hire civilian counsel at no expense to the government. Prior to convening a general court-martial, a pretrial investigation must be conducted. This investigation, known as an Article 32 hearing, is meant to ensure that there is a basis for prosecution. An investigating officer, who must be a commissioned officer, presides, and the accused has the same entitlements to counsel as in special courts-martial. However, unlike in a civilian grand jury investigation, where the accused has no access to the proceedings, the accused is afforded the opportunity to examine the evidence presented against him, cross-examine witnesses, and present his own arguments. If the investigation uncovers evidence that the accused has committed an offense not charged, the investigating officer can recommend that new charges be added. Likewise, if the investigating officer believes that evidence is insufficient to support a charge, he can recommend that it be dismissed. Once the Article 32 investigation is complete, the investigating officer makes recommendations to the convening authority (CA) via the CA's legal adviser. The legal adviser, in turn, provides the CA with a formal written recommendation, known as the Article 34, UCMJ advice, as to the disposition of the charges. The CA then determines whether to convene a court-martial or dismiss the charges.[18]

CHANGES TO THE UNIFORM CODE OF MILITARY JUSTICE

The 2014 National Defense Authorization Act made sweeping changes to the UCMJ, particularly in cases of rape and sexual assault. The changes include the elimination of the "good soldier" defense and allowing the victim to have input on whether the case is tried in military or civilian court.[19] The changes made improved the situation but left unanswered the question of whether trying sexual assault cases outside the chain of command will improve the cohesion, readiness, and morale of the troops.[20] The changes do not resolve the question whether the authority should be removed from the chain of command and given to independent military prosecutors and judges.[21]

Rear Admiral D. M. "Mac." Williams Jr., USN (Ret.), former Naval Investigative Service (NIS) Commander, believes the system does not need to be changed: "Notwithstanding all the problems that the military has had with these issues, the commanders have been making an effort to try to deal with them properly and appropriately." Williams believes more scrutiny is needed with regard to jurisdiction: "[In many cases], the military doesn't have any jurisdiction under the UCMJ. And that connection has to be demonstrated or the case gets referred to a civilian jurisdiction for them to deal with."[22]

RADM Willams's position is detailed by Judge Advocate General Maj. Steven J. Smart, U.S. Air Force. Maj. Smart holds the view that the commander-driven system is appropriate for two reasons: "First, discipline is essential to command and control which is key in maintaining a combat effective force. Second, the commander's authority over the criminal process enhances service members' responsiveness to command. Commanders need to say to subordinates, 'I have zero tolerance for drug abuse/discrimination/hazing/ sex assault/etc' and back up their words with action. Commanders sending cases to criminal trial reinforces the message."[23]

The military's unique role in protecting the national security of the United States requires the system of justice designed especially for that role, contends Smart. That military society fights wars to protect civilian society makes it different from civilian society. The Supreme Court's decision in *Parker v. Levy*, 417 U.S. 733 (1974) recognized this difference. Smart concludes "It is military discipline that transforms a collective group of individuals into combat effective units and it is the Uniform Code of Military Justice (UCMJ) that provides commanders with the means of maintaining good order and discipline."[24]

"In the UCMJ, Congress gave commanders gate-keeping authority over criminal prosecution. The military court system was created to administer the UCMJ to protect Constitutional guarantees such as right to counsel and to confront witnesses, and it also meets Constitutional requirements for substantive and procedural due process."[25] In addition, the juries or court members who are chosen according to UCMJ Article 35 tend to be more educated than civilian juries. They are chosen based upon their age, education, training, experience, length of service, and judicial temperament. Also, military courts are more transparent than civilian courts; for example, grand jury proceedings are often secret where the indictment is often sealed. By contrast, Smart states, "Article 32 hearings in the military justice system are open and the results are a matter of public record."[26]

MAJ Lillian Pfluke U.S. Army (Ret.) says,

> The chain of command is not always capable of taking optimal action, because sometimes the chain of command is involved and always the chain of command is trying to support your guys, your people, and if you have two people that are accusing each other of stuff, then it's hard to know which side to come down on. The military chain of command isn't always equipped to handle that as well as an unbiased person dealing with it may be.[27]

Pfluke states: "I think [the chain of command handling sexual; assault cases] can really be a problem. I will say it again: I think that the most important issue of the military is that the chain of command is not always an unbiased observer in this kind of thing. If so many times, both members of the incident are in the same chain of command, and then you have the whole problem of women afraid to report stuff because they have to go through their chain of command who often times will be sympathetic to the accused, to the perpetrator, or, at the very least, it will be embarrassing and difficult for someone who is trying to be professional in a professional environment to have to go to their own boss and talk about this kind of stuff."[28]

MAJ Pfluke believes that a change in the method of handling sexual assault cases is necessary and that the need is to work to move the direct chain of command out of the process. She adds,

> Even if it would save the military to get a more unbiased and unrelated person involved. Or, in more difficult cases, to get it completely out of military hands would be appropriate. Unbiased people could be set up in offices to do this. You could set up unbiased people who don't report to the chain of command. It could even be a military person if you set it up properly. Certainly for minor cases, the commanders can handle them. If you're talking about more grievous cases or more senior people, then you might have to move it out of military control completely.

CAPT Lory Manning, U.S. Navy (Ret.), says the chain of command should not be involved.

> No, [most] haven't [thought of it] because most people don't know. Congress every so often makes changes to the Uniform Code of Military Justice but it has never gone back since 1947 and revisited the circumstances under which the whole thing was written. That applies not just to sexual assault crimes, but to all kinds of crime. The CO, the Commander under the Uniform Code, can excuse or overlook murder if it is interfering with the command mission. There may be rare

occasions when that is necessary, real rare like once every thousand years or something. But it should not be within something that is handed to COs for day to day decisions. It needs to be changed. I am a supporter of Senator Gillibrand's bill and I think COs should not be mixed up in the military justice system at all, unless they are the accused or the accuser or the victim. In other words, unless they are being accused of something or something happened to them, that they should be in the decision making process at all.[29]

As to whether the chain of command should handle these kinds of cases at all, Manning replied, "No, I don't, anymore than the chain of command should handle somebody's broken arm or a thyroid condition diagnosis. They are not equipped to do it, they are not trained for it." She shared how she would you change the method of handling these cases:

I think that we ought to have something like military judges and military attorneys and we've got zillions of them. Again, back in 1947, we had a few lawyers in the military, but nothing like the numbers that we have today. It ought to be set up like a military health care as is given by the command. Military justice should be handled by a professional team with lawyers, judges, everywhere, rather like the health care system. People who are specially trained lawyers who also wear the uniform and who have an understanding what the difficulties of justice under fire are, like keeping a chain of evidence when you are at war in Afghanistan.[30]

Manning adds that Congress has to make the changes because it makes military law. The current UCMJ was set up by Congress in 1947, and the only one who can make the changes is Congress, and Congress has a problem:

Congress's problem is that the military likes having this all in their own hands with the military commander being the one who decides. They are back in that frame of mind of only the military commander really knows. And we have seen, from particularly the sexual assault cases that a lot of times the military commanders know diddly-squat. Or choose very wrongly because they do not know how to weigh the circumstances or they do know how to weigh them but they choose not to. And Congress, when they voted on Senator Gillibrand's bill, just in the past six months, had a lot of members of Congress understood that the system needed to be changed and they supported her. There will be even more should the military not fix their ability to prosecute military sexual assault crimes. It will come around again and maybe this time the military will lose. People who support Senator Gillibrand will win.[31]

Manning does not agree that the commanders need to have this responsibility because they need to have a sense of ownership. She replied, "No, and that kind of rationale is baloney." She shared her own experience as a military commander on a remote island in the middle of the

Indian Ocean, saying she was also responsible for her people's health but that does not mean she was their doctor:

> One of my sailors was badly injured in a bicycle accident and had to be flown from the Island of Diego Garcia five hours by air to Singapore to get the kind of treatment that he needed medically. I wasn't in charge of the medical treatment, I was in charge of making sure he had everything he needed in Singapore, making sure his family was notified, making sure his possessions on Diego Garcia were tended and cared for, making sure that someone was checking on him in Singapore very regularly and letting me know if he needed anything, making sure the family was kept informed. So there were plenty of responsibilities that I had and that the CO would have if he were the CO of the victim or the accused, that don't involve actually doing the surgery to save the guy's life or making the decision on whether my sailor should have been prosecuted for being a bad bicyclist. So just because you are not the one who decides whether the guy is or isn't going to court martial, does not legally take any responsibility away from you, you have plenty of it toward that person whether the victim or the accused.[32]

On the continuum of perspectives lies the issue of jurisdiction. When service members are involved in crimes, the crimes may be committed on or off base and civilian laws may be broken. Some crimes are exclusively under military authority such as failure to obey an order, but most crimes, such as assault, violate civilian and military law. The UCMJ contains the rules that guide the military criminal process. Military individuals can be tried and convicted in a court-martial, or military court, under these rules. The military court system is completely separate from the civilian court system.[33] RADM Williams believes "there must be a military connection for the military to have jurisdiction in the first instance and, I think it is appropriate for the commander to be involved in that process as he is."[34] He explains,

> I'll go back again to a case that came up when we were doing the Tailhook investigation. And there was an alleged rape. There were military officers involved. The victim was not military. It occurred off-base. When people brought the case to me, I basically said, "We're not going to look at this case. It belongs to the Commonwealth authorities. If they think there's a rape, they can deal with that case, but it happened out in the town. It wasn't related to the military. Other than the officers who were the alleged assailants were military officers." The Commonwealth attorney did not think it was the case for the Commonwealth. US Supreme Court Justice William O. Douglas was very adamant that the UCMJ had a constitutional division about how they dealt with cases. The outgrowth of that was a series of cases decided by the Supreme Court was, where there was no military connection, the military did not have jurisdiction over the case. The initial case that was decided by the Supreme Court involved a case like the one I just described. There was a sergeant on R&R [rest and recuperation] from Viet Nam and he was in Milwaukee. He raped a woman in Hawaii. He was tried by the UCMJ and was

convicted. The case went to the Supreme Court and Justice Douglas wrote the opinion.[35] The basic substance of the case was: that the military did not have jurisdiction in that case, because there was no military connection.

A case that GEN Carter F. Ham USA (Ret.) looked at, involved two military officers, they may have been off base, but it involved a group of military people. The case in Italy involved a group of military people and they were overseas additionally, so there was no U.S. court that they could go to that would have jurisdiction of the offense and that's appropriate, but the cases that the UCMJ would deal with are cases that occur that involve the military. They occur on the base or they involve two military personnel. If the two military personnel are off base, depending on the circumstances, the UCMJ might still not have jurisdiction of it. So, if there might be a military connection to that, the rationale for removing commanders from that process is that we don't trust their judgment. When Congress approves these people for promotion, confirms their appointments in that grade, they are making an affirmative determination at that time, not in the light of these cases, that they do trust this person's judgment. So what you have is a circumstance in which somebody says I don't think this is a just decision. There are always going to be those kind of cases. I don't care which side of the ledger one is on. One side or the other is unfair to prosecute the case in the first instance or unfair to reverse a finding by a court if you think there is insufficient evidence.

I have to tell you, the gentleman in Italy—when I read the letter that was allegedly written by him that was posted on the internet, the question that came up in my mind was: What was the defense counsel doing in this case, because the General laid out all the litany of things that I thought would raise reasonable doubt about the findings in the case. Now, some people may say, well it's not appropriate for him to do that, but appellate courts do that and we do not always agree with their judgment either. So, I think there must be a military connection for the military to have jurisdiction in the first instance and, I think it is appropriate for the commander to be involved in that process as he is.

Having said that, I have a good friend, BG Leon M. 'Mike' Bridges USA (Ret.), who worked at the U.S. Attorney's office in Virginia. He was the staff judge advocate for the common marketing corps when I was working for the Secretary of the Navy. He's decided that it will have the opposite effect. He's thought for a long time that commanders shouldn't be involved in that process the way they are. So, as I said before I started, there are other people who disagree with that.

Two Cases That Resulted in a Change in the UCMJ

Victims complain that the Department of Defense fails to investigate professionally, retaliates, and deprives them of due process, equal protection under the law, and First Amendment rights. When pursuing damages against the government, service members are restricted, by the Feres Doctrine. In 1950, the U.S. Supreme Court decided that the United States is not liable under the Federal Tort Claims Act for injuries to members of the armed forces sustained while on active duty and not on furlough and resulting from the negligence of others in the armed forces.[36]

Two legal cases illustrate the impetus for change in military law and culture. In 2013, Senator McCaskill put a hold on the nomination of Air Force Lt. Gen. Susan Helms for vice chief of U.S. Space Command over her involvement in a sexual assault case. In 2012, Helms used her authority to void the conviction of an officer who had been court-martialed for sexual assault.[37] In an e-mail interview follow-up, RADM Williams contended:

> Lt. Gen. Helms used her authority in reviewing a sexual assault case to reverse some of the findings against a captain. One effect of reversing some of the findings was that the captain was not required to register as a sex offender. The convictions for some other offenses remained in place and the captain was separated from the Air Force. The other Air Force case was the one in Italy. Both of these cases involved alcohol abuse by one or both parties.[38]

The second case to which Williams refers occurred on February 26, 2013, Lt. Gen. Craig Franklin, the Third Air Force commander, dismissed the sexual assault conviction of the 31st Fighter Wing's former inspector general, Lt. Col James Wilkerson. This action released the fighter pilot from jail and reinstated him into the air force. The trial at Aviano Air Base, Italy, had found Wilkerson guilty of aggravated sexual assault and sentenced him to a year in jail, forfeiture of all pay, and dismissal from the service.[39] The *Washington Post* stated, "Franklin's decision to grant clemency in February to a convicted fighter pilot at Aviano Air Base in Italy helped spark a national debate over sexual assault in the armed forces and about whether military leaders took the problem seriously enough."[40] Congress has since taken away the authority of commanders to overturn convictions such as one of the outcomes of Franklin's decision in the Wilkerson case. The *Washington Post* obtained a March 12, six-page memo wherein Franklin outlined the reasons for his decisions based in insufficient proof, such as nagging doubts about Wilkerson's accuser, and that it was difficult to believe Wilkerson could have committed "the egregious crime of sexually assaulting a sleeping woman" given that he was "a doting father and husband" who had been selected for promotion.[41] This type of reasoning is no longer legally valid. In both of those cases, Williams noted alcohol was involved:

> But in the case that Lt. Gen. Ham looked at, there was alcohol involved with both the victim and the assailant. In the case that the gentleman in Italy looked at, it was not clear to me that the commander who was court-martialed had been drinking, although there was a party at his house. My impression was that the woman who alleged that she had been assaulted, had been drinking sufficiently that the commander allowed her to stay there at night. In any event, while I'm coming back to this: when I first assumed command at the Naval Investigative Service,

in October 1980. You may recall that there were a lot of allegations about rapes at the Naval Training Center in Orlando, Florida. There were allegations that there were many, many assaults there. I asked the people in the headquarters Criminal Investigation Division to pull every case that we had worked in the prior two years. One of the things we found out was: 75 to 80 percent of the cases involved alcohol abuse. About 65 percent of the cases were reported more than 24 to 48 hours after the event. With alcohol abuse involved, it raises a whole lot of issues in determining whether there was consent. If the case was not reported until 24 to 48 hours after the event in all probability the activities, like washing clothes, destroys the evidence, the effect. Anyway, that is not directly addressing your issue about sexual assault. When I was there [NIS], there were a lot of people, several political appointees and several senior military officers, who wanted me to not allow Naval agents to investigate these offenses.[42]

Change in the Law

In the 2014 National Defense Authorization Act, the new Article 60 eliminates commanders' (convening authorities) ability to modify sentences for serious offenses by overturning a guilty verdict or reducing the finding of guilty to that of a lesser included offense.[43]

JURISDICTION FOR SEXUAL ASSAULT CASES

Depending on where the assault happens and who is involved, a sexual assault case involving military personnel can be processed in civilian court or military courts-martial or the FAP. Civilian courts will handle cases involving military personnel in which the military has no jurisdiction, for example, when the personnel are off the base. The military has jurisdiction when the assault occurs on the base or within the unit wherever the unit is stationed and the case will be heard at a court-martial. The FAP hears domestic violence cases and resolves them without taking the case to court, but the FAP does refer cases as appropriate to civilian or military courts.

The controversy about the prosecuting sexual assault cases is less about which court has jurisdiction and more about the military giving the commanders in the chain of command the primary responsibility to convene the courts-martial and be involved in the decision and the review process. The changes made to the UCMJ, particularly in cases of rape and sexual assault, in the 2014 National Defense Authorization Act improve the rights of those involved in sexual assault, but more will likely be needed to reduce the number of sexual assaults to an acceptable level.[44]

CHAPTER 5

Women

> The absence of anyone coming forward with a sexual assault case to me, doesn't mean that it is not possible that there was or could have been something going on. It just didn't come up to me.
>
> —CAPT Lory Manning, USN (Ret.)[1]

TRADITIONAL AND EVOLVING ROLES OF WOMEN IN THE MILITARY

The traditional roles for military women that placed women in noncombat units and noncombat assignments have given way. Today, women are able to serve in combat in all branches of the military and are even being assigned to special forces.[2] Secretary of the Air Force Deborah Lee James said, "Ultimately, the initiative to eliminate any remaining gender-based assignment restrictions will improve our readiness and the Air Force's ability to recruit and retain the most effective and qualified force."[3]

Women are seeing the culmination of centuries of struggle in the face of opposition from the male leaders and enlisted men. Women have always served in the wars that the United States fought. Sometimes it was disguised as male soldiers as it was during the Revolutionary and Civil Wars.[4] Sometimes it was in combat to fill in as needed. In 2011, Lieutenant Colonel Marilla Cushman, U.S. Army (Ret.), noted that in all of these years of conflict, women serving has been "about need." Brigadier General Wilma L. Vaught, U.S. Air Force (Ret.), president of Women in Military Service for America Memorial Foundation, agreed that the military came to the point of need again, "And our advancements have come because of need and they've had to use women to fulfill the need and we get a new level of things that we could do. That's where we are again."[5] Utilizing women's abilities is a readiness issue. In 2013, I wrote,

By not using women in ground combat roles, the military realized it was decreasing its fire power. Commanding officers were aware of this fact and so they did not apply the exclusion policy and assigned women to serve in combat in times of crisis and, when the crisis subsided, returned women to their noncombat positions. The policy could not keep up with the change on the battlefield and the need to deploy women to combat zones, so it had to change.[6]

By January 2013, support had increased from civilian and military leadership to remove all gender barriers, and the momentum to allow women in combat was reflected in the changed nature of war. President Obama called for equality and Secretary of Defense Leon Panetta announced that the Department of Defense (DoD) was notifying Congress of its intent to open all military units and occupations to women, ending the ground combat exclusion and eliminating the last barrier to full integration of women into the U.S. military. The new policy will be fully implemented by January 2016. There is a provision that permits an individual service to apply for a special exemption if it is determined that certain occupations or units should be closed to women.[7]

In January 2015, over 90 percent of occupations were already open to women and 15 percent of the forces are women. Juliet Beyler, the Defense department's director of officer and enlisted personnel management, said. "By removing these antiquated gender-based barriers to service, it can only strengthen the all-incrementally volunteer force and allow people to serve based on their ability and their qualifications."[8]

This major change emerged over time and, in some instances, in conjunction with women's serving where the need is great as was the case in the Revolutionary and Civil Wars, when women served disguised as men, and as medical personnel, laundresses, and cooks. In following the male soldiers, women sometimes took up arms and returned fire. "There is a paradox," notes C. Kay Larson, "that the exigencies of war usually demand more of women than what regulations state or what politicians spout."[9] Larsen believes that, to find out what women do in war, we have to look at what they do in the field during war. What actually happens in the field during the war may be different for men and women alike than what their training was. Regulations will be adapted to meet necessity. This accommodation is not characteristic of only a singular war or conflict.[10] A modern-day comparison is the heroic actions of Silver Star recipient Specialist Monica L. Brown, U.S. Army, a combat medic from the 782nd Brigade Support Battalion, 4th Brigade Combat Team, 82nd Airborne Division, who, in 2007, did not take cover but went through gunfire to assist comrades in the Jani Khail district of Paktika Province in Afghanistan. The army subsequently removed her from combat.[11]

Other major events highlight changing roles for women. During the Civil War, the government recruited women to serve as nurses, but without military status. In 1901, the Army Reorganization Act established the Army Nurse Corps and nurses became an official part of the military. In World War I and World War II, the roles of women were expanded. In World War II, women support staff and nurses were stationed near the frontlines.[12] Including women in the military was formalized through the 1948 Women's Armed Services Integration Act. The Persian Gulf War (1990–1991) demonstrated that women are essential to military readiness and are needed in combat. In the war, 41,000 women were exposed to combat. After the war, Congress repealed the Air Force and Navy exclusion laws, but did not remove the Army and the Marines exclusion policy.[13]

This progress in moving toward full equality has not been accomplished without the pain of intense and unified opposition every step of the way. The opposition included using women's gender as justification for an even more vicious assault: sexual assault.

During the March 2013 hearings, Congress heard sobering testimony about sexual assault in the military that demonstrated weakness in the current methods of handling the offense. One event exemplified the need for change. An Air Force Lieutenant General reversed the conviction of a Lieutenant Colonel, a fellow pilot, in a sexual assault case at Aviano Air Force Base. Brigette McCoy, former Specialist, U.S. Army, stated that the case "emphatically underscores several points. First, senior officers are not infallible, and in fact can be complicit in criminal injustice, and second, today's military criminal justice system is undermined by built-in bias."[14] Brian K. Lewis, former Petty Officer Third Class, U.S. Navy, Advocacy Board Member, Protect Our Defenders, added,

> Aviano Air Base commander, General Franklin's recent action to set aside the guilty verdict by a court-martial, against Lieutenant Colonel Wilkerson for aggravated sexual assault is yet another example of an action taken by a commander that will have a chilling effect on military judges and prosecutors, potentially affect future cases and inhibit victims from coming forward. A system that elevates a single individual's authority and discretion over the rule of law often precludes justice and hinders it long into the future.[15]

But what effect did the assault have on the victim? One victim who requested that her privacy be maintained (thus her statement lacks her name) testified in writing:

> It has been an incredibly hard journey back to being myself. I am still working on that. I don't know whether it is because of the assault or the legal process or both. During this entire ordeal, I kept to myself. I was ashamed and embarrassed. . . .
>
> I don't want to run into Wilkerson's friends. I work with wives of pilots who are close to Wilkerson and dread coming into work. . . .

I endured eight months of public humiliation and investigations ... And an Article 32 hearing where I was interrogated for several hours by Wilkerson's legal counsel without benefit of legal counsel myself. ...

I want the focus to be on the ethical issue of a single biased person wielding the power to derail a decision that was made in a methodical, objective manner with the swipe of a pen. I would like to use the result of my experience to change the process of law to separate sexual assault cases from the military justice system. This is the real focus now. Not my assault, because General Franklin has made sure that can't be changed. He has made sure that Colonel Wilkerson is free to do this again. What really scares me also is that Wilkerson could make Colonel now, and will be issued a position of leadership. Really? Leadership?[16]

Sexual Assaults on Women

Women are more likely to be assaulted by a fellow soldier than killed in combat, noted *Newsweek*.[17] The *Huffington Post* calculated that a servicewoman was about 180 times more likely to have become a victim of military sexual assault in 2012 than to have died while deployed during the last 11 years of combat in Iraq and Afghanistan. One in three military women has been sexually assaulted, compared to one in six civilian women, according to DoD.[18] DoD reported that in all unrestricted reports made to the department, victims are mostly female service members under the age of 25, and of a junior enlisted grade. Likewise, the demographics of subjects in all unrestricted reports made to the department are mostly male service members under the age of 35, and of an enlisted grade. Offenses originally alleged in unrestricted reports for FY2012 include crimes of rape, aggravated sexual assault/sexual assault, and abusive/wrongful sexual contact.[19]

In 2014 women comprised almost 80 percent of the 6,131 victims who filed reports, and of 9,600 (5 percent) who had experienced unwanted sexual contact, 57 percent had faced some type of retaliation. Twenty-two percent experienced sexual harassment. Women are four times more likely to report a sexual assault than men. Sexual assaults against women usually occur outside of work hours, away from their duty station, and alcohol is frequently involved.[20]

"Most assaults occur in the barracks, most victims are junior enlisted personnel, and most perpetrators are their peers or noncommissioned officers," according to Army LTC Elizabeth Robbins. She laments the circumstances that sometimes accompany sexual assaults:

It is painful to warn young soldiers, who understandably revere the brotherhood of arms, that that brotherhood ends when consuming alcohol begins. Civilians know about our fraternity from movies and history books, and in my experience all that is true. Soldiers will willingly die to protect each other, and this love rivals all other great passions. It is exhilarating to work toward meaningful goals, serving side by side with admirable people. My experience has also been that women are full and valued members of the team, whether deployed overseas or stationed at the Pentagon. But off-duty, when drinks are in hand, this can quickly change.[21]

Robbins attributes her not having been assaulted to having the philosophy that "the brotherhood of arms ends at the first drink, [and] in off-duty social settings, it is best to drink lightly and leave early."

Circumstances vary in assaults. A case at Wright-Patterson Air Force Base included in Senator Kirsten Gillibrand's 2015 report resulted in the finding, "Recommended Court-Martial—Potential Serial Sexual Predator Discharged without Trial." An Air Force assailant allegedly pinned a civilian down on the bed, penetrated her vagina with his finger, and then raped her. She sought a sexual assault examination at Miami Valley Hospital as well as told a friend that she had been raped. During the investigation, two more victims were found who provided written statements against the accused in separate incidents. At the military preliminary hearing, the investigating officer concluded: "Based on the seriousness of the offenses, I recommend the Charges be referred to a General Court-Martial." The commander with Special Court-Martial Convening Authority recommended the airman be discharged in lieu of court-martial, and the commander with General Court-Martial Convening Authority approved the discharge.[22]

Sometimes women are victims of serial assaults by either the same attacker or by different assailants. Ms. Brigette McCoy, former Specialist, U.S. Army and Gulf War-era, service-connected, disabled veteran, testified to Congress of multiple attacks perpetrated by different individuals. The first attack took place in 1988 when she was 18 and stationed in Germany. She testified, in part:

That would not be the last time I would be assaulted or harassed. . . . That . . . same year I was raped again by another soldier in my unit. Another year, I was sexually harassed by a commissioned officer in my unit.

Between 1990 and 1991, another NCO in my unit began to harass me through inappropriate touching, words, and behavior. This NCO then requested from my command that I be moved to work directly for him in a work environment where there was no access, closed and window-less, key entry coded vault.

I was given a choice to either get out or to face possible UCMJ action myself. Most women who are victims of sexual harassment or abuse are threatened and charged with UCMJ action. So I felt I had no choice. I was literally terrified, and so in that terrified position, I was paralyzed and I just chose to get out because that was the option that was given to me. Within a week, I had orders out of Germany and I was escorted by two NCO's to my plane and that was it. My career was over.

. . . I repeatedly moved from place to place and was homeless and medically disabled, but not even the Department of Veterans Affairs (VA) would recognize this and help me until some 2 decades later.

> . . . 22 years later almost to the day of my early expiration of term of service, I was awarded veteran service compensation and service connection for military sexual trauma (MST). Can you tell me why did it take so long? Why did I have to go through so much before anyone would listen to me? Why did I have to be violated again through the process of asking for help and seeking claim status?
>
> . . . I have to say I no longer have any faith or hope that the military chain of command will consistently prosecute, convict, sentence, and carry out the sentencing of sexual predators in uniform without absconding justice somehow. Only 8 percent of them are prosecuted.
>
> How many are relieved of their duties, their pensions, their careers? How many of them are placed on the national registry as sex offenders before they are returned to civilian life? Even asking that, what happens to the 92 percent that were not sentenced or prosecuted?[23]

Additional powerful women's voices can be heard through the various venues such as blogs, government platforms, or organizational structures. Stories range from the victimization of women by some in a powerful command structure who, due to their subjectivity, turn a deaf ear to her plight, or, just as bad, join the fray of active assailants. Or by a comrade in arms who in ignorance forgets he is such when he tells his rape victim, "that is how you fuck a whore."[24]

Voices of Women Attacked

So many servicewomen have been attacked and bear the scars of the attack. Mary Calvert captured some of the pain these servicewomen endured. Here are some of the words.

Kate Weber was raped one week into an Air Force deployment to Germany when she was 18. She says she was stalked and harassed after reporting the attack. "I just lost everything," Weber says. "I know he was a repeat offender the moment he touched me. He was able to get away with it because the chain of command allowed it."[25]

U.S. Army SPC Natasha Schuette was sexually assaulted by her drill sergeant during basic training at Fort Jackson, South Carolina. After reporting the assault, she suffered harassment by other drill sergeants. Schuette's assailant is serving four years in prison for assaulting her and four other trainees; she suffers from posttraumatic stress disorder (PTSD).[26]

Brittany Fintel was stationed in Bahrain when she was grabbed and pinned down on a bed by a superior. When she reported the assault, she was told she had an "adjustment disorder" and was taken off the ship; eventually she left the navy due to PTSD. "They kick the victim out. The victim is more fucked up in the head than apparently the rapist," she says.[27]

Army SGT Sophie Champoux committed suicide under suspicious circumstances after allegedly being repeatedly raped while in the military.[28]

These women give voice to the experience of many who have been sexually assaulted while serving in the military.

Military Culture in Transition

The inclusion of women in all positions is a gigantic step that is basic to a successful change in the military's culture. However, the sexual assault, abuse and discrimination that military women have endured grew out of the military's male-dominated, female subordinate culture. The military culture has its roots in the combat exclusion rules. Women were also denied access to the avenues for promotion to the top ranks. The male culture flourished. When women are admitted to the top ranks and become a major force in deciding the nature of the culture, women will have a greater chance to get fair and nondiscriminatory treatment. Changing the male-dominated military culture will require more than ending the exclusionary rules; it requires women continue to move into command positions. The DoD is acknowledging the impact of placing women in positions dedicated to the elimination of sexual assault and when it named MG Camille M. Nichols, USA, to be in charge of the Sexual Assault Prevention and Response Office.[29] The services have made progress in opening the route to command.

Besides opening combat units, each branch is making efforts. The army reports that, in 2014, 78 percent of the positions are open to women, and women serve in 95 percent of all army occupations (active-duty and the reserve components). An increasing proportion of senior-level active-duty DoD positions is filled by women. The percentage of female officers in the active army in grades O-4 (rank of major) and above increased from 11.5 percent in fiscal year 1995 to 14.6 percent in fiscal year 2013; likewise for enlisted active-duty women in grades E-7 (rank of sergeant first class) through E-9 (rank of first sergeant), it increased from 8 percent in 1995 to about 11 percent as of fiscal year 2013. Women represent about 14 percent of the active Army, 23 percent of the Army Reserve, and 16 percent of the Army National Guard as of fiscal year 2014.[30]

Women in naval active duty represent 9,334 (17 percent) officers and 2,699 (17 percent) of the reserves. The navy reports that women hold major commands such as over combatant ships, aviation squadrons, CEC commands, and Special Operations units. Eleven women are in command of combatants and 9 in aviation command. Thirty-four women are flag officers. Enlisted women also serve in other command positions.[31]

Defense Manpower Research reports that women comprise 6.2 percent of Marines and 5.8 percent officers.[32] The air force reports that, in 2008,

63,760 (19.57 percent) of the force were women; 17.98 percent of the officers were women and 19.97 percent of the enlisted corps were women. In addition, 57.04 percent of the female officers were line officers, and 42.96 percent are nonline. There are 568 (4.02 percent) female pilots, 234 (5.14 percent) female navigators, and 145 air battle managers (11.19 percent).[33]

Being in culturally subordinate positions leaves a person at an institutional disadvantage and possible sexual abuse and discrimination. The sexual abuse comes from sexual assaults, including rape, that deny a woman her right to control her body and exposes her to the risks of infection, the danger and discomfort of abortion or pregnancy, and damage in childbirth. According to the DoD *2012 Annual Report on Sexual Assault in the Military*, 26,000 service members say they were sexually assaulted in 2012. It is significant that most of these assaults were not reported; only 11 percent were. The Pentagon officially counted only 3,374 formal allegations. Of the sexual assaults reported, 88 percent were against women; 2,558 were unrestricted and 816 restricted. Unrestricted reporting results in a referral to a military criminal investigation organization, while restricted reporting allows the victim to receive confidential care.

Women's Response to Sexual Assault

Reporting

In 2012, a majority of women did not report sexual assault to a military authority. The top three reasons for not reporting were: 70 percent did not want anyone to know, 66 percent felt uncomfortable, and 51 percent did not think the report would be kept confidential. In the year before the 2012 survey, of the 6.1 percent of active-duty women who experienced unwanted sexual contact, 33 percent indicated having reported it. Primary reasons for reporting were: 72 percent indicated they thought it was the right thing to do, 67 percent indicated they wanted to seek closure, and 67 percent indicated they wanted to stop the offender from hurting others. Of the 97 percent of women who received training, 94 percent indicated reporting options were explained.[34]

In fiscal year 2014, the estimated 25 percent reporting rate (4,768 service members out of 6,131) is the highest ever recorded for the military services. The estimated gap between reporting and prevalence among service members decreased to its narrowest point since the department began tracking these data.[35]

Of women who did not report it in 2012, 47 percent gave as their reason fear of retaliation or reprisal and 43 percent had heard about the negative experiences of other victims who had reported their experience.

Retaliation—Not Just a Male Issue

In 2014, Congress and the military made illegal under the Uniform Code of Military Justice retaliating and/or threatening to retaliate against service members who have reported a crime. In spite of the change in the law, the percentage of women (62 percent) experiencing some form of retaliation, social, professional, or both, remained unchanged from the 2012 survey. While retaliation numbers are static, one in four sexual assault victims officially reported the crimes in 2014, compared to one in ten in 2012. The majority of the victims in sexual assault cases that are reported and investigated are women, junior enlisted troops, and noncommissioned officers.[36]

So, what might a commander think when no sexual assaults are reported in an environment given to their existence. One such commander, CAPT Lory Manning, U.S. Navy (Ret.), believes that she was fortunate, but adds,

> And I still wonder to this day. Did something happen and was it squelched before it could get up to me? You just don't know. Because what happens is, quite often, the person who is sexually assaulted is generally pretty junior in the chain of command and they might not even know that they could come to you directly. The perpetrator will sometimes tell a very young junior person, "You tell anybody and I'm going to kill you," and they believe it. Or "You tell anybody, you will be the one who has duty all day Christmas, every Christmas for the rest of your life." They have ways of keeping you quiet. A good commanding officer needs to be sure that people below them know that there are ways around that sort of impediment, not just with respect to sexual assault, but with anything. I guess what I am trying to say is: the absence of anyone coming forward with a sexual assault case to me, doesn't mean that it is not possible that there was or could have been something going on. It just didn't come up to me.[37]

Manning believes that there are plenty of reasons people do not come forward, not just fear of the assaulter, but of predators.

Sexual Predators

One of the problems in eliminating sexual assault, probably the most severe problem, says Manning "is the fact that there are sexual predators in the military who the military has not done near enough route out, to find, to court-martial, to get them the heck out of the military, they do not belong there." She explains,

> There are predators in the military and, all the ones that I have encountered or heard about have been men. That doesn't mean there couldn't be women also. The predators are generally competent, a little more senior than junior, they have

a good reputation in the command, and they have friends in the command. It is not just a question of them threatening the person they have assaulted, but it is also the fact that the more senior people in the command tend to see the predators as competent, as good sailors, good naval officers, good husbands, good neighbors, and the junior person is usually not known very well. It might be someone who is "newish." Some of these predators know how to pick out someone who is, maybe, not the strongest performer and how to poison the well about that person even before they begin to assault them. They trash somebody's reputation sometimes before they move in to assault them. They are well-connected and, a lot of times, the victim finds, not only that the chain of command does not believe them, but their own peers, their own friends think they screwed up.[38]

The peers are not necessarily afraid, but they just think that the person is a screw-up, because their reputation has been trashed as part of the preparation for assaulting them, explains Manning. "And the victim is afraid of losing her job, and is afraid that it will happen again. So there are many reasons that the victims do not come forward. But most of all they are afraid that they'll come forward and they won't be believed or they will be believed and still nothing will happen."

Effects on Women

The DoD concludes that the data suggest that women who experienced unwanted sexual behavior and the experiences of others who chose to report may negatively impact a service member's perceptions about the consequences associated with reporting. Of those women who did report it to a military authority: 31 percent experienced social retaliation only; 26 percent experienced a combination of professional retaliation, social retaliation, administrative action, and/or punishments; 3 percent indicated they experienced professional retaliation only; and 2 percent indicated they experienced administrative action.[39]

Whether or not women reported the assault, Jessica A., Turchik and Susan M. Wilson found that psychological effects are well documented for women and men. Findings include high rates of depression and anxiety symptoms, substance abuse and dependence, posttraumatic stress disorder (PTSD) symptoms; feelings of self-blame and shame; and difficulty with interpersonal relationships; they are more likely to report forming ideas about suicide and attempting suicide.[40]

The chain of command's failure to prosecute sexual assault cases can result in women experiencing military sexual trauma (MST). MST resulting from sexual assault is more likely to produce symptoms of PTSD than most types of military trauma including combat. MST can differ from other traumas, including sexual trauma experienced in the civilian world. As a soldier with MST said, "Going through a sexual assault is bad enough. Then to have this happen to me in my job as a soldier; it was really difficult because what happened to the unit support? Your fellow soldiers are supposed to have your back."[41]

On average, 22 veterans commit suicide daily. Senator Kirsten Gillibrand (D-NY) believes a link exists between the intolerable number of suicides and sexual assaults, harassment, and PTSD. She proposes that to stop perpetrators from continuing predatory sexual assaults against their fellow service members, a justice system is needed that ensures accountability and prevents any other service member from being victimized.[42]

WOMEN SEXUALLY ASSAULTING MEN

California's new "yes means yes" law, SB967, requires state-supported colleges to mandate continuous "affirmative consent" from all parties engaged in sexual activity. Neither silence nor a lack of protest constitutes consent, defined as "affirmative, conscious, and voluntary agreement to engage in sexual activity" that "must be ongoing throughout a sexual activity."[43] George Washington University law professor John Banzhaf says the imprecise definition of "affirmative consent" can create challenges; for example, a female student could be charged with sexual assault if she offers oral sex and her inebriated partner accepts. "This may seem bizarre that a guy who is presumably laying back and having oral sex and one assumes enjoying it—or at least tolerating it—is not consenting simply by doing that, but under that definition, if he didn't say 'yes,' she's a sexual violator."

Coercion and assault are common experiences for college men, but much more common for college women. Cindy Struckman-Johnson's 2003 study found that 58 percent of college men had been pressured for sex after saying no (since age 16), and 78 percent of women.[44] Women usually engage in less violent tactics than men such as repeated touching, emotional manipulation, intoxication, and violence. The study found that 22 percent of women and 9 percent of men had been physically restrained by a member of the other gender demanding sex.

According to Struckman-Johnson, not a huge amount of research on female perpetrators is available, but popular perceptions of men and women's sexuality may make it easier for women to rationalize sexual aggression. "Because of the idea that men are sexually oriented and wanting it all the time, it kind of lets them off the hook. . . . They get to assume they've got a ready and willing partner here who would just love to have sex with them." That may not be the case.

Women attacking men contradicts typical assumptions and cultural scripts about male aggression and female passivity. To some, such acts of aggression are contrary to the stereotypes of female behavior just as possible male response may defy gender role expectations of the male victim.

WOMEN, EQUALITY, AND PREVENTING SEXUAL ASSAULT

Sexual assault is a tragic, life-changing event for too many women in the military. The tragedy does not end when they leave the military. It follows them to civilian life and, in too many cases, results in death.

As the women in the military move toward achieving equality with men in the work that they do, the culture will change and less emphasis will be on treating women as subordinates. The developing trend that women are assuming critical leadership roles further weakens the power of those who commit sexual assaults. They will no longer believe they can "get away with it" because they have friends in the command structure who will protect them. The changes in the law and the enforcement of those changes make it more likely that the number of assaults will continue to decline.

CHAPTER 6

Men

> Men are still invisible and ignored as survivors of military sexual trauma.
>
> —Brian K. Lewis, former Petty Officer Third Class, U.S. Navy; Advocacy Board Member, Protect Our Defenders; Testimony before the U.S. Senate[1]

Men have always been the ones chosen to serve in the military. The image of a physically strong, well-trained male has always been accepted by the public to be what a soldier should look like. The image, until recently, has been that the man was white and heterosexual. The image of sailors on shore leave being surrounded by adoring females was one seen often in World War II films. Today, that image in the minds of the public is changing but not entirely. Changes in gender, race, marital status, religion, and sexuality are components that the public is forced to consider as they think of the members of today's military.[2] The presence of women is most accepted of these components, but women's battle for inclusion has been difficult and is ongoing. The presence of nonwhite service members is tolerated, but, for many, the nonwhites are invisible; the image is still strong that the soldier should be white. The marital status of the soldier is married with a family. The religion of the service member in the public's image is Christian. Islam is the religion least accepted as part of the image of the service member. The sexuality is heterosexual. Homosexuality has long been rejected by American society and it is definitely rejected for members of the military.[3]

Society's image of the U.S. military members perpetuates the misconceptions about sexual assault in the military. One misconception is that sexual assault is a women's problem and a crime that has only women as victims. The Department of Defense's (DoD) sexual assault report found that in numbers, more men were victims of assault in 2013 than women because 85 percent of service members are men and 15 percent are women. About 6.8 percent of women surveyed said they were assaulted and 1.2 percent of the men. Slightly more than 12,000 women said they were assaulted, compared with nearly 14,000 men.[4]

In December 2014, DoD asked survey questions in a new, matter-of-fact way that revealed far higher rates of penetrative sexual assault, such as rape and sodomy, than in previous years. For example, this survey asked about different physical acts and body parts without assigning sexuality, thus removing unfamiliarity with legal definitions as well. The difference was particularly significant for men who said they had been assaulted, in that the percentage of sexual assaults that were penetrative increased from 11 percent when the question was asked as it had been in previous surveys to 35 percent with the new questions. For women, penetrative assaults increased from 29 percent to 43 percent. Although a higher number of military men are sexually assaulted than military women, only about 10 percent of those men report the attacks compared to about 40 percent of women.[5]

Nate Galbreath, the senior executive adviser for the Pentagon's sexual assault prevention office, told the Associated Press, "It's disheartening that we have such a differential between the genders and how they are choosing to report . . . It's not the damsel in distress; it's your fellow service member that might need you to step in," he added, saying soldiers, sailors, and pilots should treat that request for aid just like one on the battlefield.[6]

Megan M. Schmid maintains that sexual assault by heterosexual men is an act of domination and not due to gender integration. "The fact that male-on-male sexual assault occurs in the military, where heterosexuality is assumed and indeed enforced, shows that the problem is not due to the services' sex integration. Rather, such assaults by men who consider themselves heterosexual demonstrate that sexual assault is in fact an act of domination. The DoD must recognize that military men are also victims of sexual assault and such crimes occur even when women are not present. By doing so, the DoD can help service members understand that military sexual assault is rooted in the current military culture that subordinates those seen as feminine or weak and accepts sexual violence as normal."[7]

In May 2015, the annual study examined how male service members experience sexual assault. Results indicated that men were more likely to experience repeated abuse by more than one person. Additionally, men were more likely to view the assault as hazing instead of sexual acts.[8]

SEXUAL TRAUMA

Military sexual trauma, defined as any unwanted sexual activity, including harassment, sodomy, rape, verbal remarks, grabbing and pressure for sexual favors, affects thousands of men each year. Victims are most often young, low-ranking enlistees who fall prey to peers' and superiors' desire to demean or humiliate others. The acts are rarely homosexual in nature but rather an effort to feel powerful or dominant over others.[9]

MALE ATTACKERS

Profile of the Male Attacker

The male attacker has common characteristics but there are differences. The attacker:

- Has a rank above the victim
- Is in the same unit as the victim
- Is a single individual, but the assault may involve several members
- Is often a sexual predator who believes he is protected by the system
- Takes advantage of the victim's fear of being called a homosexual.

Male Repeat Offenders

In 1994 the navy put in place the Sexual Assault Victim Intervention program. Studies of incoming male navy recruits showed that from 13 percent to 15 percent self-reported perpetrating premilitary rape or attempted rape. Terri J. Rau et al. stated, "High rates of pre military sexual assault among male Navy recruits are of great concern because men who have previously engaged in sexual aggression are likely to do so again."[10] One study found that men who reported a premilitary history of rape perpetration were almost 10 times more likely to commit or attempt rape during their first year of military service when compared with those who did not report a history. The effectiveness of the program was assessed with respect to men's factual knowledge about rape, their approval of rape myths, and their empathy for rape victims. These criteria have been shown to predict male sexual assault perpetration. Results were promising in that results showed an increase in men's rape knowledge, a reduction in their endorsement of rape myths, and an increase in their empathy for rape victims.

WOMEN ATTACKERS

In 2010, a Gallup Survey of Sexual Assault in the air force produced a profile of "the most common assailant is that of a female acquaintance that ignores the efforts to communicate lack of consent and commits a sexual contact offense."[11] The survey found that, of 1,355 active-duty air force males who were sexually assaulted in the 12-month period before the survey, women committed 61.3 percent, and, of those, about half were members of the military. Of those incidences, 28.1 percent were sexual acts as defined by the 2008 Uniform Code of Military Justice, meaning that the male victim was forced to penetrate the female assailant's vagina with his penis, his finger, or any other object without his consent. Only 5.8 percent of male victims reported the assaults, and only 4 percent of those assaults were committed by more than one person.

MALE VICTIMS OF SEXUAL ASSAULT

So often female victims are profiled as the victims of sexual assault but the pain of men who have been brutally assaulted hurts even more because society tends to believe they should be able to defend themselves. In the age of "Don't Ask, Don't Tell," the fear of being called a homosexual kept many of them from coming forward.

Greg Jeloudov was 35 and new to America when he decided to join the army. Like most soldiers, he was driven by both patriotism for his adopted homeland and the pragmatic notion that the military could be a first step in a career that would enable him to provide for his new family. Instead, Jeloudov arrived at Fort Benning, Georgia, for basic training in May 2009, in the middle of the economic crisis and rising xenophobia. The soldiers in his unit, responding to his Russian accent and New York City address, called him a "champagne socialist" and a "commie faggot." He was, . . . "in the middle of the viper's pit." Less than two weeks after arriving on base, he was gang-raped in the barracks by men who said they were showing him who was in charge of the United States. When he reported the attack to unit commanders, he says they told him, "It must have been your fault. You must have provoked them."[12]

Jeremiah Arbogast attempted suicide. He told the Senate Armed Services Committee's subcommittee on personnel, "Choosing death was my way of taking responsibility for my circumstances. I felt my death would spare my wife, daughter and myself the dishonor the rape brought upon us."

Two months after the attack, after incessant nightmares, anxiety, depression, and confusion, Arbogast confronted a base social worker who reported the attack to the Naval Criminal Investigative Service (NCIS), which investigates crimes involving Naval or Marine Corps personnel.

Arbogast's attacker was arrested and charged sexual assault, sodomy, and other charges, but a week in court resulted in praise of his 23 years of service; he received a bad conduct discharge and no jail time. The rapist was ordered to NCIS headquarters for fingerprinting, but he had dulled the skin on his fingertips. He refused to register on the sex offender database by simply saying, "No, I don't have to."[13]

In late September 1999, Steve Stovey was sailing to Hawaii, where he would be joined by his father on a Tiger Cruise, a navy tradition in which family members accompany sailors on the final leg of a deployment. Parents and kids get to see how sailors live and work; they watch the crew test air and sea weapons. The West Coast part of the cruise is usually Pearl Harbor to San Diego. Stovey, on the morning of September 20, was ambushed by three men in a remote storage area of the ship, where he had been sent to get supplies. They threw a black hood over his head, strangled and sodomized him, then left him for dead on a stack of boxes.

Stovey told no one. He was certain that his attackers, whose faces he had not glimpsed, would kill him if he did. Stovey might have killed himself were it not for his father's arrival. They spent five days on board ship, almost certainly being watched by the three attackers. "I just kept it inside. I couldn't tell him."[14]

Complexities abound when military men are assaulted. Before the repeal of "Don't ask, don't tell" in 2011, male-on-male rape victims could be discharged for having engaged in homosexual conduct. According to *GQ*, "Military culture is built upon a tenuous balance of aggression and obedience. The potential for sexual violence exists whenever there is too much of either. New recruits, stripped of their free will, cannot question authority."[15] Sexual assault is not about the sex, but about power and control.

In some cases in *GQ*, careers were lost and lives turned upside down, such as was the life of Kole Welsharmy from 2002 to 2007. He had let the assault go, because he wanted to be an officer. Six weeks later he was told, "You've tested positive [for HIV]." Welsharmy stated that he was removed from the military and signed out within a day. "It was a complete shock."

In another *GQ* case, a Mr. Welch discussed why he did not report the assault, but then took drastic action to address the assault: "Hell no, I didn't report this. Who was I going to report it to? He had serious rank over me. After they ordered me to return to work with him, I stabbed myself in the neck so I could go home."

In 2010, the Department of Veterans Affairs screened about 50,000 male veterans positive for military sexual trauma, up from just over 30,000 in 2003. "For the victims, the experience is a special kind of hell—a soldier can't just quit his job to get away from his abusers," wrote Jesse Ellison.[16]

REPORTING

Why Male Reluctance

Although women comprise about 15 percent of the force, they are significantly more likely to be sexually assaulted in the military than men, because assaults against men have been greatly underreported. "For that reason, the majority of formal complaints of military sexual assault have been filed by women, even though the majority of victims are thought to be men," James Dao reported.[17]

An additional reason for men's reluctance is denial, men do not acknowledge being a victim. Reasons for their denial are feelings of shame, embarrassment, and fear of negative reactions from others.

Male reluctance to report is complemented by a hostile military culture slow to recognize men can suffer sexual trauma. The organization Protect our Defenders told *Baltimore Sun*, "Male victims face more obstacles, more prejudice against them, more disbelief, more efforts to silence and humiliate them."[18] A Pentagon prevention program faced challenges, according to the *Baltimore Sun*. Nate Galbreath, civilian adviser to Sexual Assault Prevention and Response program, reported, "You have an environment that values strength and values the warrior ethos, . . . [a]nd, of course, when any man is sexually assaulted, they really wonder whether or not they fit into this warrior culture. But what we're trying to get across to men is that warriors not only know how to fight, they also know how to ask for help."[19] Yet, conflict of interest elements weigh in such as the accused is often a higher-ranking, longer-serving, more experienced member with significant responsibilities. The victim is frequently newer and younger with less training and responsibility, and often perceived to be of less value.

The DoD found three reasons that men did not report unwanted sexual contact: (1) fear of punishment for themselves or others for other violations, such as underage drinking (22 percent), (2) afraid that they would not be believed (17 percent), and (3) belief that their performance evaluation or chance for promotion would be compromised (16 percent).[20] Although reporting has been fraught with challenges for women, men's reluctance to report contributes to the appearance that sexual assault is more of a women's issue. Other reasons exist for men's unwillingness to report. Brian Lewis, cofounder and president of the advocacy group Men Recovering from Military Sexual Trauma, said many men are afraid to come forward because programs or policies are not in place to help them. Lewis told *Stars and Stripes*, " 'In the military, a culture of manliness is expected of the men who serve in uniform, and being the victim of this type of crime can have some serious repercussions' on a man's status within his unit."[21] Disparities do not end with those discussed here. The *Sun* found that when men do report, military authorities are less likely to identify a suspect, to refer charges to court-martial, or to discharge the assailant than when the victim is a woman. Despite male reluctance to report, DoD found the vast majority of women and men indicated training explained the reporting options (94 percent) and explained the points of contact for reporting and resources available (92 percent women and 93 percent men).[22] Numerically, more men are sexually assaulted in the military than women, because 85 percent of the people in the military are men. A higher percentage of women are assaulted but numerically more men are assaulted.

"It is very difficult for the women who have been sexually assaulted to come forward. It is even harder for a guy to do so. Most of the sexual assaults on men are not by gay men, they are straight men who are bullying, harassing, hazing, that kind of thing. It is meted out as a power play, as a punishment in all of the cases. And the men are afraid that they will be seen as not real men," according to CAPT Lory Manning, U.S. Navy (Ret.).[23] She added that men "absolutely feared that they might be labeled as gay?"

Fear of being labeled has happened to women, added Manning.

> Some of this has changed since "Don't ask, Don't tell." The sexual predator would hit on a woman and if she said, "No, I don't want to sleep with you," He'd say, "You must be gay then. I'll just have to tell everybody that you are gay." So it was used as a threat before the end of "Don't ask, Don't tell." "Sleep with me or I am going to tell everyone you are gay, and then you will be thrown out of the military, because everybody will believe me, not you." Now, it is okay, you can be gay and stay in the military. But a lot of people consider that to be their own business and don't necessarily want it widespread. Or some of the guys are straight and don't want to be labeled as gay.[24]

"The question is, 'Is our population in the military ready to talk about this?' " asks Nate Galbreath. "We want to get them there. But it's going to be bit by bit. Because it's very, very hard for people to think about someone who is a soldier and is strong" as a victim of sexual assault.[25] Often misuse of alcohol by victim and perpetrator alike makes an assault possible, causing the victim to fall asleep.

DoD Response to Male Sexual Assault

The DoD is aware of male reluctance to report and has within its 2014 Response System policy reforms to encourage more reporting from male victims. For example, the DoD Safe Helpline operated through nonprofit organization, RAINN, works in part to meet the unique needs of male survivors in anonymity and security. Many men find talking to staff first makes it easier later to tell friends or family. Services include frequently asked questions or FAQs geared to male victims, informative military and civilian referral data bases, and a mobile phone app.[26]

In 2013, DoD added a chat room support resource, Safe Helproom. Statistics indicate progress with a 45 percent increase in new Web site visitors for FY2013–FY2014 and a 251 percent increase for FY2012–FY2014.

The number of searches increased by 264 percent from FY2012 to FY2013 and 214 percent from FY2013 to FY2014. Across all three fiscal years 45,446 database searches were conducted, which indicates the service is a reliable information source. From FY2013 to FY2014, total number of Safe Helpline phone users increased by 70.5 percent while total number of online user contacts increased by 31 percent. Men and women most often discussed reporting options, emotional and social consequences, and mental health services. In 2014, almost half discussed barriers to reporting such as not wanting anyone to know, feeling uncomfortable making a report, and retaliation.[27]

Nonetheless in 2015, the Government Accounting Office (GAO) concluded that DoD is without a plan for how it will use data in making decisions about program development, risking leaving important issues unaddressed, such as those related to male victims. Although medical and mental health care are available for all victims, DOD's Health Affairs office has not systematically identified whether male victims have any gender-specific needs. Sexual assault policies specify that care be sensitive to gender-specific issues. GAO noted that men who are victims may have different responses to the trauma than women, such as questioning their masculinity and their sexuality.[28]

Second, GAO reported that although DoD has recognized that a cultural change is needed, it had not taken adequate steps to further change. DoD has noted that military culture can pose challenges to effectively implementing a prevention program. For example, in 2008, DoD recognized that it would need to address the "unofficial" culture that is, for example, defined by exaggerated characteristics of stereotypical masculinity, and is linked to values and customs that perpetuate rape. GAO contends that important practices for implementing cultural changes include establishing and measuring progress toward performance goals and training employees as a means to effect the desired change, and concluded, "DOD has not established goals or metrics to gauge sexual assault–related issues for male servicemembers, and has also generally not portrayed male sexual assault victims in its sexual assault prevention training material."[29] The services are realizing that training approaches should differ for men and women, after initially thinking all the training materials should be gender-neutral.[30]

Another medium that is helping to change the culture by bringing new attention to male victims is the documentary, "Justice Denied"[31] and the advocacy of Service Women's Action Network (SWAN), an advocacy group that has sharply criticized the Pentagon's handling of sexual assault. Although more than half of all sexual violence happens to men, SWAN believes all soldiers deserve better, and "that our troops deserve to serve in a military without fear of rape, sexual harassment or sexual assault, and without fear of retaliation for reporting. In order to accomplish this, SWAN advocates for better victims protections, professionalized and impartial prosecution of crimes, and increasing individual and institutional accountability by allowing service members to sue in civil court."[32]

Nate Galbreath described to the *Baltimore Sun* an apparent "sea change" under the leadership of Secretary of Defense Chuck Hagel and his predecessor Leon Panetta begun in 2013: a special victim's counsel, a trained attorney to represent him or her in any legal proceedings; training of enlisted personnel on recognizing and stopping rape; teaching commanders on how to respond to allegations; and the 2011 repeal of "don't ask, don't tell," because the ban on openly gay service members most likely chilled reporting by male victims, gay and straight.[33]

MSA is particularly distressing to male service members. A number of MSA survivors are males who were sexually assaulted by other men. The psychological consequences of MSA are typically worse for men. Following the assault, heterosexual male survivors often report concerns regarding their masculinity and sexual orientation. Although the assault was clearly an act of power and dominance, male survivors often feel that they were targeted for being effeminate or standing out in some way. It is important to provide psychoeducation on male rape myths and emphasize that the assault was not consensual. Health care providers should also underscore that, even if the MSA survivor experienced some sexual arousal during the assault, it does not imply willing participation.

Effects

The Center for Deployment Psychology noted that males are sexually assaulted by women less often, but the impact is still significant. The center stated that military sexual assault is particularly distressing to men and the psychological consequences are typically worse for men. Men are often less willing to seek support, feel isolated, feel alienated from others, become emotionally vulnerable, and are overwhelmed by intense emotions. After an assault by another male, heterosexual male survivors often report concerns about their masculinity and sexual orientation, feeling they were targeted for being effeminate or standing out in some way. In these cases, it is important to emphasize that the assault was not consensual. Nor experiencing some sexual arousal during the assault implies willing participation.[34] Involuntary sexual arousal is often out of the victim's control because, in many cases, the responses are muscular or involuntary, stated Afterdeployment.org. These reactions are not measures of pleasure or interest. In cases where the assault is somewhat physically pleasurable does not indicate that the victim asked for, wanted, or consented to the assault.[35]

Afterdeployment.org added that many sexual assaults of men involve more than one attacker, weapons, or forced participation. In summary, male survivors contend with issues of:

Legitimacy (Men can't be sexually assaulted; No one will believe me)
Masculinity (I must not be a real man if I let this happen to me; My manhood has been stolen)
Strength and power (I should have been able to fend them off; I shouldn't have let this happen)
Sexual orientation (Am I gay?; Will others think I'm gay and only pretended not to like it?)[36]

Although men suffer many of the same effects that women do, Jessica A., Turchik and Susan M. Wilson found only a few studies have specifically focused on male service members' responses. An early study (1984) examined 13 clinical records of active-duty Navy and Marine Corps victims of male sexual assault. They experienced high rates of depression, anger, somatic disturbances, sexual problems, and interpersonal relationship difficulties. A later study (2007) found that a large sample of male veterans had various mental and physical problems, such as posttraumatic stress disorder, alcohol abuse, and dissociative disorders. Turchik and Wilson concluded that one effect that may be unique for men is confusion concerning sexual identity, masculinity, and sexual orientation, especially if the offender is a man.[37]

MEN BECOMING VISIBLE

The pain of sexual assault was suffered in silence by too many men in the military. The strong societal bias against homosexuality kept heterosexual males from reporting the attack. The presence of "Don't Ask, Don't Tell" served as a further deterrent even for those who did not have homosexual experience; just the threat of being "outed" unjustifiably was enough of a threat to compel silence.

With the repeal of "Don't Ask, Don't Tell," the threat value of "outing" is reduced. With the weakening of the jurisdiction of the chain of command in sexual assault cases, the possibility of unjust outcomes is reduced. Sexual assaults will not be eliminated, but with proper support and effective investigation and prosecution of sexual assault cases involving military men, the number of assaults can be sharply reduced.

CHAPTER 7

Sexual Assaults on Gay, Lesbian, Bisexual, and Transgendered Service Members

No research has ever shown that open homosexuality impairs military readiness.

—Government Accountability Office and Department of Defense[1]

THE MILITARY AND HOMOSEXUALITY

Lesbians, gays, bisexuals, and transgendered[2] persons, historically, have been rejected by American society including the U.S. military. Lesbian, gay, and bisexual individuals have served in the military covertly for decades, despite exclusionary and pseudoinclusionary policies. The 2000 census revealed nearly one million gay and lesbian Americans were veterans.[3]

Since early twentieth century, consensual same-sex or LGB relationships have been against military policy. In 1982, the Department of Defense Directive 1332.14 stated, "Homosexuality is incompatible with military service" and if service members either stated they were homosexual or engaged in homosexual acts, policy dictated discharge. In the 1980s and 1990s, the public scrutinized the policy.[4]

The first "permission" for homosexuals[5] to serve did not come until 1993 when "Don't Ask, Don't Tell" (DADT) was approved. DADT became the official U.S. policy on service by gays and lesbians in the military (see Appendix G). It was instituted by the Clinton administration on February 28, 1994, when the Department of Defense Directive 1304.26 issued on December 21, 1993, took effect.[6] The policy prohibited military personnel from discriminating against or harassing closeted homosexual or bisexual service members or applicants closeted, while, at the same time, barring openly gay, lesbian, or bisexual persons from military service.

A 2010 Williams Institute Study found that an estimated 48,500 lesbians, gay men, and bisexuals were serving on active duty or in the ready reserve in the U.S. military and an additional 22,000 were in the standby and retired reserve forces, accounting for approximately 2.2 percent of military personnel. Approximately 13,000 LGB people were serving on active duty (comprising 0.9 percent of all active duty personnel) while nearly 58,000 were serving in the various guard and reserve forces (3.4 percent). While women comprise only about 14 percent of active-duty personnel, they comprise more than 43 percent of LGB men and women serving on active duty.[7]

DADT was very costly for the military. The DADT policy has cost the military between $290 million and more than $0.5 billion. The military spends an estimated $22,000 to $43,000 per person to replace those discharged under DADT.[8]

DADT remained the policy for homosexual military personnel until it was repealed on September 20, 2011. Even today after the repeal, the road to inclusion and acceptance remains difficult.

When gay and lesbian service members were discovered, they were discharged. In the years 1980 to 1994 alone, there were 19,905 homosexual conduct administrative separation discharges.[9] There were 13,000 more discharged from 1993 to 2009 following the initiation of DADT, stated Derek J. Burks.[10] The number of discharges alone would cause unease regardless of a service member's sexual orientation.

In 2008, the Servicemembers Legal Defense Network reported that women especially were caught in the crosshairs of the DADT: "Women make up 15 percent of the armed forces, so to find they represent nearly 50 percent of Army and Air Force discharges under 'Don't Ask, Don't Tell' is shocking. . . . 'Don't Ask, Don't Tell' is often used as a weapon of vengeance against service members."[11]

Those investigated on the charge of sexual assault are nearly always men (90 percent), compared with women (2 percent). These findings show that male victims are assaulted by other men. The majority of victims (88 percent) were women compared to men (12 percent). The findings show that men do not report assault at the same rate as women. Rowan Scarborough reported in the *Washington Times* that an unfounded inference is sometimes made that male-on-male assaults indicate the assaults are caused by homosexual orientation. Aron Belkin, head of the Palm Center, which studies gays and lesbians in the military, said "Very few" male-on-male perpetrators are gay. The assaults rather are "somewhat similar to prison rape."[12] When Burk asked a military member whether fear of getting labeled a homosexual contributes to the low male reporting rates by heterosexual men who are attacked, she replied,

"Yes, even since the passage of Don't Ask Don't Tell." For LGB service members, Burks believes, "In a military context influenced by sexual stigma, heterosexism, and mandated secrecy about sexual orientation, LGB service members have an increased likelihood of sexual victimization from sexual assault and sexual harassment."[13] Burks maintains that the military has started to address incidents of sexual assault and harassment, but more attention is needed on sexual orientation as a significant risk factor. Homosexual victims may experience internalized homophobia and feel that the assault was a punishment for being gay. Heterosexual victims may face confusion about their sexuality and masculinity, especially if their body sexually responded.[14] Regardless of sexual orientation, heterosexual and LGB individuals face sexual orientation challenges related to sexual assault.

Sexual Predators

Sexual predators affect both men and women in the military but the LGBT service members are especially vulnerable. CAPT Lory Manning, U.S. Navy (Ret.), says that under DADT, the sexual predator would hit on a woman and, if she said, "No, I don't want to sleep with you," He'd say, "You must be gay then. I'll just have to tell everybody that you are gay." So it was used as a threat before the end of DADT. "Sleep with me or I am going to tell everyone you are gay, and then you will be thrown out of the military, because everybody will believe me, not you."[15]

The LGBT service members are most vulnerable to the sexual predator because they are less likely to report the assault than others. This reluctance to report enables sexual predators to be serial predators. Another reason the sexual predator is able to assault repeatedly has been the method of investigating these assaults. The sexual predator has often escaped detection because there has been more focus on investigating the victim than the perpetrator. The military and civil authorities are recognizing that approach was a mistake, which permitted the sexual predator to become a serial sexual assault offender. Research has shown that in some "semi-closed settings," like college campuses, as many as 90 percent of sexual assaults come from serial predators. Some Pentagon officials believe this theory could apply to military bases, and they are working with consulting psychologists who have worked on such studies. "We think it tends to be, more often than we've believed before, 'serial predators' with more than one victim," MGen. Margaret Woodward, former director of the U.S. Air Force's Sexual Assault Prevention and Response Office, said. "If you get rid of just one of these predators, it's pretty significant."[16]

Military law enforcement investigators are increasingly trained now to look into an assault suspect's past for possible evidence or clues of habitual behavior. Previously, it was the victim's behavior just prior to the assault that was put under the microscope."Obviously you're going to investigate the incident, but we need to investigate the alleged offender, too," stated Dr. David Lisak, a clinical psychologist working with the Pentagon to train prosecutors.

> Are there any other victims? Investigators are now going away from a bias toward investigating the victim. If you go into the case with the mind-set that false allegations are rare but that perpetrators will perpetrate more than one crime—now that's power. You may actually find incidents in the perpetrator's past. It's easier to prove five assaults than one. Investigations that reveal other victims will bolster credibility in a "he said, she said" scenario.[17]

SEXUAL ASSAULTS AND LGBT SERVICE MEMBERS

Women service members are subject to pressure. Lesbian baiting or pressuring a woman for sex and harassing her by threatening to call her a lesbian to intimidate her is used toward women who do not conform to gender types or refuse sex with men.[18]

Men faced the fear of having their sexual orientation disclosed through sometimes vicious assaults. Chad blogs about his experience that took place after a brutal hazing while stationed at Fort Bragg in North Carolina:

> My attacker mounted me and started acting like he was anally raping me. He then removed my undershorts and penetrated me with a small stick, causing permanent deformity to my body.
>
> He kept repeating "You like that, don't you faggot. Yeah, that's right. I know what you are." I was terrified. I knew that if I reported it I would face the risk of discharge because of my sexuality. I kept quiet.[19]

TRANSGENDERED TROOPS

The repeal of DADT has benefited openly gay service members, but openly transgendered individuals (whose gender identity differs from their gender at birth) have not benefited. The National Transgender Discrimination Survey and the U.S. Census Bureau data show approximately 134,300 transgendered veterans, and that military service is more common among transgendered people than among the general population.[20] In 2014, the Palm Center research institute reported that over 15,000 transgendered troops serve secretly.[21] Movement to review existing medical policy appears to be in progress. On February 23, 2015, Defense Secretary Ash Carter said that transgendered people should be allowed to serve openly as long as they are able to do so. President Barack Obama supported changing the decades-old policy, which was last reviewed in 2011.

Over 90 percent of transgendered individuals report harassment, work mistreatment, or discrimination, or used avoidance techniques, such as hiding their identities. Of the 26 percent of transgendered veterans who have experienced physical assault, 64 percent attempted suicide, and 16 percent have been raped.[22] Department of Defense (DoD) regulations prohibit transgendered individuals from serving in the military. Instruction 6130.03 specifies change of sex and hermaphroditism as medically disqualifying. Psychosexual conditions such as transsexualism or transvestism disqualify an individual from serving. Lastly, conduct such as cross-dressing can disqualify.[23] The ban has existed in medical fitness standards and conduct codes since the 1960s; it appears based in part in the psychiatric establishment's long-held belief that people who identify with a gender different from the one assigned at birth suffer from a mental disorder. In addition, the ban also was based on the assumption that providing hormone treatment and sex reassignment surgeries would be too difficult, disruptive, and expensive. This reasoning was rejected as inconsistent with modern medical practice and the scope of health care services routinely provided to nontransgendered military personnel.[24] The Service Women's Action League states that the military view is narrow.

Transgendered persons have a particularly difficult time when they serve. The American Military Partner Association (AMPA) report features testimony of transgendered service members and family members. Common threads include going without necessary medical and mental health care out of fear of exposure and ignorance. The threat of discharge is ever present for the families because at any time possible discharge from the military could occur because they are "transgendered or gender non-conforming." The examples that follow depict a capsule in time.[25] The basis for sexual assault is perceived or desired power over another individual. When transgendered individuals are perceived differently, discrimination occurs, which is sometimes the basis for sexual assault.

Army service member Number 1:

The fear, pain, and frustration is so overwhelming that it has led me to contemplate suicide. Unlike a few service members who left and transitioned, and despite the reoccurring nightmares I still have, I cannot transition out of fear I'll be discharged for my gender identity. I still hold deeply strong feelings about wanting to continue to serve in the Army, but I want to serve in a safe environment that leadership keeps talking about.

Army service member Number 2:

From the time I drive on-post until the time I drive off, I have to pretend to be someone that I am not. I have to smile in the face of my co-workers and friends and pretend that everything is okay, when in all actuality it is killing me inside. Just small things such as having to answer to the wrong pronouns, and using the female latrines set off my anxiety. I go to work every day in the same uniform as my brothers and sisters and work just as hard as them, only to know that if I admit to being who I am I could be discharged.

Navy service member:

I am forced to be two separate people. I have a wife and children that see me as the man I am and love me for all of my faults and strengths. I have a career that I love very much and yet, not only do I have to hide the most obvious part of me, lie to close friends, and act like one of the girls who looks like a boy, but I have to live in fear. I have to ignore the looks and stares as I walk by a new female check-in in my berthing on my way to my bunk. I have to ignore the awkwardness that comes when someone calls me "sir," then only to be corrected by someone around me after I have returned a greeting. I am scared to answer the question at medical if I am my child's father when picking up medicine for them.

Air force service member:

There is an awards ball coming up and I have to be at the function. This means I must be in a mess dress. The thought of wearing that skirt sends me into a panic and depression like I can't even explain. For my daily uniform, I wear the men's Airmans Battle Uniform (ABU) and even the men's jacket. There are so many constant reminders in the military that I cannot be myself, and it is very disappointing. I was very pleased that DADT fell, and that I could legally marry my wife and provide benefits for her. However, transgendered service members are still living in fear. I am still living in fear of being found out. Nobody should have to live in fear of who they are to defend their country.

Civilian society also discriminates. Carolyn Martin found that transgendered individuals are subject to abuse on a regular basis such as innuendo, verbal harassment, discrimination, and assault. In 2013, the National Center for Transgender Equality and the National Gay and Lesbian Task Force study on transgendered discrimination revealed near universal problems at the workplace. Ninety percent of transgendered individuals have encountered harassment or mistreatment at work. Forty-seven percent of workers have experienced an adverse job outcome, including 44 percent who were passed over for a job, 23 percent who were denied a promotion, and 26 percent who were fired because they were transgendered. Martin concluded, "The magnitude of such abuse is difficult to ascertain due to low reporting rates. Those involved in such abuse have a multitude of reasons for not reporting the abuse to mainstream agencies that deal with such issues."[26]

SIGNS OF PROGRESS TOWARD INCLUSION

Repeal of DADT

President Obama signed legislation on December 22, 2010, that repealed DADT, but the repeal did not take effect, until September 20, 2011 (see Appendix B). After the repeal, previously discharged service members have the opportunity to re-enlist. Gay men and lesbians for the first time ever are able to openly join the military. Currently serving members have the freedom to disclose their orientation.[27]

The repeal of DADT was an important step toward equal rights for LGB individuals, but much is left to accomplish in efforts to change the culture through policy enforcement. In 2013, Heather Wilder and Jami Wilder concluded, "the culture of the armed forces, for the past 18 years, has been an unwelcoming and unsafe place for LGB service members."[28]

Societal homophobia sometimes grounds itself in perceptions that suggest all same-sexual activity, including assault, results from homosexual orientation. Still, insight into military and societal cultures can be gained through examination of such observations. If nothing else, an examination reveals the intensity that the proposed repeal of the law, Don't Ask Don't Tell, invited at the time. In 2009, the Family Research Council analysis found "a significant problem of homosexual misconduct in the military. This problem can only become worse if the current law is repealed and homosexuals are openly welcomed (and even granted special protections) within the military, as homosexual activists are demanding."[29]

In 2013, Family Research Council Vice President Jerry Boykin linked the trend of increased number of sexual assaults to the DADT repeal, suggesting the "sexualization of our military with social engineering" was partly responsible, according to the *HuffPost Gay Voices*. Citing close living quarters as a reason for "inviting this kind of behavior,"[30] Lila Shapiro reported that the first academic study of the military's new open-service policy, conducted in 2012, found no negative consequences in spite of the "fierce" debate over the repeal of the 1993 policy. Supporters of the law believed consequences would be disastrous.[31] A letter, signed by over 1,000 military officers, argued that repeal would undermine recruiting efforts, negatively affect "troop readiness" and "eventually break the All-Volunteer Force."[32]

The research of Nathaniel Frank, Palm Center, takes issue with Boykin and others who hold these positions. Frank reminds that the study of openly gay service is extensive, and includes over half a century of evidence. In 1957, the secretary of the navy appointed a panel to investigate its homosexual exclusion policy. The result, the Crittenden report, stated, "the number of cases of blackmail as a result of past investigations of homosexuals is negligible" and "no factual data exist to support the contention that homosexuals are a greater risk than heterosexuals."[33] The military's researchers have consistently found that openly gay service does not undermine cohesion. Further, the military has repeatedly strived to condemn or suppress these conclusions. Yet no research has ever shown that open homosexuality impairs military readiness, according to the Government Accountability Office and DoD.[34]

Significant progress took place in 2013 for the employment rights of transgendered or gender-nonconforming individuals, according to attorney Lauren R. S. Mendonsa. For the first time, the Senate passed a version of the Employment Nondiscrimination Act (ENDA) that included explicit protection for transgendered individuals. This legislative action was important because transgendered individuals experience unemployment rates double than those among the general population. In 2013, less than one-fifth of all states had laws that bar discrimination on the basis of gender identity. The trend is to expand such rights. Mendonsa believed that these laws are a step toward leveling the playing field for transgendered individuals seeking employment and eradicating workplaces that tolerate harassment of people based on their perceived or actual gender identity.[35]

Full Benefits

Gay and lesbian military spouses soon will have the same benefits as traditional spouses to include military health coverage, base shopping, travel reimbursements for military moves, and the larger "with dependent" housing allowances or, when available, access to base housing instead.

Twenty-one years after presidential candidate Bill Clinton vowed to be the first commander in chief to allow homosexuals to serve their country openly—and had to compromise on that promise—gay and lesbian members serve openly and have now won full equality in military benefits.[36]

The final hurdle was defeat of the Defense of Marriage Act (DOMA), which had defined marriage for the purpose of federal benefits as solely between a man and woman. The U.S. Supreme Court on Wednesday, June 26, 2013, in a 5–4 decision, struck down DOMA as unconstitutional.

Writing for the court majority in *U.S. v Windsor*, Justice Anthony Kennedy said DOMA "violates basic due process and equal protection principles" and deviates "from the tradition of recognizing and accepting state definitions of marriage" to "deprive same-sex couples of the benefits and responsibilities that come with federal recognition of their marriages."

Three of four dissenting justices wrote separate opinions including Chief Justice John Roberts who said Congress acted constitutionally in passing DOMA in the interest of uniformity and stability in defining marriage. He also said no part of the majority opinion stops states from continuing to define marriage, as most still do, as only between a man and a woman.

After the ruling, Defense Secretary Chuck Hagel issued a statement that it changed the "law of the land" and the DoD "intends to make the same benefits available to all military spouses—regardless of sexual orientation—as soon as possible."[37]

POLICY

Although the U.S. military has grappled successfully with equality issues in the areas of race, sexual orientation, and women, it "faces yet another equal opportunity, equal-protection-under-the law battle, gender identity," stated Endia T. Mendez. DoD Instruction (DoDI) 6130.03, "Medical Standards for Appointment, Enlistment, or Induction in the Military Service," covers a wide range of impairments, deformities, diseases, disorders, learning, and psychiatric and behavioral issues. The instruction is used to "establish policy, assign responsibilities, and prescribe procedures for physical and medical standards for appointment, enlistment, or induction in the Military Services. . . . [and] medical standards, which, if not met, are grounds for rejection for military service. Other standards may be prescribed for a mobilization for a national emergency."[38]

Three sections are applicable specifically to transgendered persons and concern the altering of female and male genitalia. Specifically, regarding male genitalia, the instruction states a "history of penis amputation" by listing a "history of major abnormalities or defects of the genitalia, such as change of sex, hermaphroditism, pseudohermaphroditism, or pure gonadal dysgenesis" as disqualifiers for service in the military. Denial of entry of transsexuals is included under the category of psychosexual conditions, "current or history of psychosexual conditions, including but not limited to transsexualism, exhibitionism, transvestism, voyeurism, and other paraphilias."[39]

Transgendered persons remain excluded from military service, but, on March 6, 2015, the army announced that dismissals of transgendered soldiers must be approved by an assistant secretary of the army, a senior-level official. Previously, such dismissals could be approved by lower-level officials. It is the latest sign that the military is taking a hard look at its long-standing policy barring transgendered service members. In late January 2015, new Defense Secretary Ashton Carter, during a town hall meeting in Kandahar, Afghanistan, expressed an openness to permitting transgendered people to openly serve in the military.[40] In another sign that transgendered persons are closer to full acceptance, Bradley Manning, who is now Chelsea Manning, has been approved for hormone therapy. In a first for the army, Chelsea Manning, the convicted national-security secrets leaker, has been approved for hormone therapy for transition to a woman at the army's Fort Leavenworth prison.[41]

Post DADT

Equality under the law gained, how are the benefactors getting along? Although Jeremy Johnson considers his current navy environment friendly since his reenlistment, whether or not he should "come out" may already be decided for him. He says, "my DD 214 (discharge paper) is part of my official record and still says 'homosexual admission' at the bottom. Anyone who reviews my record will see this and immediately be informed of something I may have otherwise chosen to leave unannounced. . . . That bold statement in my record says my personal life is subject to scrutiny. If I wanted to remain closeted at every command from now on . . . I couldn't control that. The personnel office and my Commanding Officer have access to this information."[42]

Johnson says the repeal brings an ethical dilemma, and poses the question whether the DoD is obligated to upgrade his discharge or rewrite history? He questions whether to expect such is fair. And finally, he asks, "Is it such an indignity to face . . . that is, being 'outed' by my past for the rest of my career? . . . Shouldn't they want me to blend in, and not let my LGBT status influence my career (positively or negatively)?" Perhaps DADT is only a beginning as Johnson notes.[43]

THE TIDE HAS TURNED

On May 29, 2015, President Barack Obama proclaimed June 2015 as Lesbian, Gay, Bisexual, and Transgender Pride Month and called upon the people of the United States to eliminate prejudice everywhere it exists, and to celebrate the great diversity of the American people. The president said,

> From the moment our Nation first came together to declare the fundamental truth that all men are created equal, courageous and dedicated patriots have fought to refine our founding promise and broaden democracy's reach. Over the course of more than two centuries of striving and sacrifice, our country has expanded civil rights and enshrined equal protections into our Constitution. Through struggle and setback, we see a common trajectory toward a more free and just society. But we are also reminded that we are not truly equal until every person is afforded the same rights and opportunities—that when one of us experiences discrimination, it affects all of us—and that our journey is not complete until our lesbian, gay, bisexual, and transgendered (LGBT) brothers and sisters are treated like anyone else under the law.
>
> * * * *

> All people deserve to live with dignity and respect, free from fear and violence, and protected against discrimination, regardless of their gender identity or sexual orientation. During Lesbian, Gay, Bisexual, and Transgender Pride Month, we celebrate the proud legacy LGBT individuals have woven into the fabric of our Nation, we honor those who have fought to perfect our Union, and we continue our work to build a society where every child grows up knowing that their country supports them, is proud of them, and has a place for them exactly as they are.[44] (See Appendix D.)

For LGBT military service members, the tide has turned.

CHAPTER 8

The Impact of Sexual Assault on the Military

Sexual assault is not about . . . presence in the military, it is about power and violence. The offenders that commit these crimes take away an individual's trust, faith, and their judgment. It does not stop there; it negatively influences the cohesion and readiness of an organization, placing others in harm's way.
—MAJ Wendy Brinson, U.S. Army[1]

CULTURE, PREVENTION, JUSTICE

Sexual assault is impacted by all aspects of the military: the culture, prevention policies, and the system of justice. In the past, the culture, policies, and system did not do enough and, in some cases, did not work for the reduction or elimination of sexual assault.

CULTURE

For the male-dominated military culture that existed in 1976, male prejudice against women at the academies proved to be a major obstacle.[2] Students, faculty, and staff of the military academies ostracized the female cadets.[3] MAJ Lillian Pfluke, U.S. Army (Ret.), a member of the West Point's first class of women, compares today with her experience.

I don't think you can compare the kinds of just overt, blatant harassment that we were put under to what goes on today. Back then, it was okay. Everybody did it. It was okay to do it. Many people were very, very resistant to the idea of women being there at all. And so we were ostracized, not only by our own students and our own classmates, but also by the faculty and also by the staff. Certainly, every once in a while, someone would do a random act of kindness, but, most of the time, you were reminded every single day that you weren't welcome there.[4]

When the male-dominated culture of the U.S. military permitted, and even condoned, the behaviors of the naval aviators at the 1991 Tailhook Convention, the sexual acts conveyed an attitude of disrespect and devaluing of women, even women in the military. The behavior at Tailhook '91 was not unlike the behavior at past conventions. The difference was that, in 1991, someone complained; Paula Coughlin took her complaint to her commanding officer.[5] Only when her complaint became public were the sexual behaviors denounced. Tailhook '91 became a scandal.

When the military banned and could punish homosexuals for even attempting to join the military, the strong heterosexual bias was confirmed. When "Don't Ask, Don't Tell" was passed in 1994, the homosexual military person could be in the military, but still was not accepted and was made more of a target for harassment.[6]

A culture that places the mission above justice for the individual, that stresses readiness, cohesion, and morale above justice, is out of step with the realities of today's mobile society. Placing the unit commander and the chain of command in charge of achieving unit readiness, cohesion, and morale to accomplish the mission and, at the same time, making the commander responsible for judging cases of wrongdoing that occur in the unit do not promote readiness, cohesion, or morale. CAPT Lory Manning U.S. Navy (Ret.), says the military has "a very broken military justice system."[7] The Uniform Code of Military Justice (UCMJ) gives commanders the discretion to give the mission priority over justice, something that was true when the UCMJ was written after World War II. Manning says that the UCMJ gives military commanders the sort of discretion they needed under World War II battlefield conditions "when you were probably remote, like on some island in the middle of the Pacific or out in the middle of a battlefield somewhere in Europe or Italy or Northern Africa, when communication systems were light years away from what we have now. Now, even if you are on a ship in the middle of the Antarctic, you can pick up a phone and call somebody. Under some World War II situations, commander discretion was a very necessary thing, but it is just not the case anymore."

Manning says, "Most people don't even understand that I am talking about commanders. That was written in there [UCMJ] trusting the discretion of the CO to know when he is in battlefield conditions and then and only then, to have to make the tough decision about mission versus justice. Now, even in Iraq or Afghanistan, that this is not the case anymore, that the commander needs that kind of discretion. The commander ought to be told that justice comes first."[8]

Another problem created by the broken justice system is the sexual predator. Manning says sexual predators are rampant in the military and some are serial rapists. The predator operates in different ways:

> The sexual predator would hit on a woman [or man] and if she said, "No, I don't want to sleep with you," He'd say, "You must be gay then. I'll just have to tell everybody that you are gay." So it was used as a threat before the end of "Don't ask, Don't tell." "Sleep with me or I am going to tell everyone you are gay, and then you will be thrown out of the military, because everybody will believe me, not you."[9]

Manning points out with the repeal of "Don't Ask, Don't Tell"; "Now, it is okay, you can be gay and stay in the military. But a lot of people consider that to be their own business and don't necessarily want it widespread. Or some of the guys are straight and don't want to be labeled as gay."[10]

A second method the sexual predator employs, Manning says, is:

> Quite often, the person who is sexually assaulted is generally pretty junior in the chain of command and they might not even know that they could come to you directly. The perpetrator will sometimes tell a very young junior person, "You tell anybody and I'm going to kill you," and they believe it. Or "You tell anybody, you will be the one who has duty all day Christmas, every Christmas for the rest of your life." They have ways of keeping you quiet. "A good commanding officer needs to be sure that people below them know that there are ways around that sort of impediment, not just with respect to sexual assault, but with anything."[11]

The culture, even though changes are occurring, is a major factor in measuring the impact of sexual assault. The current military justice system is embedded in the culture and places unfair responsibility on the commanding officers to do something that they are not trained to do. Their training involves the ability to command their units as they perform the missions assigned to them. They are not trained to be lawyers and judges, just as they are not trained as doctors and surgeons. If a member of their unit is injured, that member is treated by trained medical personnel. If a member or members of their unit is accused of sexual assault or has been sexually assaulted, the case should be handled by impartial, trained legal personnel. The current system does not routinely permit this.[12]

Sexual Assault Effects on Service Members

Sexual victimization among service members is linked to significant physical and psychological consequences for the victim. In addition, violence within the ranks represents a threat to good order and discipline and undermines the command structure.[13]

Psychological consequences of sexual assault for the individual include: posttraumatic stress disorder (PTSD), depression, suicide, substance abuse, and insomnia, all which do not contribute to a ready force. In addition, victims suffer immediate physical harm resulting from the assault itself, increased risks of sexually transmitted illnesses, pregnancy, and chronic health problems. Psychological consequences are numerous due to the nature of the trauma with an emphasis on the trauma context. Since it is an interpersonal assault, it is a personal, intentional violation of an individual's boundaries and personal rights. In the military context, sexual assault is disturbing, stated the Center for Deployment Psychology. Victims are violated within a small community by someone who should be trustworthy. Assault is incompatible with the independent and self-sufficient spirit needed to thrive in the military. Victims often know their assailant and work or live in the same environment. Work and social environments converge, making reporting difficult. Power differentials, peer chastisement, and rank progression are some resulting concerns.[14]

Sexual assault during military service differs from civilian assaults. Military service emphasizes loyalty and community. The victim may experience a heightened sense of shock and betrayal when a colleague commits the offense. When someone from within the chain of command assaults a service member, which occurs in about one-quarter of reported cases, the victim may have no way to escape, thus may remain vulnerable to repeated assaults and other abuses. Possible significant negative influence on career trajectories may occur, and retention may decline.[15]

Societal Effects of Sexual Assault

In addition to consequences for the victim, sexual assault has costs for society. Coreen Farris, Terry L. Schell, and Terri Tanielian utilized a 2002 figure that calculated the cost of each societal sexual assault to be $129,908. They extrapolated these numbers to the Sexual Assault Prevention and Response Office (SAPRO), which estimates that, of all military sexual assault cases (disclosed and undisclosed), the total cost of military sexual assault was approximately $2.9 billion in FY2010.[16]

Effects on the Military

"The issue of sexual assault in our armed forces undermines . . . trust. So not only is it a crime, not only is it shameful and disgraceful, but it also is going to make and has made the military less effective than it can be. And as such, it is dangerous to our national security," President Obama said.[17] He went on to say that sexual assault violates the trust the armed forces is based on, thereby threatening our national security.

Sexual assault negatively affects the military's strength, readiness, and morale. Posttraumatic stress and military sexual trauma negatively affect military readiness because of possible devastating consequences to those assaulted while serving. Lives are ruined and subsequent monetary losses are incurred. Robyn A. Diehl points out how sexual assault affects national security, "Although essential, allocating countless resources to understanding rape within the ranks undermines the mission and weakens the military."[18] Sexual assault in the military poses an even greater threat and possible consequences. Diehl contends that the military exists to protect the American public from enemies both foreign and domestic and when attention and efforts are focused on eliminating sexual assault, other efforts can suffer.

Defense Secretary Ash Carter echoed these philosophies, "Sexual assaults and retaliation against people who report them undermine the military's values of honor and trust. . . . The values of honor and trust are the lifeblood of our military, and every act of sexual assault directly undermines those values. So too does every act of retaliation against those who report these crimes."[19]

PREVENTION AND ELIMINATION OF SEXUAL ASSAULT

Current efforts to prevent and eliminate sexual assault in the military are not working. In fact, the methods being employed are counterproductive and work against prevention.

Zero Tolerance and Prevention

After the Tailhook '91 scandal, the navy publicized a "zero tolerance" policy. This was the part of the navy's effort to prevent and eliminate sexual assault and harassment. "Zero tolerance" is defined as: the act of punishing all criminal or unacceptable behavior severely, even if it is not very serious.[20] It is also "the policy of applying laws or penalties to even minor infringements of a code in order to reinforce its overall importance and enhance deterrence."[21] The military's use of the phrase "zero tolerance" dates back at least to 1989, when Navy Secretary H. Lawrence Garrett III declared that his branch had "zero tolerance" for sexual assault. In 1991, the year of the Tailhook scandal, it appeared in *New York Times*.[22] Eric Schmitt, who covered the Tailhook scandal extensively, wrote: "Mr. Garrett, who proclaimed his distaste for lewd behavior with a 'zero tolerance' policy issued when he became Navy Secretary, has said that he spent 30 to 45 minutes on the patio but was unaware there was anything amiss inside until three weeks later."[23] The disconnect between the policy and Garrett's behavior is part of the clash between policy and culture. Lawrence

Downes writing in the *New York Times* in 2013 is critical of the military's zero tolerance: "If the military could agree to stop using the phrase, and start reforming itself instead, that'd be great."[24] Defense Secretary Chuck Hagel finally said on May 17, 2013, "It's not good enough to say we have a zero tolerance policy. How does that translate into changing anything?"[25] In 2012, the Editorial Board of the *Washington Post* commented: "One area that clearly demands immediate attention is how the military punishes those who are accused or convicted of sex crimes. Analysis by the Service Women's Action Network of 2011 reported that Defense Department statistics showed that 10 percent of accused sex offenders were never held accountable because they were allowed to resign. Even more startling is its finding that one in every three convicted sex offenders was allowed to remain in the service. So much for zero tolerance."[26]

The zero tolerance policy is widely misunderstood and the military does little to correct the misunderstanding. "Zero tolerance" seems to mean that "any instance of sexual assault is not acceptable and appropriate action will be taken." It also seems to mean that zero tolerance involves taking appropriate actions to prevent sexual assaults. The true meaning of "zero tolerance" is: " the act of punishing all criminal or unacceptable behaviour severely, even if it is not very serious."[27] zero tolerance is also "the policy of applying laws or penalties to even minor infringements of a code in order to reinforce its overall importance and enhance deterrence."[28] Bruce Schneier contends that these so-called zero tolerance policies are actually zero-discretion policies. They are policies that must be followed, no situational discretion allowed.[29] Schneier says, "These policies enrage us because they are blind to circumstance."[30] Whether applied with no discretion or with discretion, the military's zero tolerance policy has not prevented sexual assaults.

The truth is zero tolerance operating within the chain of command structure has influenced the outcome of sexual assault cases. A commanding officer faced with the loss of a member of the unit does not want to weaken the readiness of the unit by having a "good soldier" found guilty of a crime that would result in a less than honorable discharge from the service. Until Senator Claire McCaskill's bill eliminated it, one defense that a person accused of sexual assault could use was the "good soldier" defense.[31] Another problem with zero tolerance is the reluctance of the person assaulted to report the assault because the penalty for the assault might mean that the person who committed the assault might be disciplined in a way that the person assaulted did not want.

The zero tolerance policy should be eliminated in sexual assault cases because it does not prevent or help eliminate sexual assaults. In certain cases, it makes the securing of justice difficult if not impossible.

Training and Prevention

After Tailhook '91, the navy turned its focus to training as a way to reduce sexual assaults. Rear Admiral Duvall M. "Mac" Williams, the Commander of the Naval Investigative Service (NIS) at the time, describes the initiative on training:

> The first time I met with Admiral Kelso about the Tailhook incident and the investigation, he called the Chief of Naval Education and Training, Vice Admiral [Jack] Fetterman, and the Chief of Naval Personnel, Vice Admiral [Ronald] Zlatoper. He directed both of them to develop education and training programs to address the treatment of women in the Navy. I thought Admiral Kelso had the right resolve and that is education and training programs.[32]

Williams describes the process:

> The training programs that I was developing at the Naval Investigative Service were for female and male sailors because it is not just women that are being sexually assaulted, there are men who are sexual assault victims too. We were trying to address all of them, but clearly there was a lot of effort that we put in to developing training programs for young female sailors about behavior, places to go, not to go. Some of the training was localized to the facilities where they were. When Admiral [Paul David] Miller was commander of the Atlantic fleet, we developed a training program for him. He kept looking at his ledger, his blotter every morning and seeing all these reports of sailors being assault in various sections of Virginia Beach and so we put together training programs for sailors about where you go, where you don't go. If you are going to go out and you are going to be drinking and that results in these kinds of compromise situations, make sure you have got somebody with you who has not. We had training and education programs for sailors to talk to them about these issues and I think that is the way to deal with it. That's the way they dealt with racial integration in the military and that's the way they ought to deal with this.[33]

The training programs instituted by RADM Williams and others undoubtedly made a difference in some cases, but, to prevent sexual assaults, the training programs need to be constantly updated in order to keep up with the changing times. Training is important but it alone has not been able to prevent the unacceptable numbers of sexual assaults.

Policy and Prevention

The zero tolerance policy has not worked and should be eliminated, but policy is necessary to prevent and eliminate sexual assault. In May 2015, the military has issued an updated policy. The goal for prevention is to deliver consistent and effective prevention methods and programs.

The objective is "cultural imperatives of mutual respect and trust, professional values, and team commitment are reinforced to create an environment where sexual assault is not condoned, tolerated, or ignored."[34] If this objective is achieved, it will reduce sexual assault in the military.

SEXUAL ASSAULT AND READINESS, COHESION, AND MORALE

The military has the responsibility to perform its missions through the chain of command. To perform a mission, a unit must be ready. Readiness involves training and understanding of the mission; cohesion involves unit members bonding together; and morale, or esprit de corps, is the capacity of a group's members to maintain belief in an institution or goal, particularly in the face of opposition or hardship.

The arguments for and against trying sexual assault cases, either in or out of the chain of command, focus on the cohesion and readiness of the troops. Those who believe that the sexual assault cases should stay in the chain of command contend that removing jurisdiction from the chain of command will undermine military readiness. Lawrence Korb, a senior fellow at the Center for American Progress and a former assistant secretary of defense in the Reagan administration, and Major General Dennis Laich (Ret.), who served in the army for 35 years, argue that not only is there no empirical evidence to support this claim among our allies who have removed the issue from the chain of command, but this line of reasoning ignores that military readiness has already been undermined by the way in which commanders are handling the situation.[35] Successful examples of removal policies are in place in Canada, New Zealand, Australia, Israel, Germany, and the United Kingdom. The decision in these countries rests with professional military prosecutors.[36]

Korb and Laich state that the apocalyptic claims about military readiness are like the claims that military leaders made when women were admitted to the military and when the ban against gays and lesbians serving openly was lifted. Additionally, in many cases, people in the chain of command are responsible for the violence, and the same people are now responsible for ultimately deciding the cases.

In its Sexual Assault Prevention and Response program, "Together We Can Prevent Sexual Assault," the navy acknowledges that sexual assault has negative impact on readiness, cohesion, and morale.[37] Since the 2012, Sexual Assault Prevention Report that detailed the 26,000 cases of sexual assault in the military, the military's efforts have intensified to reduce the effects of sexual assault on a unit's mission, and on readiness, cohesion, and morale.[38] In May 2015, Army MG Jeffrey J. Snow stated that the unprecedented attention that leadership has focused on the crime has trends going in the right direction. Still, while there is progress, no one is doing a victory lap, he said, noting that much remains to be done to reach out to victims and to put in place programs that prevent the crime in the first place. Defense secretaries Leon Panetta, Chuck Hagel, and Ash Carter have made combating sexual assault a priority for the department. This has led to a strategic plan with clear lines of effort and objectives. "We've developed measures to determine whether it is working, and when it is not, we've taken steps to address it."[39]

JUSTICE IN CASES OF SEXUAL ASSAULT

The problem of achieving justice in sexual assault cases is demonstrated by the 26,000 sexual assaults that occurred in the military in 2012, of which 3,374 were reported, 2,558 cases were pursued by victims, 302 went to trial, 238 were convicted, and 64 were acquitted.[40] The gap between 26,000 sexual assaults and the 2,558 pursued by victims demonstrates that justice is not sought in the majority of cases and that only 302 went to trial focuses attention on the system for achieving justice.

In the current system, the unit commanders have the responsibility for processing criminal cases including sexual assault. The commander's primary responsibility is the unit's mission. Achieving the mission is made more complicated for the unit commanders when they have the added responsibility of processing crimes that occur in the unit. When the accused and accuser are in the same unit, the task of the unit commander becomes more difficult. There is controversy whether the unit commanders and the chain of command can or should perform both responsibilities.

The positions on the role of the chain of the chain of command in sexual assault cases are essentially three: (1) having the chain of command maintain its current position in relation to processing criminal cases, including sexual assault, but provide better training for all commanders in the chain of command and improve the process of review of the decisions made in the chain of command; (2) removing the serious cases from the chain of command but not all cases; and (3) removing all cases from the chain of command.

RADM Williams, former Commander of the Naval Investigative Service (NIS), supports the first option. He believes that removing the chain of command from the task of processing cases would "probably not be helpful. . . . I think it would have other deleterious effects. Some of the commanders might welcome being excluded from the process. Some of these cases put them in somewhat awkward positions . . . Notwithstanding all the problems that the military has had with these issues, the commanders have been making an effort to try to deal with them properly and appropriately."[41]

The second option is to remove some but not all cases from the chain of command. MAJ Lillian Pfluke, U.S. Army (Ret.), advocates this option.[42] She believes that, in some cases, the chain of command is functioning adequately, but sexual assault cases should be removed from the chain of command.

> The chain of command is not always capable of [handling sexual assault cases], because sometimes the chain of command is involved and always the chain of command is trying to support your guys, your people, and if you have two people that are accusing each other of stuff, then it's hard to know which side to come down on. The military chain of command isn't always equipped to handle that as well as an unbiased person dealing with it may be.[43]

Senator Claire McCaskill (D-MO) takes the position that some of the authority of the chain of command should be removed, but not all. The changes that McCaskill supports, the elimination of the "good soldier" defense and allowing the victim to have input on whether the case is tried in military or civilian court, were included in the defense authorization bill signed by President Obama on December 23, 2013. The act includes other major sexual assault reforms: it would strip military commanders of the ability to overturn jury convictions, require a civilian review if a commander declines to prosecute a case, assign victims an independent legal counsel to protect their rights, mandate a dishonorable discharge for anyone convicted of sexual assault, criminalize retaliation against victims who report a sexual assault, and eliminate the statute of limitations in rape and sexual assault cases.[44]

The third option is gaining support: remove all cases from the chain of command. CAPT Lory Manning, U.S. Navy (Ret.), is a strong advocate for this position. She believes "we have a very broken military justice system."[45] Manning contends that when a sailor under her command was injured and needed medical attention, they did not come to her and ask her to operate. The sailor was placed in the care of the medical staff. Similarly, she does not believe that, when a sexual assault occurs, the unit commander should be asked to try the case; that role belongs to the trained legal staff.[46] Manning supports Senator Kirsten Gillibrand's (D-NY) bill that would remove the jurisdiction from the chain of command. Gillibrand has fought passionately to remove sexual assault cases from the chain of command because victims have testified that they do not trust their commanders to handle those cases effectively without retaliating.[47] Gillibrand believes that the harm caused by the current system demands the change. She points to sexual violence as the leading cause of PTSD among women veterans. It destabilizes our military and threatens unit cohesion and national security. Victims of assault are involved in two wars, the theater and within their own ranks among their fellow service members and ranking officers, an environment that enables sexual assault. Some victims have to fight all over again to have their voice heard, their assailant brought to any measure of justice, and the disability claims honored. The psychological and physical costs are high, but this crisis also erodes significant assets, making us weaker both morally and militarily.[48]

If commanders are removed from handling the sexual assault allegations, they will still be accountable to produce cohesive and ready units. Removing a commander from sexual assault cases does not remove his or her command authority in all other cases. Prohibiting sexual assault through good order and conduct will be the commander's challenge. Failure to do so should result in holding the commander accountable along with the perpetrator. Commanders monitor and teach soldiers when to kill and when to stop killing. Likewise, commanders set the climate for good order and discipline, which is about dignity and respect. They must also enforce that tone. Assault is contrary to good order and discipline. Since regulations exist to support the commander, when good, strong leadership fails, units have cohesion and readiness problems.[49]

Greater institutional accountability, more impartial prosecution of cases, and eliminating retaliation are needed to create a fair and just system that will deter sexual assaults. The system needs to encourage victims to come forward to take part in their perpetrator's prosecution to see that it is not detrimental to their safety or future, and will result in justice being done.[50]

THE IMPACT

The impact of sexual assault on the military is great and is negative. Sexual assault affects negatively the accused and the accuser, but it harms the military's mission by undermining a unit's readiness, cohesion, and morale. The Defense Authorization Act that Congress passed and President Obama signed in December 2013 made significant changes that have begun to change the landscape, but Senator Gillibrand is correct: sexual assault cases should not be decided by the chain of command.

CHAPTER 9

Approaches That Reduce or Eliminate Sexual Assault in the Military

Eradicating sexual assault from our ranks is not only essential to the long-term health and readiness of the force; it is also about honoring our highest commitments to protect our fellow soldiers, sailors, airmen and Marines.

—Defense Secretary Chuck Hagel[1]

"Get to the left" of these incidents by changing the cultural structures that allow them to occur.

—Douglas C. Lovelace Jr., Director Strategic Studies Institute and U.S. Army War College Press[2]

THE MANDATE FOR CHANGE

The 2013 Department of Defense (DoD) *Annual Report on Sexual Assault in the Military, Fiscal Year 2012* that revealed 26,000 sexual assaults occurred in the military in 2012 resulted in concerted action by the government, military, and society at large.[3] In the Senate, Senator Kirsten Gillibrand (D-NY) worked to have cases of sexual assault removed from the chain of command.[4] Senator Claire McCaskill (D-MO) believed that changes in the processing of sexual assaults were needed, but that the chain of command should still be involved in the process.[5] Senator McCaskill's bill passed the Senate 97–0 and was approved by the House with additions proposed by Representative Nita Lowey (D-NY). Lowey's amendment required military academies to provide sexual assault training to new cadets and midshipmen within 14 days of arriving at the academy. The curricula must include "a brief history of the problem of sexual assault in the Armed Forces, a definition of sexual assault, information relating to reporting a sexual assault, victims' rights, and dismissal and dishonorable discharge for offenders."[6]

The changes were included in H.R. 3304, the *National Defense Authorization Act for Fiscal Year 2014* (Appendix A). The bill was passed by the Congress and signed by President Obama on December 20, 2013.

In his statement when he signed the bill, Obama gave a strong mandate to the military:

Earlier this year I directed Secretary Hagel, Chairman Dempsey and our entire defense leadership team to step up their game exponentially in preventing and responding to the serious crime of sexual assault in our military. As Commander in Chief, I've made it clear that these crimes have no place in the greatest military on earth. Since then, our armed forces have moved ahead with a broad range of initiatives, including reforms to the military justice system, improving and expanding prevention programs, and enhancing support for victims. I commend the Pentagon leadership for their hard work on this critical issue of vital importance to our nation.

Yet, so long as our women and men in uniform face the insider threat of sexual assault, we have an urgent obligation to do more to support victims and hold perpetrators accountable for their crimes, as appropriate under the military justice system. Members of Congress, especially Senators Gillibrand and McCaskill, have rightly called attention to the urgency of eradicating this scourge from our armed forces. As a result, there were a broad range of reforms proposed in this year's National Defense Authorization Act. The White House and the Department of Defense and other relevant agencies in my Administration will continue to work with Congress to address this corrosive problem, which is a violation of the values our armed forces stand for, destroys trust among our troops, and undermines our readiness.

Today, I instructed Secretary Hagel and Chairman Dempsey to continue their efforts to make substantial improvements with respect to sexual assault prevention and response, including to the military justice system. I have also directed that they report back to me, with a full-scale review of their progress, by December 1, 2014. If I do not see the kind of progress I expect, then we will consider additional reforms that may be required to eliminate this crime from our military ranks and protect our brave service members who stand guard for us every day at home and around the world.[7] (Appendix C)

THE MILITARY'S RESPONSE

The military reacted vigorously to the president's mandate. The progress is detailed in the DoD *Annual Report on Sexual Assault in the Military Fiscal Year 2015*.[8] The Report contained data collected by the RAND Corporation that showed marked improvement from data in the 2012 report that was released in 2013. The 2014 RAND *Military Workplace Study* found the number and percentage of active-duty contacts in 2014 were 20,300, down from the 26,000 service member victims estimated in 2012.[9]

The prevalence of "unwanted sexual contact" (the definition from earlier studies) and sexual harassment in 2014 compared to the prevalence measured in 2012, 2010, and 2006 found the rates of unwanted sexual contact for active-duty women declined from 6.1 percent in 2012 to 4.3 percent in 2014 and from 1.2 percent for men in 2012 to 0.9 percent in 2014. Rates for both men and women are lower than in 2006 but about the same as in 2010.[10] In 2014, most (65 percent) of these sexual assault incidents involving active-component service members occurred on a military installation or ship.

Rank and being in the military were factors in a majority of the assaults. Eighty-nine percent of women and 81 percent of men said they were assaulted by a military person. The perpetrator had higher rank in 54 percent of the assault cases. Men had more multiple incidents and were assaulted by multiple perpetrators during a single incident.[11] Men were more likely than women to have been sexually assaulted at work or during duty hours.

An estimated 116,600 U.S. active-component service members were sexually harassed in the past year, with women experiencing significantly higher rates than men (22 percent of women and 7 percent of men). A supervisor or unit leader was reported as committing the violations in nearly 60 percent of those cases. Also, 43,900 active-component service members experienced gender discrimination in the past year.[12]

While the military's actions produced encouraging results, more needs to be done if sexual assault cases are to be further significantly reduced. The 2014 initiatives do seem able further to reduce sexual assaults.

CULTURE, PREVENTION, AND JUSTICE

To reduce or eliminate sexual assault in the military, change must take place in (1) the culture of the military, (2) the prevention programs, and (3) the justice system.

CULTURE

The culture of the military has long contributed to the existence and extent of sexual assault in the military. Society's acceptance that only the physically strong, heterosexual male could be in the military provided a culture that was exclusive and was resistant to change. It was a culture that was maintained by policy. Military policy rejected women, homosexuals. and even certain men from being members of the military. While the culture of the military has evolved over the last century, change took place in an environment of pervasive and negative opposition. When women were admitted to the service academies in 1976, the opposition to their presence was strong and unified. MAJ Lillian Pfluke, U.S. Army, (Ret.), a member of the first class of women at West Point, recalls, "[Blatant harassment] was okay. Everybody did it. It was okay to do it. Many people were very, very resistant to the idea of women being there at all. And so we were ostracized, not only by our own students and our own classmates, but also by the faculty and also by the staff."[13] The cultural resistance has decreased over the last decade as women have gained access to an increased number of positions, including combat, but it still exists.

The culture of the military has changed and is changing to address the problem of sexual assault but must change even more if the culture of the past is to be reversed fully. In the past, the culture was negative in its treatment of not only of women, but also, homosexuals, transgendered, and men. The culture has changed from the time when it was accepted as "the norm" to have unfettered sexual behavior of naval aviators at Tailhook conventions. The military has changed from the time when women were punished for seeking to be admitted to previously closed units of the military. The military changed for homosexuals from when they were banned from serving to when "Don't ask, don't tell" was established, until now when "Don't ask, don't tell" has ended. The culture, however, has not changed enough. It still favors too much the strong, heterosexual male as being compatible with the military's mission.

Changing the Military Culture

A realistic admission that the problem of sexual assaults and harassment exists and a positive attitude that change can occur is reflected in the words of Douglas C. Lovelace Jr., director of the Strategic Studies Institute and U.S. Army War College Press:

> The U.S. Army has been and is struggling with sexual harassment, assault, and rape in its ranks, but the future can be different ... [b]y changing the cultural structures that allow them to occur. This will only become more critical as the Army works on the policies that will fully integrate women into the combat arms, introducing women to sub-cultures that have, for years, equated martial virtues with masculine ones.[14]

The cultural structures are changing, in part, because of the amendment of Representative Nita Lowey (D-NY) that required the nation's military academies to incorporate sexual assault training into their ethics curricula and ensure that new cadets and midshipmen receive the training within 60 days of entering the academy.[15]

When MAJ Pfluke visited West Point in 2014, she found a new climate among the cadets:

> The military at West Point ... has always had the honor code, where a cadet will not lie, cheat, or steal, but now they are talking about living honorably. It's not enough to not lie, cheat, or steal, but you need to live honorably and living honorably includes good relations with different races, with different sexes. It includes everything from being polite to people, to being a good person, an honorable person, doing the right thing, an ethically correct person. There's tremendous emphasis on this kind of stuff.[16]

MAJ Pfluke also teaches on a U.S. army base in Germany. She found the same energy for change among those stationed there: "I'm on a military base everyday because I am teaching on a military base, so I see the young kids, and I can call them young kids, because I am 55 years old, (laughs) and they get it. They get it. They do. And their bosses get it and are really trying to make America's Army, America's military, intolerant of [sexual assault]."[17]

PREVENTION

As with any issue, preventing sexual assault is critical. The military is working through training programs to bring down the number of sexual assaults. West Point authors Robert L. Caslen Jr., Cindy R. Jebb, Daniel Gade, and Hope C. Landsem advocate addressing the culture, language, and behaviors that are the center of the sexual harassment and assault problem rather than solely addressing the aftereffects in the criminal justice system. The authors base their approach in the army's bitter experience with improvised explosive devices (IEDs). They explain. "After years of failure in preventing IEDs, the Army turned to a new technique, colloquially known as 'getting to the left of the boom,' ... [which] means taking away the conditions that result in the willingness of the populace to emplace IEDs in the first place. Likewise, the Army must 'get to the left of Sexual Harassment/Assault Response and Prevention (SHARP).' "[18]

Caslen et al. present five recommendations that grew out of West Point prevention efforts, past and present.

> Principle 1: Leaders identify and break chains of circumstance;
> Principle 2: Education is preferable to litigation;
> Principle 3: What's electronic is public;
> Principle 4: Don't ignore pornography; and,
> Principle 5: Unit climate is the commander's responsibility.

They contend, senior commanders should hold junior commanders responsible for their unit climates when evidence exists that bad unit climates have led to sexual assault or harassment incidents. Commanders should personally lead some of this training, and not be afraid to treat all unit functions as opportunities to promote positive cultures.[19]

CAPT Lory Manning, U.S. Navy (Ret.), offers two words as the most important issue as she sees it, facing the military as it deals with sexual assault: "Stopping it." She expands, "The biggest thing they have to do is stop it before it happens. Develop a culture so that it is unthinkable for a member of the military to assault, not only another member of the military, but anybody. And, to tell them that if they do that, we don't want you." Manning outlines the steps, to develop this culture when it is so ingrained:

> First, [the military] has to make it unacceptable culturally. That's the most important thing. It has to develop for those times when it happens anyway, a system that believes the victim, that believes the person who's come forward and says, "I was sexually assaulted," that does a proper criminal investigation, that does not let that person's peers razz them because they've come forward to report it. A lot of these military installations are small and they're isolated and even when you are trying to keep something close hold, the rumor mills gets it out there. They got to be supportive of those who come forward and handle it properly. . . . The military needs a system that handles it in a just way.[20]

Training

As a result of the 2012 study of commanders' related misconduct during the air force's basic training for new enlisted personnel, the U.S. Government Accountability Office (GAO) concluded that the air force had implemented most recommendations. In addition, the DoD had made a number of efforts to prevent, investigate, and respond to sexual assault occurrences. Yet, DoD data show that recruits and other junior enlisted service members appear particularly vulnerable to sexual assault and related misconduct. In 2014 GAO recommended that DoD develop and implement a tool, for example a survey or leverage existing military training surveys, like the air force or the navy used, that would provide more comprehensive and detailed information to decision makers about sexual assault and other sexual misconduct that occur during initial military training, including basic and subsequent career-specific military training. Without these surveys, service officials may not have the comprehensive and detailed data needed to improve their sexual assault and sexual misconduct prevention programs. In addition, training leadership may have difficulty in determining the best corrective actions.[21]

Current Intervention Strategy

Since identifying a potential assailant of sexual assault is difficult and treatment after the assault has more impact, "educating a perpetrator about the issues and consequences of committing a sexual assault have a minimal if any impact toward prevention," stated George Vukotich.[22]

Early prevention methods emphasized personal safety and low risk taking. In 2004 as military culture changed, the approach changed to making everyone aware. For example, discriminatory behaviors such as those related to women and gays had to change such as posting of centerfolds or using derogatory language. Vukotich found that the present emphasis on bystander intervention training is moving military members from an awareness level into taking a proactive stance when they see behaviors and actions that are inappropriate

Sexual Harassment

In the service academy culture, sexual harassment is the more prevalent and corrosive problem than sexual assault, creating an environment where sexual assault is more likely to happen.[23] But wherever harassment occurs, it provides fodder for an unsafe and unprofessional environment. Although much of the solution to preventing sexual harassment rests with cadets and midshipmen themselves, they must understand that the obligation not to engage in or tolerate sexually harassing behavior is a values and leadership issue. As officers, quality command climate is essential.

Command Climate

Command climate is vital in all environments. In an interview, RADM D. M. "Mac" Williams Jr. U.S. Navy (Ret.), former NIS Commander, illustrates sexual harassment cases with an example when he was the staff judge advocate with the submarine corps, and they had some submarine tenders that had integrated crews. The cases when there was some inappropriate conduct are the kind of things that get handled by commanders in non-judicial punishment, Article 15:

> The commanding officers who had those kind of instances right after they assumed command, where they dealt with them very firmly, did not have other problems during their command tours with that kind of behavior. The commanding officers who did not do that, who did not deal with it firmly, resulted in, I don't want to use the term "death spiral." The conduct was not prohibited immediately and so what happened was, you began to get more and more of it. And the situation got progressively worse and ultimately they ended up with sexual assaults and other things of that nature that were far worse than any of the original behavior. But I think if the military approaches this with an aggressive education and training program, that's the way to deal with it.

Williams concludes that he has not kept abreast of what the military is doing in relation to education training, but that when he was Naval Investigative Service (NIS) commander, a lot of the complaints got started because, if a woman complained that she had been sexually assaulted and was not dealt with appropriately, she felt re-victimized. He explains the training programs put in place:

> We tried to address [re-victimization] with training programs for the agents, training programs for people at medical facilities where they might be initially brought for examination or treatment. All of that factors in here. I think the military is better suited than the civilian community to deal with these things in an education and training way because they can deal with all aspects of it from like training the agents, training the medical people, training the individuals about their behavior. Notwithstanding my comments about alcohol abuse, when I was young in the military, all the clubs had big happy hours and there was a lot more alcohol abuse than there is now. Over time, the military has been very aggressive about discouraging that kind of conduct which is also helpful in these things, but again, I think it is a general societal issue that is occurring elsewhere, where there are young people of the same age at colleges and universities.[24]

Addressing Alcohol as a Problem

Understanding that misuse of alcohol aids cause of sexual assault can be a valuable preventative tool in the effort to change the military culture. One-third of active-duty service members reported binge drinking. The National Institute on Alcohol Abuse defines "binge drinking" as when men consume five or more drinks or when women consume four or more drinks within approximately two hours or on the same occasion. Binge drinking is common among active-duty service members.[25] Alcohol misuse has been linked to sexual assault perpetration and heightened vulnerability to sexual assault. Research with college heterosexual males shows increased general aggression in young men, particularly men predisposed to behaving aggressively during alcohol misuse. Farris and Hepner reason that indirect evidence suggests that alcohol use increases the risk of committing sexual assault. Young men are more likely to misinterpret the sexual intent of women, take longer than men who have not consumed alcohol to identify that a sexual encounter in an audio track has turned into a date rape, and are more likely to indicate that they would sexually assault someone in a situation similar to a hypothetical date rape scenario.

Farris and Hepner found that alcohol use in civilian women can increase vulnerability when ingested in a setting with a nearby potential attacker. High doses of alcohol may cause users to become incapacitated or unconscious. Resisting or avoiding an assault is problematic. At lower doses, alcohol use may reduce attention to risk indicators thereby not allowing a timely exit. Individuals who see another person drinking alcohol may attribute more sexual intentions to that person than they do to someone who is not drinking alcohol. The misperception increases the risk of offending.[26]

Power of one person over another is the precursor to sexual assault, according to my military friend. But she goes on to explain the mix included in the cause, one of which is alcohol consumption.

Is [power] what causes it? I can't say what causes it. I don't think anyone can know what causes it. There are predators. In the military; a lot of it is young people are out there. They are drinking alcohol often times. They are engaged in different kinds of behaviors that young people do when they are acting up. You see the same thing on college campuses. The majority of the sexual assaults in the military are close to the same age group, the same age cohort. Often times, alcohol is involved. So, they are drinking too much. They are not predators in cases like that. There are people who are predators, both in the civilian community and the military. But the majority of our sexual assaults don't involve predatory behavior. They are young and stupid behavior. It's not right. It's simply not right, but we are looking at the kinds of environment that allow sexual assault to happen. Increased use of alcohol, which oftentimes can be a huge factor [is a factor in one type of environment].

Lessons from the Past: Alcohol, Training through the Chain of Command

In an interview, RADM Williams shared his experiences with investigating the problem of alcohol abuse in the navy[27]:

When I first assumed command at the Naval Investigative Service (NIS), in October 1980, you may recall that there were a lot of allegations about rapes at the Naval Training Center in Orlando Florida. There were allegations that there were many, many assaults there. I asked the people in the headquarters Criminal Investigation Division to pull every case that we had worked in the prior two years. One of the things we found out was: 75 to 80% of the cases involved alcohol abuse. About 65% of the cases were reported more than 24 to 48 hours after the event. With alcohol abuse involved, it raises a whole lot of issues in determining whether there was consent. If the case was not reported until 24 to 48 hours after the event in all probability the activities, like washing clothes, destroys the evidence, the effect.[28]

When I was there, there were a lot of people, several political appointees and several senior military officers, who wanted me to not allow Naval agents to investigate these offenses because they were in addition to allegations of sexual assault. They were all kind of allegations of re-victimizing the victim by the way they were treated. What we did in response to all of that was: we developed training programs for agents and for people who would be the first people who would come into contact with victims of sexual assault on how to deal with it. We also developed a training program for young sailors about how not to put themselves in circumstances that increase the likelihood of these kinds of events. Also, in addition, although I didn't elect the requirement that naval agents could not investigate these cases, I did re-assign two female agents, one African-American and one Caucasian, who had background in doing these kinds of cases. I talked to both of them about it. I re-assigned them and they were fine with doing that. Yes, we tried, through the chain of command, to develop training programs that would address these issues.[29]

Now, this also would apply that Admiral Kelso took in the Tailhook scenario. The first time I met with him about the Tailhook incident and the investigation, he called the people at Personnel and he called the Chief of Naval Education and Training. Vice Admiral [Jack] Fetterman was Chief of Naval Education and Training and Vice Admiral [Ronald] Zlatoper was the Chief of Naval Personnel and he directed both of them to develop education and training programs to address the treatment of women in the Navy and dealing with these kinds of issues. I think the political overlay that is on these circumstances to a certain extent distorts it somewhat.[30]

I think there are a number of people who would argue that having the chain of command involved in this process showed that they could take action like GEN [Carter F.] Ham USA (Ret.) or the other general took is not helpful but they're the people who are responsible for maintaining good order and discipline in the unit. I think removing the chain of command in these kinds of cases will probably have a detrimental effect. It may have a positive effect in other ways, but overall, I think it will be detrimental because they are responsible for maintaining good order and discipline in the unit. In the case of GEN Ham, my understanding was, there was another designated driver in that case that was not aware that there was another female who was the designated driver in that case, who didn't recognize that there was anything untoward or that there was a sexual assault in the back seat.[31] Now that maybe have been because of the influence of alcohol on the two participants, I don't know. But I think the fact that this person was there was influential in GEN Ham's decision, but nonetheless—this is a circumstance.[32]

Williams concluded that Admiral Kelso had the right resolve and that is education and training programs. In addition, the training programs for men and women that he was developing at the NIS were effective. He explained,

[B]ut clearly there was a lot of effort that we put in to developing training programs for young female sailors about behavior, places to go, not to go. Some of the training was localized to the facilities where they were. When Admiral [Paul David] Miller was commander of the Atlantic fleet, we developed a training program for him. He kept looking at his ledger, his blotter every morning and seeing all these reports of sailors being assault in various sections of Virginia Beach and so put together training programs for sailors about where you go, where you don't go. If you are going to go out and you are going to be drinking and that results in these kinds of compromise situations, make sure you have got somebody with you who's not. We had training and education programs for sailors to talk to them about these issues and I think that is the way to deal with it. That's the way they dealt with racial integration in the military and that's the way they ought to deal with this. But again, I think this is a general societal issue. There are lot of cases that are being reported in the military, but I don't think there are any more cases in the military than there are in colleges and universities, but the circumstances lend themselves better to be reported and there are a lot of emphasis by the military on reporting these cases, so people can deal with them.[33]

ROTC and Student Groups Partnerships

As a part of the initiative to prevent sexual assaults in the military and college campuses. Reserve Officers' Training Corps (ROTC) units housed on college campuses have formed cooperative relationships with college sexual assault prevention groups. The effort was given added impetus by the launching of the "It's on Us" campaign (Appendix E). On September 19, 2014, President Obama and Vice President Joe Biden rolled out the campaign.[34] The president said,

> A lot of the people in this room have been on the front lines in fighting sexual assault for a long time. And . . . I want to thank all the survivors who are here today, and so many others around the country. . . . I'm sure [you] took strength from a community of people—some who came before, some who were peers—who were able to summon the courage to speak out about the darkest moment of their lives. They endure pain and the fear that too often isolates victims of sexual assault. So when they give voice to their own experiences, they're giving voice to countless others—women and men, girls and boys—who still suffer in silence.
>
> So to the survivors who are leading the fight against sexual assault on campuses, your efforts have helped to start a movement. I know that, . . . there are times where the fight feels lonely, and it feels as if you're dredging up stuff that you'd rather put behind you. But we're here to say, today, it's not on you. This is not your fight alone. This is on all of us, every one of us, to fight campus sexual assault. You are not alone, and we have your back, and we are going to organize campus by campus, city by city, state by state. This entire country is going to make sure that we understand what this is about, and that we're going to put a stop to it.
>
> And this is a new school year. We've been working on campus sexual assault for several years, but the issue of violence against women is now in the news every day. We started to I think get a better picture about what domestic violence is all about. People are talking about it. Victims are realizing they're not alone. Brave people have come forward, they're opening up about their own experiences.
>
> And so we think today's event is all that more relevant, all that more important for us to say that campus sexual assault is no longer something we as a nation can turn away from and say that's not our problem. This is a problem that matters to all of us.
>
> An estimated one in five women has been sexually assaulted during her college years—one in five. Of those assaults, only 12 percent are reported, and of those reported assaults, only a fraction of the offenders are punished. And while these assaults overwhelmingly happen to women, we know that men are assaulted, too. Men get raped. They're even less likely to talk about it. We know that sexual

assault can happen to anyone, no matter their race, their economic status, sexual orientation, gender identity—and LGBT victims can feel even more isolated, feel even more alone.

For anybody whose once-normal, everyday life was suddenly shattered by an act of sexual violence, the trauma, the terror can shadow you long after one horrible attack. It lingers when you don't know where to go or who to turn to. It's there when you're forced to sit in the same class or stay in the same dorm with the person who raped you; when people are more suspicious of what you were wearing or what you were drinking, as if it's your fault, not the fault of the person who assaulted you. It's a haunting presence when the very people entrusted with your welfare fail to protect you.

Students work hard to get into college. I know—I'm watching Malia right now, she's a junior. She's got a lot of homework. And parents can do everything they can to support their kids' dreams of getting a good education. When they finally make it onto campus, only to be assaulted, that's not just a nightmare for them and their families; it's not just an affront to everything they've worked so hard to achieve—it is an affront to our basic humanity. It insults our most basic values as individuals and families, and as a nation. We are a nation that values liberty and equality and justice. And we're a people who believe every child deserves an education that allows them to fulfill their God-given potential, free from fear of intimidation or violence. And we owe it to our children to live up to those values. So my administration is trying to do our part.

First of all, three years ago, we sent guidance to every school district, every college, every university that receives federal funding, and we clarified their legal obligations to prevent and respond to sexual assault. And we reminded them that sexual violence isn't just a crime, it is a civil rights violation. And I want to acknowledge Secretary of Education Arne Duncan for his department's work in holding schools accountable and making sure that they stand up for students.

Number two, in January, I created a White House task force to prevent—a Task Force to Protect Students from Sexual Assault. Their job is to work with colleges and universities on better ways to prevent and respond to assaults, to lift up best practices. And we held conversations with thousands of people—survivors, parents, student groups, faculty, law enforcement, advocates, academics. In April, the task force released the first report, recommending a number of best practices for colleges and universities to keep our kids safe. And these are tested, and they are common-sense measures like campus surveys to figure out the scope of the problem, giving survivors a safe place to go and a trusted person to talk to, training school officials in how to handle trauma. Because when you read some of the accounts, you think, what were they thinking? You just get a sense of too many people in charge dropping the ball, fumbling something that should be taken with the most—the utmost seriousness and the utmost care.

Number three, we're stepping up enforcement efforts and increasing the transparency of our efforts. So we're reviewing existing laws to make sure they're adequate. And we're going to keep on working with educational institutions across the country to help them appropriately respond to these crimes.

So that's what we have been doing, but there's always more that we can do. And today, we're taking a step and joining with people across the country to change our culture and help prevent sexual assault from happening. Because that's where prevention—that's what prevention is going to require—we've got to have a fundamental shift in our culture.

As far as we've come, the fact is that from sports leagues to pop culture to politics, our society still does not sufficiently value women. We still don't condemn sexual assault as loudly as we should. We make excuses. We look the other way. The message that sends can have a chilling effect on our young women.

And I've said before, when women succeed, America succeeds—let me be clear, that's not just true in America. If you look internationally, countries that oppress their women are countries that do badly. Countries that empower their women are countries that thrive.

And so this is something that requires us to shift how we think about these issues. One letter from a young woman really brought this point home. Katherine Morrison, a young student from Youngstown, Ohio, she wrote, "How are we supposed to succeed when so many of our voices are being stifled? How can we succeed when our society says that as a woman, it's your fault if you are at a party or walked home alone. How can we succeed when people look at women and say 'you should have known better,' or 'boys will be boys'?"

... Women make up half this country; half its workforce; more than half of our college students. They are not going to succeed the way they should unless they are treated as true equals, and are supported and respected. And unless women are allowed to fulfill their full potential, America will not reach its full potential. So we've got to change.

This is not just the work of survivors, it's not just the work of activists. It's not just the work of college administrators. It's the responsibility of the soccer coach, and the captain of the basketball team, and the football players. And it's on fraternities and sororities, and it's on the editor of the school paper, and the drum major in the band. And it's on the English department and the engineering department, and it's on the high schools and the elementary schools, and it's on teachers, and it's on counselors, and it's on mentors, and it's on ministers.

It's on celebrities, and sports leagues, and the media, to set a better example. It's on parents and grandparents and older brothers and sisters to sit down young people and talk about this issue.

And it's not just on the parents of young women to caution them. It is on the parents of young men to teach them respect for women. And it's on grown men to set an example and be clear about what it means to be a man.

It is on all of us to reject the quiet tolerance of sexual assault and to refuse to accept what's unacceptable. And we especially need our young men to show women the respect they deserve, and to recognize sexual assault, and to do their part to stop it. Because most young men on college campuses are not perpetrators. But the rest—we can't generalize across the board. But the rest of us can help stop those who think in these terms and shut stuff down. And that's not always easy to do with all the social pressures to stay quiet or go along; you don't want to be the guy who's stopping another friend from taking a woman home even if it looks like she doesn't or can't consent. Maybe you hear something in the locker room that makes you feel uncomfortable, or see something at a party that you know isn't right, but you're not sure whether you should stand up, not sure it's okay to intervene.

And I think Joe said it well—the truth is, it's not just okay to intervene, it is your responsibility. It is your responsibility to speak your mind. It is your responsibility to tell your buddy when he's messing up. It is your responsibility to set the right tone when you're talking about women, even when women aren't around—maybe especially when they're not around.

And it's not just men who should intervene. Women should also speak up when something doesn't look right, even if the men don't like it. It's all of us taking responsibility. Everybody has a role to play.

And in fact, we're here with Generation Progress to launch, appropriately enough, a campaign called "It's On Us." The idea is to fundamentally shift the way we think about sexual assault. So we're inviting colleges and universities to join us in saying, we are not tolerating this anymore—not on our campuses, not in our community, not in this country. And the campaign is building on the momentum that's already being generated by college campuses by the incredible young people around the country who have stepped up and are leading the way. I couldn't be prouder of them.

And we're also joined by some great partners in this effort—including the Office of Women's Health, the college sports community, media platforms. We've got universities who have signed up, including, by the way, our military academies, who are represented here today. So the goal is to hold ourselves and each other accountable, and to look out for those who don't consent and can't consent. And anybody can be a part of this campaign.

So the first step on this is to go to ItsOnUs.org—that's ItsOnUs.org. Take a pledge to help keep women and men safe from sexual assault. It's a promise not to be a bystander to the problem, but to be part of the solution. I took the pledge. Joe took the pledge. You can take the pledge. You can share it on social media, you can encourage others to join us.

And this campaign is just part of a broader effort, but it's a critical part, because even as we continue to enforce our laws and work with colleges to improve their responses, and to make sure that survivors are taken care of, it won't be enough unless we change the culture that allows assault to happen in the first place.

And I'm confident we can. I'm confident because of incredible young people like Lilly who speak out for change and empower other survivors. They inspire me to keep fighting. I'm assuming they inspire you as well. And this is a personal priority not just as a President, obviously, not just as a husband and a father of two extraordinary girls, but as an American who believes that our nation's success depends on how we value and defend the rights of women and girls.

So I'm asking all of you, join us in this campaign. Commit to being part of the solution. Help make sure our schools are safe havens where everybody, men and women, can pursue their dreams and fulfill their potential.[35]

The It's on Us campaign is an important part of preventing sexual assault and sexual harassment in the military because those future commanding officers in ROTC will enter the service with a different understanding of what the climate should be: a climate that embraces diversity and diverse lifestyles as part of an efficient mission prepared military.

Eliminating sexual assault in the military will probably not happen, but it can be greatly reduced, as the 2014 data show, by taking preventative measures and working to reduce the impact of elements that often facilitate assault.

JUSTICE

What can produce justice for those who are sexually assaulted is the question that is being asked. Certain policies that originally were put in place to solve the problem have not worked. One of those policies is zero tolerance. It sounds good from a public image perspective but it cannot and has not been a positive in the efforts against sexual assault. Zero tolerance impinges on unit readiness, cohesion, and morale because if strictly enforced, unit numbers are decreased through enforcement of the zero tolerance penalties. If not strictly enforced, it harms unit morale and the troops lose faith in their commanders. If not strictly enforced, it emboldens the sexual predator that CAPT Manning has correctly identified.[36] Zero tolerance should be repealed as part of the military justice system.

Sexual assault cases will not be resolved properly until "a very broken military justice system" is rethought.[37] The system is broken because the Uniform Code of Military Justice (UCMJ) was devised in a different time and different circumstances right after World War II. The times and circumstances today provide instant communication and rapid movement from place to place. These make it no longer necessary to have commander decide the outcome of a sexual assault case. Right after World War II, there were not many lawyers in the military; today there are a sufficient number to relieve the commanders of their judicial responsibilities. Manning says, "The justice system ought to be set up like a military health care as is given by the command. Military justice should be handled by a professional team with lawyers, judges, everywhere, rather like the health care system. People who are specially trained lawyers who also wear the uniform and who have an understanding what the difficulties of justice under fire are, like keeping a chain of evidence when you are at war in Afghanistan."[38]

What can produce justice for those who are sexually assaulted? Three solutions that have been advocated are: (1) leave the chain of command in charge of processing cases, as Williams advocates, but do a better job of training military personnel and commanders in ways to prevent sexual assault and how to produce just decisions; (2) remove sexual assault and other major crimes from the chain of command, but leave everything, as Pfluke suggests; and (3) remove all cases from the chain of command, as Manning advocates, and establish a court system for the military similar to the civilian court system. Current momentum is away from leaving all cases with the chain of command, but it is unclear how far it will change. The issue will be decided by Congress through legislation. Positive change is abolishing the "good soldier" defense and giving the sexual assault victim the right to try the case outside the chain of command.

Justice for those involved in sexual assault depends on the quality of the investigation of the offense. The investigation must be accurate, thorough, and timely. Some progress was made in 2014 toward achieving this objective.

The DoD established the Investigative Line of Effort.

> The objective of the Investigation Line of Effort is to achieve high competence in the investigation of sexual assault. The Department established the Special Victim Investigation and Prosecution Capability, which became fully operational in January 2014. This initiative is not a specific person or team but a capability available globally throughout the Department to investigate and prosecute adult sexual assault offenses. The personnel who are part of the capability receive specialized training for their roles, which enhances the Department's ability to produce timely and accurate investigative results.[39]

Justice will depend also on the availability of well-trained legal staff as counsels and presiding judges who are committed to fair application of the law and evidence. Progress toward that goal was achieved with the initiatives reported by the Sexual Assault Prevention and Response Office by stressing accountability and advocacy/victim assistance.

> **Accountability**
>
> Holding offenders appropriately accountable is the objective of the Accountability Line of Effort, and victim participation in the military justice process is key to holding offenders appropriately accountable. As a means to provide advice and advocacy, as well as empower victims to participate in the justice system, in addition to the specialized prosecution capability noted above in the Special Victim Investigation and Prosecution Capability, the Military Departments established the Special Victims' Counsel/Victims' Legal Counsel Program, which reached full operating capability in January 2014. These programs provide victims with military judge advocates who provide independent, personalized legal advice and representation to victims of sexual assault, protecting their rights and empowering them to successfully navigate the military justice system.

At the time of publishing this report, a total of 50 initiatives were directed by the Secretary of Defense. Thirty-five of the 50 have been completed, 4 are awaiting the secretary's review, and 11 are in progress. These initiatives also include measures to be implemented by the military service academies.[40]

Advocacy/Victim Assistance

Throughout fiscal year 2014, Department efforts also focused on the delivery of consistent and effective victim support, response, and reporting options. The Department implemented provisions to expand victims' rights by giving them the opportunity to provide input during the post-trial action phase. The Department also took steps to enhance screening criteria for personnel working with victims and issued guidance regarding document retention for 50 years regardless of the type of the report. All of these efforts demonstrate the Department's continued commitment of providing victims with a dynamic sexual assault prevention and response system.[41]

Only as the person who was sexually assaulted and the person accused of the assault are assured of a just and fair process and outcome, will the justice system be judged as good. The system has a way to go to reach that goal, but the recent changes have moved it in the right direction.

THE WAY FORWARD

Sexual assault in the military has been given intense scrutiny since the 2012 Sexual Assault Prevention and Response (SAPR) report was made public in 2013. The attention has produced some positive results, but the actions must be ongoing. At the end of its annual report, SAPR Office has a section called "Way Forward." The way forward to reducing sexual assault in the military involves changing the culture, implementing effective prevention programs, and ensuring just outcomes for those involved in sexual assault cases.

The culture has always been the key element in sexual assault cases in the military and society. When attitudes justified the assault because the person assaulted "asked for it" or "the victim was dressed or behaved provocatively" then the assaults are not deterred. When a service member who is guilty of assault is excused on the "good soldier" ground, the assaults will continue. That culture is no longer accepted. Respect for all is the culture that is being developed today. Accepting diversity as promoting equality is the culture that is being developed today. The culture is changing and it is changing for the better.

Prevention is always central to reducing or eliminating a problem. Preventing a disease is as important as finding a cure. Vaccines have promoted good health and have, in some cases, eradicated a disease; smallpox is one example. Training programs and military-societal partnership are effective because society needs to be involved and change if sexual assault in the military is to be reduced or eliminated.

Ensuring just outcomes in sexual assault cases has been the concern of legislators, military leaders, and civil society. The attention has been focused on the role of the chain of command in administering justice. But they are not trained to be legal experts; they are trained to perform the military mission assigned to them. They are charged with maintaining unit cohesion, readiness, and morale. Having to be the judge in sexual assault cases detracts from and can undermine the mission. The most important components of justice for those involved in sexual assault are: (1) fair, accurate, and timely investigations; (2) competent counsel available to those involved; and (3) trained legal personnel to preside and render judgments that are based in fair and accurate application of the laws.

The way forward may see some setbacks as the military makes progress toward reducing or eliminating sexual assault, but the paths they have chosen are good ones. Together the military and society will get the mission accomplished.

APPENDIX A

2014 National Defense Authorization Act: Selected Sections on Sexual Assault

Note: *The sections of the 2014 National Defense Authorization Act selected include the changes intended to prevent and respond to sexual assault in the military.*

NATIONAL DEFENSE AUTHORIZATION

ACT FOR FISCAL YEAR 2014

REPORT

[TO ACCOMPANY S. 1197]

ON

TO AUTHORIZE APPROPRIATIONS FOR FISCAL YEAR 2014 FOR MILITARY ACTIVITIES OF THE DEPARTMENT OF DEFENSE AND FOR MILITARY CONSTRUCTION, TO PRESCRIBE MILITARY PERSONNEL STRENGTHS FOR SUCH FISCAL YEAR, AND FOR OTHER PURPOSES

TOGETHER WITH

ADDITIONAL VIEWS

COMMITTEE ON ARMED SERVICES

UNITED STATES SENATE

JUNE 20, 2013.

TITLE V—MILITARY PERSONNEL POLICY—Continued
Subtitle E—Sexual Assault Prevention and Response and Military Justice Matters

Part I—Sexual Assault Prevention and Response Prohibition on service in the Armed Forces by individuals who have been convicted of certain sexual offenses (sec. 531)

The committee recommends a provision that would amend chapter 37 of title 10, United States Code to prohibit the commissioning or enlistment in the armed forces of individuals who have been convicted of felony offenses of rape or sexual assault, forcible sodomy, incest, or of an attempt to commit these offenses.

Temporary administrative reassignment or removal of a member of the Armed Forces on active duty who is accused of committing a sexual assault or related offense (sec. 532)

The committee recommends a provision that would amend chapter 39 of title 10, United States Code, to authorize service secretaries to provide guidance for commanders regarding their authority to make a timely determination and to take action regarding whether a service member serving on active duty who is alleged to have committed specified sexual offenses under the Uniform Code of Military Justice should be temporarily reassigned or removed from a position of authority or from an assignment, not as a punitive measure, but solely for the purpose of maintaining good order and discipline within the unit.

Issuance of regulations applicable to the Coast Guard regarding consideration of request for permanent change of station or unit transfer by victim of sexual assault (sec. 533)

The committee recommends a provision that would amend section 673(b) of title 10, United States Code, to clarify that the requirement for timely determination and action on an application by a victim of certain sexual offenses for a change of station or unit transfer applies to the Coast Guard.

Inclusion and command review of information on sexual-related offenses in personnel service records of members of the Armed Forces (sec. 534)

The committee recommends a provision that would require that substantiated complaints of a sexual-related offense resulting in a court-martial conviction, non-judicial punishment, or administrative action be noted in the service record of the service member, regardless of the member's grade. The provision would also require the Secretary of Defense to prescribe regulations requiring commanders to review the history of substantiated sexual offenses of service members permanently assigned to the commander's facility, installation, or unit.

Enhanced responsibilities of Sexual Assault Prevention and Response Office for Department of Defense sexual assault prevention and response program (sec. 535)

The committee recommends a provision that would amend section 1611 (b) of the Ike Skelton National Defense Authorization Act for Fiscal Year 2011 (10 U.S.C. 1561 note) to require the Director of the Sexual Assault Prevention and Response Office (the Director) to: (1) oversee development and implementation of the comprehensive policy for the Department of Defense (DOD) sexual assault prevention and response program; (2) serve as the single point of authority, accountability, and oversight for the sexual assault prevention and response program; (3) undertake responsibility for the oversight of the implementation of the sexual assault prevention and response program by the armed forces; (4) collect and maintain data of the military departments on sexual assault; (5) provide oversight to ensure that the military departments maintain documents relating to allegations and complaints of sexual assault involving service members and courts-martial or trials of service members for sexual assault offenses; (6) act as a liaison between DOD and other federal and state agencies on programs and efforts relating to sexual assault prevention and response; (7) oversee development of strategic program guidance and joint planning objectives for resources in support of the sexual assault prevention and response program, and make recommendations on modifications to policy, law, and regulations needed to ensure the continuing availability of such resources; and (8) provide the Secretary of the Department of Veterans Affairs (VA) any records or documents on sexual assault in the armed forces, including restricted reports with the approval of the individuals who filed such reports, that are required for the purposes of the administration of the laws administered by the Secretary of the VA.

The provision would amend subtitle A of title XVI of the Ike Skelton National Defense Authorization Act for Fiscal Year 2011 (10 U.S.C. 1561 note) to require the Director to collect and maintain data from the services on sexual assaults involving service members and to develop metrics to measure the effectiveness of, and compliance with, the training and awareness objectives on sexual assault and prevention. The provision would also amend section 1631(f) of the Ike Skelton National Defense Authorization Act for Fiscal Year 2011 (10 U.S.C. 1561 note) to require the service secretaries to include in the case synopsis portion of the annual report regarding sexual assaults involving members of the armed forces the unit of each service member accused of committing a sexual assault and the unit of each service member who is a victim of a sexual assault.

Comprehensive review of adequacy of training for members of the Armed Forces on sexual assault prevention and response (sec. 536)

The committee recommends a provision that would require the Secretary of Defense to review the adequacy of: (1) the training provided to service members on sexual assault prevention and response, and (2) the training, qualifications, and experience of each service member and Department of Defense civilian employee assigned to a position that includes responsibility for sexual assault prevention and response. The provision would require the Secretary to take appropriate corrective action to address any deficiencies identified during these reviews and to report to the Committees on Armed Services of the Senate and the House of Representatives not later than 120 days after the date of enactment of this Act on the findings and responsive action, including recommendations for legislative action, on the adequacy of the training, qualifications, and experience of each service member and Department of Defense civilian employee assigned to a position that includes responsibility for sexual assault prevention and response.

Availability of Sexual Assault Response Coordinators for members of the National Guard and the Reserves (sec. 537)

The committee recommends a provision that would require service secretaries to ensure that each member of the National Guard or Reserve who is the victim of a sexual assault either during the performance of duties as a member of the National Guard or Reserve, or is a victim of a sexual assault by another member of the Guard or Reserve, has access to a Sexual Assault Response Coordinator not later than 2 business days following a request for such assistance.

Retention of certain forms in connection with Restricted Reports and Unrestricted Reports on sexual assault involving members of the Armed Forces (sec. 538)

The committee recommends a provision that would amend section 577(a) of the National Defense Authorization Act for Fiscal Year 2013 (Public Law 112–239) to require the Secretary of Defense to ensure that copies of Department of Defense Forms 2910 and 2911 filed in connection with Restricted Reports and Unrestricted Reports of sexual assault are retained for the longer of 50 years or the period that such forms are required to be retained pursuant to Department of Defense Directives.

Special Victims' Counsel for victims of sexual assault committed by members of the Armed Forces (sec. 539)

The committee recommends a provision that would require the service secretaries to implement a program to provide a Special Victims' Counsel to service members who are victims of a sexual assault committed by a member of the armed forces. The Special Victims' Counsel would provide legal advice and assistance to the victim in connection with criminal and civil legal matters related to the sexual assault.

Sense of Congress on commanding officer responsibility for command climate free of retaliation (sec. 540)
The committee recommends a provision that would express the sense of Congress that: (1) commanding officers are responsible for establishing a command climate in which sexual assault allegations are properly managed and fairly evaluated and a victim can report criminal activity, including sexual assault, without fear of retaliation, including ostracism and group pressure from other members of the command; (2) the failure of commanding officers to maintain such a command climate is an appropriate basis for relief from their command positions; and (3) senior officers should evaluate subordinate commanding officers on their performance in establishing a command climate free of retaliation.

Commanding officer action on reports on sexual offenses involving members of the Armed Forces (sec. 541)
The committee recommends a provision that would require commanding officers to immediately refer to the appropriate military criminal investigation organization reports of sexual-related offenses involving service members in the commander's chain of command.

Department of Defense Inspector General investigation of allegations of retaliatory personnel actions taken in response to making protected communications regarding sexual assault (sec. 542)
The committee recommends a provision that would amend section 1034 (c)(2)(A) of title 10, United States Code, to require the Inspector General to review and investigate allegations of retaliatory personnel actions for making a protected communication regarding violations of law or regulation that prohibit rape, sexual assault, or other sexual misconduct.

Advancement of submittal deadline for report of independent panel on assessment of military response systems to sexual assault (sec. 543)
The committee recommends a provision that would amend section 576(c)(1)(B) of the National Defense Authorization Act for Fiscal Year 2013 (Public Law 112–239) to provide that the panel established to conduct an independent review and assessment of the systems used to investigate, prosecute, and adjudicate crimes involving sexual assault and related offenses under the Uniform Code of Military Justice would terminate no later than one year after the first meeting of the panel.

Assessment of clemency in the military justice system and of database of alleged offenders of sexual assault as additional duties of independent panel on review and assessment of systems to respond to sexual assault cases (sec. 544)

The committee recommends a provision that would amend section 576(d) of the National Defense Authorization Act for Fiscal Year 2013 (Public Law 112–239) to require the panel established to conduct an independent review and assessment of the systems used to investigate, prosecute, and adjudicate crimes involving adult sexual assault and related offenses under the Uniform Code of Military Justice to also include an assessment of: (1) the opportunities for clemency provided in the military and civilian systems, the appropriateness of clemency proceedings in the military system, the manner in which clemency is used in the military system, and whether clemency in the military justice system could be reserved until the end of the military appeals process; and (2) the means by which the name, if known, and other necessary identifying information of an alleged offender that is collected as part of a restricted report of a sexual assault could be compiled into a protected, searchable database accessible only to military criminal investigators, Sexual Assault Response Coordinators, or other appropriate personnel for the purpose of identifying subjects of multiple accusations of sexual assault and encouraging victims to make an unrestricted report to facilitate increased prosecution of serial offenders.

Assessment of provisions and proposed provisions of law on sexual assault prevention and response as additional duties of independent panels for review and assessment of Uniform Code of Military Justice and judicial proceedings of sexual assault cases (sec. 545)

The committee recommends a provision that would amend section 576(d) of the National Defense Authorization Act for Fiscal Year 2013 (Public Law 112–239) to require the panel established to conduct an independent review and assessment of the systems used to investigate, prosecute, and adjudicate crimes involving adult sexual assault and related offenses under the Uniform Code of Military Justice to assess: (1) the effectiveness of the provisions of law on sexual assault prevention and response in the National Defense Authorization Act for Fiscal Year 2014; and (2) the potential effectiveness of the provisions of law on sexual assault prevention and response that were offered but not adopted during the markup by the Senate Committee on Armed Services of the bill to enact the National Defense Authorization Act for Fiscal Year 2014. The provision would also require the panel established to conduct an independent review and assessment of judicial proceedings conducted under the Uniform Code of Military Justice (UCMJ) involving adult sexual assault and related offenses to: (1) monitor and assess the implementation of the provisions of law on judicial proceedings in connection with sexual assault in the National Defense Authorization Act for Fiscal Year 2014; and (2) assess the potential effectiveness of provisions of law on judicial proceedings that were offered but not adopted during the markup by the Senate Committee on Armed Services of the bill to enact the National Defense Authorization Act for Fiscal Year 2014.

Assessment of compensation and restitution of victims of offenses under the Uniform Code of Military Justice as additional duty of independent panel on review and assessment of judicial proceedings of sexual assault cases (sec. 546)

The committee recommends a provision that would amend section 576(d) of the National Defense Authorization Act for Fiscal Year 2013 (Public Law 112–239) to require the panel established to conduct an independent review and assessment of judicial proceedings conducted under the Uniform Code of Military Justice (UCMJ) involving adult sexual assault and related offenses to assess the adequacy of the provision of compensation and restitution for victims of offenses under the UCMJ and to develop recommendations on expanding such compensation and restitution.

Part II—Related Military Justice Matters

Elimination of five-year statute of limitations on trial by court-martial for additional offenses involving sex-related crimes (sec. 551)

The committee recommends a provision that would amend Article 43 of the Uniform Code of Military Justice (section 843 of title 10, United States Code) to eliminate the 5 year statute of limitations on trial by court-martial for sexual assault and sexual assault of a child.

Review of decisions not to refer charges of certain sexual offenses to trial by court-martial (sec. 552)

The committee recommends a provision that would require review of decisions not to refer charges of rape or sexual assault, forcible sodomy, or attempts to commit these offenses to trial by courtmartial. In any case in which the staff judge advocate recommends that the charges be referred to trial by court-martial and the convening authority decides not to refer the charges to trial by courtmartial, the convening authority would be required to forward the case file to the service secretary for review. In cases where the staff judge advocate recommends that the charges not be referred to trial by court-martial and the convening authority agrees, the convening authority would be required to forward the case file to a superior commander authorized to exercise general court-martial convening authority for review.

Defense counsel interview of complaining witnesses in presence of trial counsel or outside counsel (sec. 553)

The committee recommends a provision that would amend Article 46 of the Uniform Code of Military Justice (section 846 of title 10, United States Code) to require that, upon notice by trial counsel to defense counsel that trial counsel intends to call a complaining witness to testify at an investigation under Article 32, Uniform Code of Military Justice (section 842 of title 10, United States Code) or court-martial, the defense counsel must make all requests to interview the complaining witness through the trial counsel, and, if requested by the complaining witness, the defense counsel interview shall take place only in the presence of the trial counsel, counsel for the witness, or outside counsel.

Mandatory discharge or dismissal for certain sex-related offenses under the Uniform Code of Military Justice and trial of such offenses by general courts-martial (sec. 554)

The committee recommends a provision that would amend Article 56 of the Uniform Code of Military Justice (UCMJ) (section 856 of title 10, United States Code) to require that the punishment for convictions of violations of Articles 120, 120b, or 125 of the Uniform Code of Military Justice (sections 920, 920b, or 925 of title 10, United States Code), include, at a minimum, a dismissal or dishonorable discharge. The provision would also amend Article 18 of the Uniform Code of Military Justice (section 818 of title 10, United States Code) to provide that only general courts-martial have jurisdiction over charges of violations of articles 120, 120b, or 125 of the UCMJ.

Limitation on authority of convening authority to modify findings of a court-martial (sec. 555)

The committee recommends a provision that would amend article 60 of the Uniform Code of Military Justice (section 860 of title 10, United States Code) to limit the authority of a convening authority to modify the findings of a court-martial to qualified offenses for which the maximum sentence of confinement that could be adjudged does not exceed 1 year and the sentence adjudged by the court-martial does not include a punitive discharge or confinement for more than 6 months. Qualified offenses do not include offenses under Articles 120, 120a, 120b, and 120c of the Uniform Code of Military Justice (sections 920, 920a, 920b, and 920c of title 10, United States Code).

The provision would also require the convening authority to explain, in writing, any action to modify the findings or sentence of a court-martial and require the written explanation to be made a part of the record of trial.

Participation by complaining witnesses in clemency phase of courts-martial process (sec. 556)

The committee recommends a provision that would amend Article 60(b) of the Uniform Code of Military Justice (section 860(b) of title 10, United States Code) to: (1) afford a complaining witness an opportunity to respond to any clemency matters submitted by an accused to the convening authority that refer to the complaining witness; (2) afford a complaining witness an opportunity to submit matters to the convening authority in any case in which findings and sentence have been adjudged for an offense involving the complaining witness; and (3) prohibit the convening authority from considering matters that go to the character of a complaining witness unless the matters were presented at the court-martial.

Secretary of Defense report on modifications to the Uniform Code of Military Justice to prohibit sexual acts and contacts between military instructors and trainees (sec. 557)

The committee recommends a provision that would require the Secretary of Defense to submit to the Committees on Armed Services of the Senate and the House of Representatives a report on whether legislative action is required to modify the Uniform Code of Military Justice (chapter 47 of title 10, United States Code) to prohibit sexual acts and contacts between military instructors and their trainees.

Sense of Senate on disposition of charges involving certain sexual misconduct offenses under the Uniform Code of Military Justice through courts-martial (sec. 558)

The committee recommends a provision that would express the sense of the Senate that charges of rape, sexual assault, forcible sodomy, or attempts to commit these offenses should be disposed of by court-martial rather than by non-judicial punishment or administrative action, and that the disposition authority should include in the case file a justification in any case where these charges are disposed of by non-judicial punishment or administrative action.

Sense of Senate on the discharge in lieu of court-martial of members of the Armed Forces who commit sexual-related offenses (sec. 559)

The committee recommends a provision that would express the sense of the Senate that: (1) the armed forces should be sparing in discharging in lieu of court-martial service members who have committed rape, sexual assault, forcible sodomy, or attempts to commit such offenses, and should do so only when the facts of the case clearly warrant such discharge; (2) whenever possible, victims of these offenses should be consulted about the discharge of the service member; (3) commanding officers should consider the views of these victims when determining whether to discharge service members in lieu of court-martial; and (4) discharges of service members in lieu of court-martial for the specified offenses should be characterized as Other Than Honorable.

Source: National Defense Authorization Act for Fiscal Year 2014 Report, enacted December 26, 2013, http://www.dtic.mil/dtic/tr/fulltext/u2/a592402.pdf.

APPENDIX B

Repeal of "Don't Ask, Don't Tell"

Note: After being in force since 1993, the "Don't Ask, Don't Tell" policy was repealed in 2010.

Don't Ask. Don't Tell Repeal Act of 2010
Public Law 111–321
111th Congress

An Act

To amend the Small Business Act with respect to the Small Business Innovation Research Program and the Small Business Technology Transfer Program, and for other purposes.

Be it enacted by the Senate and House of Representatives of the United States of America in Congress assembled.

SECTION 1. SHORT TITLE

This Act may be cited as the "Don't Ask, Don't Tell Repeal Act of 2010."

SEC. 2. DEPARTMENT OF DEFENSE POLICY CONCERNING HOMOSEXUALITY IN THE ARMED FORCES.

(a) COMPREHENSIVE REVIEW ON THE IMPLEMENTATION OF A REPEAL OF 10 U.S.C. 654.—

(1) IN GENERAL.—On March 2, 2010, the Secretary of Defense issued a memorandum directing the Comprehensive Review on the Implementation of a Repeal of 10 U.S.C. 654 (section 654 of title 10, United States Code)

(2) OBJECTIVES AND SCOPE OF REVIEW.—The Terms of Reference accompanying the Secretary's memorandum established the following objectives and scope of the ordered review:

(A) Determine any impacts to military readiness, military effectiveness and unit cohesion, recruiting/retention, and family readiness that may result from repeal of the law and recommend any actions that should be taken in light of such impacts.

(B) Determine leadership, guidance, and training on standards of conduct and new policies.

(C) Determine appropriate changes to existing policies and regulations, including but not limited to issues regarding personnel management, leadership and training, facilities, investigations, and benefits.

(D) Recommend appropriate changes (if any) to the Uniform Code of Military Justice.

(E) Monitor and evaluate existing legislative proposals to repeal 10 U.S.C. 654 and proposals that may be introduced in the Congress during the period of the review.

(F) Assure appropriate ways to monitor the workforce climate and military effectiveness that support successful follow-through on implementation. (G) Evaluate the issues raised in ongoing litigation involving 10 U.S.C. 654. Don't Ask, Don't Tell Repeal Act of 2010. 10 USC 654 note. Dec. 22, 2010 [H.R. 2965]

(b) EFFECTIVE DATE.—The amendments made by subsection (f) shall take effect 60 days after the date on which the last of the following occurs:

(1) The Secretary of Defense has received the report required by the memorandum of the Secretary referred to in subsection (a).

(2) The President transmits to the congressional defense committees a written certification, signed by the President, the Secretary of Defense, and the Chairman of the Joint Chiefs of Staff, stating each of the following:

(A) That the President, the Secretary of Defense, and the Chairman of the Joint Chiefs of Staff have considered the recommendations contained in the report and the report's proposed plan of action.

(B) That the Department of Defense has prepared the necessary policies and regulations to exercise the discretion provided by the amendments made by subsection (f).

(C) That the implementation of necessary policies and regulations pursuant to the discretion provided by the amendments made by subsection (f) is consistent with the standards of military readiness, military effectiveness, unit cohesion, and recruiting and retention of the Armed Forces.

(c) NO IMMEDIATE EFFECT ON CURRENT POLICY.—Section 654 of title 10, United States Code, shall remain in effect until such time that all of the requirements and certifications required by subsection

(b) are met. If these requirements and certifications are not met, section 654 of title 10, United States Code, shall remain in effect.

(d) BENEFITS.—Nothing in this section, or the amendments made by this section, shall be construed to require the furnishing of benefits in violation of section 7 of title 1, United States Code (relating to the definitions of "marriage" and "spouse" and referred to as the "Defense of Marriage Act").

(e) NO PRIVATE CAUSE OF ACTION.—Nothing in this section, or the amendments made by this section, shall be construed to create a private cause of action.

(f) TREATMENT OF 1993 POLICY.—

(1) TITLE 10.—Upon the effective date established by subsection (b), chapter 37of title 10, United States Code, is amended—

(A) by striking section 654; and

(B) in the table of sections at the beginning of such chapter, by striking the item relating to section 654.

(2) CONFORMING AMENDMENT.—Upon the effective date established by subsection (b), section 571 of the National Defense Authorization Act for Fiscal Year 1994 (10 U.S.C. 654 note) is amended by striking subsections (b), (c), and (d).

Approved December 22, 2010.

Source: "Don't Ask. Don't Tell Repeal Act of 2010," Public Law 111-121, 111th Congress, http://www.gpo.gov/fdsys/pkg/PLAW-111publ321/pdf/PLAW-111publ321.pdf.

APPENDIX C

President Obama's Charge to the Military on Sexual Assault

Note: *After Congress passed the National Defense Authorization Act of 2014, President Obama charged the military leaders with the task of implementing the changes.*

Obama Directs Review of Sexual Assault Prevention Progress

Earlier this year I directed Secretary Hagel, Chairman Dempsey and our entire defense leadership team to step up their game exponentially in preventing and responding to the serious crime of sexual assault in our military. As Commander in Chief, I've made it clear that these crimes have no place in the greatest military on earth. Since then, our armed forces have moved ahead with a broad range of initiatives, including reforms to the military justice system, improving and expanding prevention programs, and enhancing support for victims. I commend the Pentagon leadership for their hard work on this critical issue of vital importance to our nation.

Yet, so long as our women and men in uniform face the insider threat of sexual assault, we have an urgent obligation to do more to support victims and hold perpetrators accountable for their crimes, as appropriate under the military justice system. Members of Congress, especially Senators Gillibrand and McCaskill, have rightly called attention to the urgency of eradicating this scourge from our armed forces. As a result, there were a broad range of reforms proposed in this year's National Defense Authorization Act. The White House and the Department of Defense and other relevant agencies in my Administration will continue to work with Congress to address this corrosive problem, which is a violation of the values our armed forces stand for, destroys trust among our troops, and undermines our readiness.

Today, I instructed Secretary Hagel and Chairman Dempsey to continue their efforts to make substantial improvements with respect to sexual assault prevention and response, including to the military justice system. I have also directed that they report back to me, with a full-scale review of their progress, by December 1, 2014. If I do not see the kind of progress I expect, then we will consider additional reforms that may be required to eliminate this crime from our military ranks and protect our brave service members who stand guard for us every day at home and around the world.

Source: American Forces Press Service, "Obama Directs Review of Sexual Assault Prevention Progress," American Forces Press Service, U.S. Department of Defense, December 20, 2013, http://www.defense.gov/news/newsarticle.aspx?id=121378.

APPENDIX D

President Obama Proclaims June 2015 as LGBT Month

Note: *This proclamation issued by President Obama on May 29, 2015, honors the LGBT community for its contributions to American society in the face of discrimination and establishes June 2015 as LGBT pride month.*

President Proclaims June as LGBT Pride Month

From the moment our Nation first came together to declare the fundamental truth that all men are created equal, courageous and dedicated patriots have fought to refine our founding promise and broaden democracy's reach. Over the course of more than two centuries of striving and sacrifice, our country has expanded civil rights and enshrined equal protections into our Constitution. Through struggle and setback, we see a common trajectory toward a more free and just society. But we are also reminded that we are not truly equal until every person is afforded the same rights and opportunities—that when one of us experiences discrimination, it affects all of us—and that our journey is not complete until our lesbian, gay, bisexual, and transgender (LGBT) brothers and sisters are treated like anyone else under the law.

Across our Nation, tremendous progress has been won by determined individuals who stood up, spoke out, and shared their stories. Earlier this year, because of my landmark Executive Order on LGBT workplace discrimination, protections for Federal contractors went into effect, guarding against discrimination based on sexual orientation and gender identity. The Federal Government is now leading by example, ensuring that our employees and contractors are judged by the quality of their work, not by who they love. And I will keep calling on the Congress to pass legislation so that all Americans are covered by these protections, no matter where they work.

In communities throughout the country, barriers that limit the potential of LGBT Americans have been torn down, but too many individuals continue to encounter discrimination and unfair treatment. My Administration supports efforts to ban the use of conversion therapy for minors because the overwhelming scientific evidence demonstrates that it can cause substantial harm. We understand the unique challenges faced by sexual and gender minorities—especially transgender and gender non-conforming individuals—and are taking steps to address them. And we recognize that families come in many shapes and sizes. Whether biological, foster, or adoptive, family acceptance is an important protective factor against suicide and harm for LGBTQ youth, and mental health experts have created resources to support family communication and involvement.

For countless young people, it is not enough to simply say it gets better; we must take action too. We continue to address bullying and harassment in our classrooms, ensuring every student has a nurturing environment in which to learn and grow. Across the Federal Government, we are working every day to unlock the opportunities all LGBT individuals deserve and the resources and care they need. Too many LGBT youth face homelessness and too many older individuals struggle to find welcoming and affordable housing; that is why my Administration is striving to ensure they have equal access to safe and supportive housing throughout life. We are updating our National HIV/AIDS Strategy to better address the disproportionate burden HIV has on communities of gay and bisexual men and transgender women. We continue to extend family and spousal benefits to legally married same-sex couples. And because we know LGBT rights are human rights, we are championing protections and support for LGBT persons around the world.

All people deserve to live with dignity and respect, free from fear and violence, and protected against discrimination, regardless of their gender identity or sexual orientation. During Lesbian, Gay, Bisexual, and Transgender Pride Month, we celebrate the proud legacy LGBT individuals have woven into the fabric of our Nation, we honor those who have fought to perfect our Union, and we continue our work to build a society where every child grows up knowing that their country supports them, is proud of them, and has a place for them exactly as they are.

NOW, THEREFORE, I, BARACK OBAMA, President of the United States of America, by virtue of the authority vested in me by the Constitution and the laws of the United States, do hereby proclaim June 2015 as Lesbian, Gay, Bisexual, and Transgender Pride Month. I call upon the people of the United States to eliminate prejudice everywhere it exists, and to celebrate the great diversity of the American people.

IN WITNESS WHEREOF, I have hereunto set my hand this twenty-ninth day of May, in the year of our Lord two thousand fifteen, and of the Independence of the United States of America the two hundred and thirty-ninth.

BARACK OBAMA

Source: "President Proclaims June as LGBT Pride Month," DoD News, Defense Media Activity, Department of Defense, May 29, 2015, http://www.defense.gov/news/newsarticle.aspx?id=128938.

APPENDIX E

President Obama Initiates the "It's on Us" Campaign

***Note:** These remarks by President Obama to roll out the "It's on Us" campaign highlight the partnerships that have been established on campuses between military units, like Reserve Officer's Training Corps (ROTC), and on-campus anti-sexual assault groups.*

Remarks by the President at "It's on Us" Campaign Rollout

THE PRESIDENT: Welcome to the White House, everybody. And thank you to Joe Biden not just for the introduction, not just for being a great Vice President—but for decades, since long before he was in his current office, Joe has brought unmatched passion to this cause. He has. (Applause.)

And at a time when domestic violence was all too often seen as a private matter, Joe was out there saying that this was unacceptable. Thanks to him and so many others, last week we were able to commemorate the 20th anniversary of the law Joe wrote, a law that transformed the way we handle domestic abuse in this country—the Violence Against Women Act.

And we're here to talk today about an issue that is a priority for me, and that's ending campus sexual assault. I want to thank all of you who are participating. I particularly want to thank Lilly for her wonderful presentation and grace. I want to thank her parents for being here. As a father of two daughters, I on the one hand am enraged about what has happened; on the other hand, am empowered to see such an incredible young woman be so strong and do so well. And we're going to be thrilled watching all of the great things she is going to be doing in her life. So we're really proud of her.

I want to thank the White House Council on Women and Girls. Good Job. Valerie, thank you. (Applause.) I want to thank our White House Advisor on Violence Against Women—the work that you do every day partnering with others to prevent the outrage, the crime of sexual violence.

We've got some outstanding lawmakers with us. Senator Claire McCaskill is right here from the great state of Missouri, who I love. (Applause.) And we've got Dick Blumenthal from the great state of Connecticut, as well as Congresswoman Susan Davis. So thank you so much, I'm thrilled to have you guys here. (Applause.)

I also want to thank other members of Congress who are here and have worked on this issue so hard for so long. A lot of the people in this room have been on the front lines in fighting sexual assault for a long time. And along with Lilly, I want to thank all the survivors who are here today, and so many others around the country. (Applause.) Lilly I'm sure took strength from a community of people—some who came before, some who were peers—who were able to summon the courage to speak out about the darkest moment of their lives. They endure pain and the fear that too often isolates victims of sexual assault. So when they give voice to their own experiences, they're giving voice to countless others—women and men, girls and boys—who still suffer in silence.

So to the survivors who are leading the fight against sexual assault on campuses, your efforts have helped to start a movement. I know that, as Lilly described, there are times where the fight feels lonely, and it feels as if you're dredging up stuff that you'd rather put behind you. But we're here to say, today, it's not on you. This is not your fight alone. This is on all of us, every one of us, to fight campus sexual assault. You are not alone, and we have your back, and we are going to organize campus by campus, city by city, state by state. This entire country is going to make sure that we understand what this is about, and that we're going to put a stop to it.

And this is a new school year. We've been working on campus sexual assault for several years, but the issue of violence against women is now in the news every day. We started to I think get a better picture about what domestic violence is all about. People are talking about it. Victims are realizing they're not alone. Brave people have come forward, they're opening up about their own experiences.

And so we think today's event is all that more relevant, all that more important for us to say that campus sexual assault is no longer something we as a nation can turn away from and say that's not our problem. This is a problem that matters to all of us.

An estimated one in five women has been sexually assaulted during her college years—one in five. Of those assaults, only 12 percent are reported, and of those reported assaults, only a fraction of the offenders are punished. And while these assaults overwhelmingly happen to women, we know that men are assaulted, too. Men get raped. They're even less likely to talk about it. We know that sexual assault can happen to anyone, no matter their race, their economic status, sexual orientation, gender identity—and LGBT victims can feel even more isolated, feel even more alone.

For anybody whose once-normal, everyday life was suddenly shattered by an act of sexual violence, the trauma, the terror can shadow you long after one horrible attack. It lingers when you don't know where to go or who to turn to. It's there when you're forced to sit in the same class or stay in the same dorm with the person who raped you; when people are more suspicious of what you were wearing or what you were drinking, as if it's your fault, not the fault of the person who assaulted you. It's a haunting presence when the very people entrusted with your welfare fail to protect you.

Students work hard to get into college. I know—I'm watching Malia right now, she's a junior. She's got a lot of homework. And parents can do everything they can to support their kids' dreams of getting a good education. When they finally make it onto campus, only to be assaulted, that's not just a nightmare for them and their families; it's not just an affront to everything they've worked so hard to achieve—it is an affront to our basic humanity. It insults our most basic values as individuals and families, and as a nation. We are a nation that values liberty and equality and justice. And we're a people who believe every child deserves an education that allows them to fulfill their God-given potential, free from fear of intimidation or violence. And we owe it to our children to live up to those values. So my administration is trying to do our part.

First of all, three years ago, we sent guidance to every school district, every college, every university that receives federal funding, and we clarified their legal obligations to prevent and respond to sexual assault. And we reminded them that sexual violence isn't just a crime, it is a civil rights violation. And I want to acknowledge Secretary of Education Arne Duncan for his department's work in holding schools accountable and making sure that they stand up for students.

Number two, in January, I created a White House task force to prevent—a Task Force to Protect Students from Sexual Assault. Their job is to work with colleges and universities on better ways to prevent and respond to assaults, to lift up best practices. And we held conversations with thousands of people—survivors, parents, student groups, faculty, law enforcement, advocates, academics. In April, the task force released the first report, recommending a number of best practices for colleges and universities to keep our kids safe. And these are tested, and they are common-sense measures like campus surveys to figure out the scope of the problem, giving survivors a safe place to go and a trusted person to talk to, training school officials in how to handle trauma. Because when you read some of the accounts, you think, what were they thinking? You just get a sense of too many people in charge dropping the ball, fumbling something that should be taken with the most—the utmost seriousness and the utmost care.

Number three, we're stepping up enforcement efforts and increasing the transparency of our efforts. So we're reviewing existing laws to make sure they're adequate. And we're going to keep on working with educational institutions across the country to help them appropriately respond to these crimes.

So that's what we have been doing, but there's always more that we can do. And today, we're taking a step and joining with people across the country to change our culture and help prevent sexual assault from happening. Because that's where prevention—that's what prevention is going to require—we've got to have a fundamental shift in our culture.

As far as we've come, the fact is that from sports leagues to pop culture to politics, our society still does not sufficiently value women. We still don't condemn sexual assault as loudly as we should. We make excuses. We look the other way. The message that sends can have a chilling effect on our young women.

And I've said before, when women succeed, America succeeds—let me be clear, that's not just true in America. If you look internationally, countries that oppress their women are countries that do badly. Countries that empower their women are countries that thrive.

And so this is something that requires us to shift how we think about these issues. One letter from a young woman really brought this point home. Katherine Morrison, a young student from Youngstown, Ohio, she wrote, "How are we supposed to succeed when so many of our voices are being stifled? How can we succeed when our society says that as a woman, it's your fault if you are at a party or walked home alone. How can we succeed when people look at women and say 'you should have known better,' or 'boys will be boys'?"

And Katherine is absolutely right. Women make up half this country; half its workforce; more than half of our college students. They are not going to succeed the way they should unless they are treated as true equals, and are supported and respected. And unless women are allowed to fulfill their full potential, America will not reach its full potential. So we've got to change.

This is not just the work of survivors, it's not just the work of activists. It's not just the work of college administrators. It's the responsibility of the soccer coach, and the captain of the basketball team, and the football players. And it's on fraternities and sororities, and it's on the editor of the school paper, and the drum major in the band. And it's on the English department and the engineering department, and it's on the high schools and the elementary schools, and it's on teachers, and it's on counselors, and it's on mentors, and it's on ministers.

It's on celebrities, and sports leagues, and the media, to set a better example. It's on parents and grandparents and older brothers and sisters to sit down young people and talk about this issue. (Applause.)

And it's not just on the parents of young women to caution them. It is on the parents of young men to teach them respect for women. (Applause.) And it's on grown men to set an example and be clear about what it means to be a man.

It is on all of us to reject the quiet tolerance of sexual assault and to refuse to accept what's unacceptable. And we especially need our young men to show women the respect they deserve, and to recognize sexual assault, and to do their part to stop it. Because most young men on college campuses are not perpetrators. But the rest—we can't generalize across the board. But the rest of us can help stop those who think in these terms and shut stuff down. And that's not always easy to do with all the social pressures to stay quiet or go along; you don't want to be the guy who's stopping another friend from taking a woman home even if it looks like she doesn't or can't consent. Maybe you hear something in the locker room that makes you feel uncomfortable, or see something at a party that you know isn't right, but you're not sure whether you should stand up, not sure it's okay to intervene.

And I think Joe said it well—the truth is, it's not just okay to intervene, it is your responsibility. It is your responsibility to speak your mind. It is your responsibility to tell your buddy when he's messing up. It is your responsibility to set the right tone when you're talking about women, even when women aren't around—maybe especially when they're not around. And it's not just men who should intervene. Women should also speak up when something doesn't look right, even if the men don't like it. It's all of us taking responsibility. Everybody has a role to play.

And in fact, we're here with Generation Progress to launch, appropriately enough, a campaign called "It's On Us." The idea is to fundamentally shift the way we think about sexual assault. So we're inviting colleges and universities to join us in saying, we are not tolerating this anymore—not on our campuses, not in our community, not in this country. And the campaign is building on the momentum that's already being generated by college campuses by the incredible young people around the country who have stepped up and are leading the way. I couldn't be prouder of them.

And we're also joined by some great partners in this effort—including the Office of Women's Health, the college sports community, media platforms. We've got universities who have signed up, including, by the way, our military academies, who are represented here today. So the goal is to hold ourselves and each other accountable, and to look out for those who don't consent and can't consent. And anybody can be a part of this campaign.

So the first step on this is to go to ItsOnUs.org—that's ItsOnUs.org. Take a pledge to help keep women and men safe from sexual assault. It's a promise not to be a bystander to the problem, but to be part of the solution. I took the pledge. Joe took the pledge. You can take the pledge. You can share it on social media, you can encourage others to join us.

And this campaign is just part of a broader effort, but it's a critical part, because even as we continue to enforce our laws and work with colleges to improve their responses, and to make sure that survivors are taken care of, it won't be enough unless we change the culture that allows assault to happen in the first place.

And I'm confident we can. I'm confident because of incredible young people like Lilly who speak out for change and empower other survivors. They inspire me to keep fighting. I'm assuming they inspire you as well. And this is a personal priority not just as a President, obviously, not just as a husband and a father of two extraordinary girls, but as an American who believes that our nation's success depends on how we value and defend the rights of women and girls.

So I'm asking all of you, join us in this campaign. Commit to being part of the solution. Help make sure our schools are safe havens where everybody, men and women, can pursue their dreams and fulfill their potential.

Thank you so much for all the great work. (Applause.)

Source: "Remarks by the President at 'It's on Us' Campaign Rollout," Office of the Press Secretary, The White House, September 19, 2014, https://www.whitehouse.gov/the-press-office/2014/09/19/remarks-president-its-us-campaign-rollout.

APPENDIX F

Selected Sections of the Uniform Code of Military Justice Law, 1949

Note: *These articles are selected from the original Uniform Code of Military Justice law that was enacted in 1949. The law is often referred to as Morgan's Law because the chairman of the Committee on a Uniform Code Of Military Justice was Professor Edmund M. Morgan Jr., Professor of Law, Harvard University.*

UNIFORM CODE
of
MILITARY JUSTICE

Text, References and Commentary
based on the Report of the
Committee on a Uniform Code of
Military Justice to
The Secretary of Defense
1949

Abbreviations

The following abbreviations are used in the references and commentaries to this Code:

"AW" refers to the Articles of War, 41 Stat. 787 to 811 as amended, 10 U.S.C. sl 1471-1593 (1946) as amended by Pub. L. 759, 80th Cong., 2nd Sess. (1948).

"AGN" refers to the Articles for the Government of the Navy, Rev. Stat. 1624 as amended, 34 U.S.C. 8 1200 (1946).

"Proposed AGN" refers to S.1338, 80th Cong., 1st Sess. (1947).
"McM" refers to The Manual for Courts-Martial, U.S. Army (1949).
"Nc&BW" refers to Naval Courts and Boards, U.S. Navy (1937).
"Naval Justice" refers to Naval Justice, U.S. Navy (1945).
"Keeffe Report" refers to the Report of the General Court Martial Sentence Review Board to the Secretary of the Navy, U.S. Navy (1945).

UNIFORM CODE OF MILITARY JUSTICE
Part. I. General Provisions

PART. 1. Definitions. The following terms when used in this Code shall be construed in the sense indicated in this Article, unless the context shows that a different sense is intended, namely: (1) "Department" shall be construed to refer, severally, to the Department of the Army, the Department of the Navy, and the Department of the Air Force, and, except when the Coast Guard is operating as a part of the Navy, the Treasury Department; (2) "Armed force" shall be construed to refer, severally, to the Army, the Navy, the Air Force, and except when operating as a part of the Navy, the Coast Guard; (3) "Navy" shall be construed to include the Marine Corps and, when operating as a part of the Navy, the Coast Guard; (4) "The Judge Advocate General" shall be construed to refer, severally, to The Judge Advocates General of the Army, Navy, and Air Force, and, except when the Coast Guard is operating as a part of the Navy, the General Counsel of the Treasury Department; (5) "officer" shall be construed to refer to a commissioned officer including a commissioned warrant officer; (6) "Superior officer" shall be construed to refer to an officer superior in rank or command; (7) "Cadet" shall be construed to refer to a cadet of the United States Military Academy or of the United States Coast Guard Academy; (8) "midshipman" shall be construed to refer to a midshipman at the United States Naval Academy and any other midshipman on active duty in the naval service; (9) "enlisted person" shall be construed to refer to any person who is serving in an enlisted grade in any armed force; (PO) "military" shall be construed to refer to any or all of the armed forces; (1%) "Accuser" shall be construed to refer to a person who signs and swears to the charges and to any other person who has an interest other than an official interest in the prosecution of the accused; (12) "Law officer" shall be construed to refer to an official of a general court-martial detailed in accordance with Article 26; (1-3) "Law specialist" shall be construed to refer to an officer of the Navy or Coast Guard designated IOF special duty (law); (14) "Legal officer" shall be construed to refer to any officer in the Navy or Coast Guard designated to perform legal duties for a command.

ART. 2. Persons Subject to the Code. The following persons are subject to this Code: (1) All persons belonging to a regular component of the armed forces, including those awaiting discharge after expiration of their terms of enlistment; all volunteers and inductees, from the dates of their muster or acceptance into the armed forces of the United States; and all other persons lawfully called, drafted, or ordered into, or to duty in or for training in, the armed forces, from the dates they are required by the terms of the call, draft, or order to obey the same; (2) Cadets, aviation cadets, and midshipmen; (3) Reserve personnel who are voluntarily on inactive duty training authorized by written orders; (4) Retired personnel of a regular component of the armed forces who are entitled to receive pay; (5) Retired personnel of a reserve component who are receiving hospital benefits from an armed force; (6) Members of the Fleet Reserve and Fleet Marine Corps Reserve; (7) All persons in custody of the armed forces serving a sentence imposed by a court-martial; (8) Personnel of the Coast and Geodetic Survey, Public Health Service, and other organizations, when serving with the armed forces of the United States; (9) Prisoners of war in custody of the armed forces; (10) In time of war, all persons serving with or accompanying an armed force in the field; (11) All persons serving with, employed by, accompanying, or under the supervision of the armed forces without the continental limits of the United States and the following territories: that part of Alaska east of longitude one hundred and seventy-two degrees west, the Canal Zone, the main group of the Hawaiian Islands, Puerto Rico, and the Virgin Islands; (12) All persons within an area leased by the United States which is under the control of the Secretary of a Department and which is without the continental limits of the United States and the following territories: that part of Alaska east of longitude one hundred and seventy-two degrees west, the Canal Zone, the main group of the Hawaiian Islands, Puerto Rico, and the Virgin Islands.

ART. 3. Jurisdiction to Try Certain Personnel.—(a) Reserve personnel of the armed forces who are charged with having committed, while in a status in which they are subject to this Code, any offense against this Code may be retained in such status or, whether or not such status has terminated, placed in an active duty status for disciplinary action, without their consent, but not for a longer period of time than may be required for such action. (b) All persons discharged from the armed forces subsequently charged with having fraudulently obtained said discharge shall be subject to trial by court-martial on said charge and shall be subject to this Code while in the custody of the armed forces for such trial. Upon conviction of said charge they shall be subject to trial by court-martial for all offenses under this Code committed prior to the fraudulent discharge. (c) Any person who has deserted from the armed forces shall not be relieved from amenability to the jurisdiction of this Code by virtue of a separation from any subsequent period of service.

ART. 4. Dismissed Officer's Right to Trial by Court-Martial. (a) When any officer, dismissed by order of the President, makes a written application for trial by court-martial, setting forth, under oath, that he has been wrongfully dismissed, the President, as soon as practicable, shall convene a general court-martial to try such officer on the charges on which he was dismissed. A court-martial so convened shall have jurisdiction to try the dismissed officer on such charges, and he shall be held to have waived the right to plead any statute of limitations applicable to any offense with which he is charged. The court-martial may, as part of its sentence, adjudge the affirmance of the dismissal, but if the court-martial acquits the accused or if the sentence adjudged, as finally approved or affirmed, does not include dismissal or death, the Secretary of the Department shall substitute for the dismissal ordered by the President a form of discharge authorized for administrative issuance. (b) If the President fails to convene a general court-martial within six months from the presentation of an application for trial under this Article, the Secretary of the Department shall substitute for the dismissal ordered by the President a form of discharge authorized for administrative issuance. (c) Where a discharge is substituted for a dismissal under the authority of this Article, the President alone may reappoint the officer to such commissioned rank and precedence as in the opinion of the President such former officer would have attained had he not been dismissed. The reappointment of such a former officer shall be without regard to position vacancy and shall affect the promotion status of other officers only insofar as the President may direct. All time between the dismissal and such reappointment shall be considered as actual service for all purposes, including the right to receive pay and allowances. (d) When an officer is discharged from any armed force by administrative action or is dropped from the rolls by order of the President, there shall not be a right to trial under this Article.

ART. 5. Territorial Applicability of the Code. This Code shall be applicable in all places.

ART. 6. Judge Advocates and Legal Officers. (a) The assignment for duty of all judge advocates of the Army and Air Force and law specialists of the Navy and Coast Guard shall be subject to the approval of The Judge Advocate General of the armed force of which they are members. The Judge Advocate General or senior members of his staff shall make frequent inspections in the field in supervision of the administration of military justice. (b) Convening authorities shall at all times communicate directly with their staff judge advocates or legal officers in matters relating to the administration of military justice; and the staff Judge advocate or legal officer of any command is authorized to communicate directly with the staff judge advocate or legal officer of a superior or subordinate command, or with The Judge Advocate General. (c) No person who has acted as member, law officer, trial counsel, assistant trial counsel, defense counsel, assistant defense counsel, or investigating officer in any case shall subsequently act as a staff judge advocate or legal officer to any reviewing authority upon the same case.

Part. 11. Apprehension and Restraint

ART. 7. Apprehension. (a) Apprehension is the taking into custody of a person. (b) Any person authorized under regulations governing the armed forces to apprehend persons subject to this Code may do so upon reasonable belief that an offense has been committed and that the person apprehended committed it. (c) All officers, warrant officers, petty officers, and noncommissioned officers shall have authority to quell all quarrels, frays, and disorders among persons subject to this Code and to apprehend persons subject to this Code who take part in the same.

ART. 8. Apprehension of Deserters. It shall be lawful for any civil officer having authority to apprehend offenders under the laws of the United States or of any State, District, Territory or possession of the United States summarily to apprehend a deserter from the armed forces of the United States and deliver him into the custody of the armed forces of the United States.

ART. 9. Imposition of Restraint. (a.) Arrest is the restraint of a person by an order directing him to remain within certain specified limits not imposed as a punishment for an offense. Confinement is the physical restraint of a person. (b) An enlisted person may be ordered into arrest or confinement by any officer by an order delivered in person or through other persons subject to this Code. A commanding officer may authorize warrant officers, petty officers, or noncommissioned officers to order enlisted persons of his command or subject to his authority into arrest or confinement. (c) An officer, a warrant officer, or a civilian subject to this Code may be ordered into arrest .or confinement only by a commanding officer to whose authority he is subject, by an order delivered in person or by another officer. The authority to order such persons into arrest or confinement may not be delegated. (d) No person shall be ordered into arrest or confinement except for probable cause. (e) Nothing in this Article shall be construed to limit the authority of persons authorized to apprehend offenders to secure the custody of an alleged offender until proper authority may be notified.

ART. 10. Restraint of Persons Charged .with Offenses. Any person subject to this Code charged with an offense under this Code shall be ordered into arrest or confinement, as circumstances may require; but when charged only with an offense normally tried by a summary court-martial, such person shall not ordinarily be placed in confinement. When any person subject to this Code is placed in arrest or confinement prior to trial, immediate steps shall be taken to inform him of the specific wrong of which he is accused and to try him or to dismiss the charges and release him.

ART. 11. Reports and Receiving of Prisoners. (a) No provost marshal, commander of a guard, or master at arms shall refuse to receive or keep any prisoner committed to his charge by an officer of the armed forces, when the committing officer furnishes a statement, signed by him, of the offense charged against the prisoner. (b) Every commander of a guard or master at arms to whose charge a prisoner is committed shall, within twenty four hours after such commitment or as soon as he is relieved from guard, report to the commanding officer the name of such prisoner, the offense charged against him, and the name of the person who ordered or authorized the commitment.

ART. 12. Confinement with Enemy Prisoners Prohibited. No member of the armed forces of the United States shall be placed in confinement in immediate association with enemy prisoners or other foreign nationals not members of the armed forces of the United States.

ART. 13. Punishment Prohibited Before Trial. Subject to the provisions of Article 57, no person, while being held for trial or the results of trial, shall be subjected to punishment or penalty other than arrest or confinement upon the charges pending against him, nor shall the arrest or confinement imposed upon him be any more rigorous than the circumstances require to insure his presence, but he may be subjected to punishment during such period for minor infractions of discipline.

ART. 14. Delivery of Offenders to Civil Authorities. (a) Under such regulations as the Secretary of the Department may prescribe, a member of the armed forces accused of an offense against civil authority may be delivered, upon request, to the civil authority for trial. (b) When delivery under this Article is made to any civil authority of a person undergoing sentence of a court-martial, such delivery, if followed by conviction in a civil tribunal, shall be held to interrupt the execution of the sentence of the court-martial, and the offender after having answered to the civil authorities for his offense shall, upon request, be returned to military custody completion of the said court-martial sentence.

ART. 15. Commanding Officer's Non-Judicial Punishment. (a) Under such regulations as the President may prescribe any commanding officer may, in addition to or in lieu of admonition or reprimand, impose one of the following disciplinary punishments for minor offenses without the intervention of a court-martial—(1) upon officers and warrant officers of his command : (A) withholding of privileges for a period not to exceed two consecutive weeks; or (B) restriction to certain specified limits, with or without suspension from duty, for a period not to exceed two consecutive weeks; or (c) if imposed by an officer exercising general court-martial jurisdiction, forfeiture of one-half of his pay per month for a period not exceeding three months. (2) upon other military personnel of his command: (A) withholding of privileges for a period not to exceed two consecutive weeks; or (B) restriction to certain specified limits, with or without suspension from duty, for a period not to exceed two consecutive weeks; or (c) extra duties for a period not to exceed two consecutive weeks, and not to exceed two hours per day, holidays included; or (D) reduction to next inferior grade if the grade from which demoted was established by the command or an equivalent or lower command; or (E) confinement for a period not to exceed seven consecutive days; confinement on bread and water or diminished rations for a period not to exceed five consecutive days; or (Q) if imposed by an officer exercising special court-martial jurisdiction, forfeiture of one-half of his pay for a period not exceeding one month. (b) The Secretary of a Department may, by regulation, place limitations on the powers granted by this Article with respect to the kind and amount of punishment authorized, the categories of commanding officers authorized to exercise such powers, and the applicability of this Article to an accused who demands trial by court-martial. (c) An officer in charge may, for minor offenses, impose on enlisted persons assigned to the unit of which he is in charge, such of the punishments authorized to be imposed by commanding officers as the Secretary of the Department may by regulation specifically prescribe.

d) A person punished under authority of this Article who deems his punishment unjust or disproportionate to the offense may, through the proper channel, appeal to the next superior authority. The appeal shall be promptly forwarded and decided, but the person punished may in the meantime be required to undergo the punishment adjudged. The officer who imposes the punishment, his successor in command, and superior authority shall have power to suspend, set aside, or remit any part or amount of the punishment and to restore all rights, privileges, and property affected. (e) The imposition and enforcement of disciplinary punishment under authority of this Article for any act or omission shall not be a bar to trial by court-martial for a serious crime or offense growing out of the same act or omission, and not properly punishable under this Article; but the fact that a disciplinary punishment has been enforced may be shown by the accused upon trial, and when so shown shall be considered in determining the measure of punishment to be adjudged in the event of a finding of guilty.

ART. 16. Courts-Martial Classified. There shall be three kinds of courts-martial in each of the armed forces, namely: (1) General courts-martial, which shall consist of a law officer and any number of members not less than five; (2) Special courts-martial, which shall consist of any number of members not less than three; and (3) Summary courts-martial, which shall consist of one officer.

ART. 17.—Jurisdiction of Courts-Martial in General.—(a) Each armed force shall have court-martial jurisdiction over all persons subject to this Code. The exercise of jurisdiction by one armed force over personnel of another armed force shall be in accordance with regulations prescribed by the President. (b) In all cases, departmental review subsequent to that by the officer with authority to convene a general court-martial for the command which held the trial, where such review is required under the provisions of this Code, shall be carried out by the armed force of which the accused is a member.

ART. 18. Jurisdiction of General Courts-Martial. Subject to Article 17, general courts-martial shall have jurisdiction to try persons subject to this Code for any offense made punishable by this Code and may, under such limitations as the President may prescribe, adjudge any punishment not forbidden by this Code. General courts-martial shall also have jurisdiction to try any person who by the law of war is subject to trial by a military tribunal and may adjudge any punishment permitted by the law of war.

ART. 19. Jurisdiction of Special Courts-Martial. Subject to Article 17, special courts-martial shall have jurisdiction to try persons subject to this Code for any non-capital offense made punishable by this Code and, under such regulations as the President may prescribe, for capital offenses. Special courts-martial may, under such limitations as the President may prescribe, adjudge any punishment not forbidden by this Code except death, dishonorable discharge, dismissal, confinement in excess of six months, hard labor without confinement in excess of three months, forfeiture of pay exceeding two-thirds pay per month, or forfeiture of pay for a period exceeding six months. A bad conduct discharge shall not be adjudged unless a complete record of the proceedings and testimony before the court has been made.

ART. 20. Jurisdiction of Summary Courts-Martial. Subject to Article 17, summary courts-martial shall have jurisdiction to try persons subject to this Code except officers, warrant officers, cadets, aviation cadets, and midshipmen for any non-capital offense made punishable by this Code, but no person who objects thereto shall be brought to trial before a summary court-martial unless he has been permitted to refuse punishment under Article 15. Where such objection is made by the accused, trial shall be ordered by special or general court-martial, as may be appropriate. Summary courts-martial may, under such limitations as the President may prescribe, adjudge any punishment not forbidden by this Code except death, dismissal, dishonorable or bad conduct discharge, confinement in excess of one month, hard labor without confinement in excess of forty-five days, restriction to certain specified limits in excess of two months, or forfeiture of pay in excess of two-thirds of one month's pay.

ART. 21. Jurisdiction of Courts-Martial Not Exclusive. The provisions of this Code conferring jurisdiction upon courts-martial shall not be construed as depriving military commissions, provost courts, or other military tribunals of concurrent jurisdiction in respect of offenders or offenses that by statute or by the law of war may be tried by such military commissions, provost courts, or other military tribunals.

ART. 22. Who May Convene General Courts-Martial. (a) General courts-martial may be convened by—(1) the President of the united

States; (2) the Secretary of a Department; (3) the commanding officer of a Territorial Department, an Army Group, an Army, an Army Corps, a division, a separate brigade, or a corresponding unit of the Army; (4) the Commander in Chief of a Fleet; the commanding officer of a naval station or larger shore activity of the Navy beyond, the continental limits of the United States; "(5) the commanding officer of an Air Command, an Air Force, an air division, or a separate wing of the Air Force; (6) such other commanding officers as may be designated by the Secretary of a Department; or (7) any other commanding officer in any of the armed forces when empowered by the President. (b) When any such commanding officer is an accuser, the court shall be convened by superior competent authority, and may in any case be convened by such authority when deemed desirable by him."

ART. 23. Who May Convene Special Courts-Martial. (a) Special courts-martial may be convened by—(1) any person who may convene a general court-martial; (2) the commanding officer of a district, garrison, fort, camp, station, Air Force base, auxiliary airfield, or other place where members of the Army or Air Force are on duty; (3) the commanding officer of a brigade, regiment, detached battalion, or corresponding unit of the Army; (4) the commanding officer of a wing, group, or separate squadron of the Air Force; (5) the commanding officer of any naval or Coast Guard vessel, shipyard, base, or station; or of any marine brigade, regiment or barracks; (6) the commanding officer of any separate or detached command or group of detached units f any of the armed forces placed under a single commander for this purpose; or (7) the commanding officer or officer in charge of any other command when empowered by the Secretary of a Department. (b) When any such officer is an accuser, the court shall be convened by superior competent authority, and may in any case be convened by such authority when deemed advisable by him.

ART. 24. Who May Convene Summary Courts-Martial. (a) Summary courts-martial may be convened by—(1) any person who may convene a general or special court-martial; (2) the commanding officer of a detached company, or other detachment of the Army; (3) the commanding officer of a detached squadron or other detachment of the Air Force; or (4) the commanding officer or officer in charge of any other command when empowered by the Secretary of a Department. (b) When but one officer is present with a command or detachment he shall be the summary court-martial of that command or detachment and shall hear and determine all summary court-martial cases brought before him. Summary courts-martial may, however, be convened in any case by superior competent authority when deemed desirable by him.

ART. 25. Who May Serve on Courts-Martial. (a) Any officer on active duty with the armed forces shall be competent to serve on all courts-martial for the trial of any person who may lawfully be brought before such courts for trial. (b) Any warrant officer on active duty with the armed forces shall be competent to serve on general and special courts-martial for the trial of any person, other than an officer, who may lawfully be brought before such courts for trial. (c) Any enlisted person on active duty with the armed forces who is not a member of the same unit as the accused shall be competent to serve on general and special courts-martial for the trial of any enlisted person who may lawfully be brought before such courts for trial, but he shall be appointed as a member of a court only if, prior to the convening of such court, the accused has requested in writing that enlisted persons serve on it. After such a request, no enlisted person shall be tried by a general or special court-martial the membership of which does not include enlisted persons in a number comprising at least one-third of the total membership of the court, unless competent enlisted persons cannot be obtained on account of physical conditions or military exigencies. Where such persons cannot be obtained, the court may be convened and the trial held without them, but the convening authority shall make a detailed written statement, to be appended to the record, stating why they could not be obtained.

ART. 26. Law Officer of a General Court-Martial. (a) The authority convening a general court martial shall appoint as law officer thereof an officer who is a member of the bar of a Federal court or of the highest court of a State of the United States and who is certified to be qualified for such duty by The Judge Advocate General of the armed force of which he is a member. No person shall be eligible to act as law officer in a case when he is the accuser or a witness for the prosecution or has acted as investigating officer or as counsel in the same case. (b) The law officer shall not consult with the members of the court, other than on the form of the findings as provided in Article 39, except in the presence of the accused, trial counsel, and defense counsel, nor shall he vote with the members of the court.

ART. 27. Appointment of Trial Counsel and Defense Counsel. (a) For each general and special court-martial the authority convening the court shall appoint a trial counsel and a defense counsel, together with such assistants as he deems necessary or appropriate. No person who has acted as investigating officer, law officer, or court member in any case shall act subsequently as trial counsel, assistant trial counsel, or, unless expressly requested by the accused, as defense counsel or assistant defense counsel in the same case. No person who has acted for the prosecution shall act subsequently in the same case for the defense, nor shall any person who has acted for the defense act subsequently in the same case for the prosecution. (b) Any person who is appointed as trial counsel or defense counsel in the case of a general court martial—(1) shall be a judge advocate of the Army or the Air Force, or a law specialist of the Navy or Coast Guard, or a person who is a member of the bar of a Federal court or of the highest court of a State; and (2) shall be certified as competent to perform such duties by The Judge Advocate General of the armed force of which he is a member. (c) In the case of a special court-martial—(1) if the trial counsel is certified as competent to act as counsel before a general court-martial by The Judge Advocate General of the armed force of which he is a member, the defense counsel appointed by the convening authority shall be a person similarly certified; and (2) if the trial counsel is a judge advocate, or a law specialist, or a member of the bar of a Federal court or the highest court of a State, the defense counsel appointed by the convening authority shall be one of the foregoing.

Source: Uniform Code of Military Justice, 1949, http://www.loc.gov/rr/frd/Military_Law/pdf/morgan.pdf.

APPENDIX G

Department of Defense Directive, Number 1304.26, December 21, 1993

(Establishing "Don't Ask, Don't Tell")

Note: *This Department of Defense Directive issued by Secretary of Defense Les Aspin established "Don't Ask, Don't Tell."*

Department of Defense
DIRECTIVE NUMBER 1304.26
December 21, 1993
Incorporating Change 1, March 4, 1994
ASD (P&R)

SUBJECT: Qualification Standards for Enlistment, Appointment, and Induction

References: (a) Title 10, United States Code

(b) DoD Instruction 1205.1, "Implementation of the Universal Military Training and Service Act with Respect to Medical and Dental Registrants," September 2, 1960

(c) Title 32, United States Code

(d) Compact of Free Association between the United States and the Government of the Federated States of Micronesia and the Government of the Marshall Islands, 99 Stat. 1770 (1986) (reprinted as amended at 48 U.S.C.A. 1681 note)

(e) DoD Directive 1145.1, "Qualitative Distribution of Military Manpower," January 22, 1986

(f) DoD Directive 6130.3, "Physical Standards for Enlistment, Appointment, and Induction," March 31, 1986

1. PURPOSE

This Directive:

1.1. Establishes basic entrance qualification standards for enlistment, appointment, and induction into the Armed Forces in accordance with Section 113 of reference (a) and delegates the authority to specify certain of those standards to the Secretaries of the Military Departments.

1.2. Establishes the age, citizenship, education, aptitude, physical fitness, dependency status, moral character, and other disqualifying conditions that are causes for rejection for military service. Other standards may be prescribed in the event of mobilization or national emergency.

1.3. Sets standards designed to ensure that individuals under consideration for enlistment, appointment, or induction are able to perform military duties successfully, and to select those who are the most trainable and adaptable to Service life.

2. *APPLICABILITY AND SCOPE*

This Directive applies to:

2.1. The Office of the Secretary of Defense and the Military Departments. The term "Military Services," as used herein, refers to the Army, the Navy, the Air Force, the Marine Corps, and the Coast Guard (by agreement with the Secretary of Transportation when it is not operating as a Military Service in the Navy) and their National Guard and Reserve components.

2.2. Applicants for initial enlistment into the Regular Armed Forces and the Reserve components.

2.3. Applicants for appointment as commissioned or warrant officers in the Active and Reserve components.

2.4. Applicants for reenlistment following release from active duty into subsequent Active or Reserve components (including the Army National Guard of the United States and the Air National Guard of the United States) after a period of more than 6 months has elapsed since discharge.

2.5. Applicants for the Scholarship or Advanced Course Reserve Officers Training Corps (ROTC), and all other Armed Forces special officer personnel procurement programs, including the Military Service Academies.

2.6. All individuals being inducted into the Armed Forces.

3. *DEFINITION*

Reserve Components. Includes the Army National Guard of the United States, the Army Reserve, the Naval Reserve, the Marine Corps Reserve, the Air National Guard of the United States, the Air Force Reserve, and the Coast Guard Reserve.

4. *POLICY*

It is DoD policy to:

4.1. Encourage to the maximum extent practical the use of common entrance qualification standards.

4.2. Avoid inconsistencies and inequities based on gender, race, religion, or ethnicity in the application of these standards by the Military Services.

4.3. Judge the suitability of persons to serve in the Armed Forces on the basis of their adaptability, potential to perform, and conduct.

5. *RESPONSIBILITIES*

5.1. The Assistant Secretary of Defense for Personnel and Readiness shall:

5.1.1. Review, coordinate, approve, and issue modifications to the standards in enclosure 1.

5.1.2. Ensure that the U.S. Military Entrance Processing Command assists the Services in implementing these standards.

5.2. The Assistant Secretary of Defense for Health Affairs shall act as an advisor to the Assistant Secretary of Defense for Personnel and Readiness (ASD(P&R)) on the physical and medical aspects of these standards.

5.3. The Assistant Secretary of Defense (Reserve Affairs) shall act as an advisor to the ASD(P&R) on the Reserve enlistment and appointment standards.

5.4. The Secretaries of the Military Departments:

5.4.1. Shall ensure conformance with this Directive.

5.4.2. Shall recommend to the ASD(P&R) suggested changes to this Directive.

5.4.3. Shall review all standards on an annual basis.

5.4.4. Shall establish procedures to grant waivers to the standards in individual cases for appropriate reasons.

5.4.5. Shall establish other standards as necessary to implement this Directive.

5.4.6. May issue generalized exceptions to these standards as permitted by law, with approval from the ASD(P&R).

6. PROCEDURES

The standards in enclosure 1 shall be used to determine the entrance qualifications for all individuals being enlisted, appointed, or inducted into any component of the Military Services.

7. EFFECTIVE DATE AND IMPLEMENTATION

This Directive is effective February 28, 1994. Forward one copy of the implementing documents to the Assistant Secretary of Defense for Personnel and Readiness within 30 days of the signature date.

Enclosures - 1

E1. Qualification Standards for Enlistment, Appointment, and Induction

E1. ENCLOSURE 1

QUALIFICATION STANDARDS FOR ENLISTMENT, APPOINTMENT, AND INDUCTION

E1.1. GENERAL ELIGIBILITY CRITERIA

E1.1.1. Entrance Considerations. Accession of qualified individuals shall be a priority when processing applicants for the Military Services.

E1.1.2. Eligibility. Eligibility shall be determined by the applicant's ability to meet all requirements of this Directive, to include obtaining waivers. Applicants shall not be enlisted, appointed, or inducted unless fully qualified

E1.2. BASIC ELIGIBILITY CRITERIA

E1.2.1. Age

E1.2.1.1. For service in the Active and Reserve components, the minimum age for enlistment is 17 years and the maximum age is 35 years. (See 10 U.S.C., 510, reference (a).) The maximum age for a prior service enlistee is determined by adding the individual's years of prior service to 35. The Secretaries of the Military Departments concerned shall establish age standards for enlistment in the Reserve components (10 U.S.C., 510, reference (a)).

E1.2.1.2. Age limitations for appointment as a commissioned or warrant officer normally depend on the Service concerned. In prescribing the age qualification for appointment as a Reserve officer, the Secretary of the Military Department concerned may not prescribe a maximum standard of less than 47 years for the initial appointment of a person who will serve as a medical, dental, or nurse officer in a specialty designated by the Secretary concerned as critically needed in wartime. (See DoD Instruction 1205.1 (reference (b)).

E1.2.1.3. By law (10 U.S.C., 532, reference (a)), persons appointed as commissioned officers must be able to complete 20 years of active commissioned service before their 55th birthday to receive a Regular commission. The Secretary of the Military Department concerned may defer the retirement for certain health profession officers on a case-by-case basis (10 U.S.C., 1251, reference (a)).

E1.2.2. Citizenship

E1.2.2.1. To be eligible for enlistment in the Regular Army or Air Force, an individual must be an American citizen, or lawfully admitted to the United States for permanent residence (10 U.S.C., 3253 and 8253, reference (a)). There is no equivalent statute limiting enlistment in the Regular Navy and Marine Corps, but they usually apply the same citizenship requirements as those required for the Army and Air Force.

E1.2.2.2. To be eligible for enlistment in the Reserve components, an individual must be a citizen of the United States or lawfully admitted to the United States for permanent residence (10 U.S.C., 510, reference (a)).

E1.2.2.3. To be eligible for appointment as a commissioned or warrant officer, U.S. citizenship is required except for Reserve appointment where an individual must be lawfully admitted to the United States for permanent residence (Sections 532 and 591 of reference (a)). For regular appointment, when tendered, U.S. citizenship is required. Law requires National Guard officers to be U.S. citizens (32 U.S.C., 313, reference (c)).

E1.2.2.4. Citizens of the Federated States of Micronesia or the Republic of the Marshall Islands also are eligible for enlistment in the Active and Reserve components. (See the Compact of Free Association (reference (d)).)

E1.2.3. Education

E1.2.3.1. Possession of a high school diploma is desirable, although not mandatory, for enlistment in any component of the Military Services. Section 520 of reference (a) states, "A person who is not a high school graduate may not be accepted for enlistment in the Armed Forces unless the score of that person on the Armed Forces Qualification Test is at or above the thirty first percentile; however, a person may not be denied enlistment in the Armed Forces solely because of his not having a high school diploma if his enlistment is needed to meet established strength requirements." Alternative credential holders (i.e., General Education Development certificates and certificates of attendance and completion) and nongraduates may be assigned lower enlistment priority based on their first-term attrition rates.

E1.2.3.2. Educational requirements for appointment as a commissioned or warrant officer are determined by each Military Service. Generally, a bachelors degree is a required prerequisite for a commission or appointment. In addition, special occupations (e.g., physician, chaplain) may require additional vocational credentials, which are determined by the Secretary of the Military Department concerned.

E1.2.4. Aptitude

E1.2.4.1. Overall aptitude requirements for enlistment and induction are based on applicant scores on the Armed Forces Qualification Test (AFQT) derived from the Armed Services Vocational Aptitude Battery. Applicant scores are grouped into percentile categories. Persons who score in AFQT Category V (percentiles 1-9) are, by law (10 U.S.C., 520 and DoD Directive 1145.1 (references (a) and (e)), ineligible to enlist. By law (10 U.S.C., 520, reference (a)), the number of persons who enlist during any fiscal year who score in AFQT Category IV (percentiles 10 to

30) may not exceed 20 percent of the total number of persons enlisted. The Secretary of Defense delegates to the Secretaries of the Military Departments the authority to specify more restrictive aptitude standards for enlistment.

E1.2.4.2. Generally, for officers and warrant officers, no single test or instrument is used as an aptitude requirement for appointment.

E1.2.5. Physical Fitness

E1.2.5.1. DoD Directive 6130.3 (reference (f)) establishes the standards for entrance under the authority of 10 U.S.C. (reference (a)).

E1.2.5.2. The pre-accession screening process should be structured to identify individuals with any medical condition that disqualifies an applicant for military service. Specifically, each applicant shall be independently evaluated by an authorized physician or a physician at a Military Entrance Processing Station to ensure the applicant is:

E1.2.5.2.1. Free of contagious or infectious diseases;

E1.2.5.2.2. Free of medical conditions or physical defects that would require excessive time lost from duty or would likely result in separation from the Service for medical unfitness;

E1.2.5.2.3. Medically capable of satisfactorily completing required training;

E1.2.5.2.4. Medically adaptable to the military environment;

E1.2.5.2.5. Medically capable of performing duties without aggravation of existing physical defects or medical conditions.

E1.2.6. Dependency Status

E1.2.6.1. Title 10 U.S.C. (reference (a)) does not specifically address eligibility requirements for single parents.

E1.2.6.2. The Military Services may not enlist married individuals with more than two dependents under the age of 18 or unmarried individuals with custody of any dependents under the age of 18. However, the Secretary of the Military Department concerned may grant a waiver for particularly promising entrants.

E1.2.6.3. The Military Services shall specify the circumstances under which individuals who have dependents may become commissioned officers or warrant officers; variations in policy are affected by the commissioning source (e.g., Service Academy vs. ROTC or Officer Candidate School; ROTC scholarship status, etc.).

E1.2.7. Moral Character. Persons entering the Armed Forces should be of good moral character. The underlying purpose of moral character enlistment standards is to minimize entrance of persons who are likely to become disciplinary cases or security risks or who disrupt good order, morale, and discipline. The Military Services also have a responsibility to parents who expect that their sons and daughters will not be placed into close association with persons who have committed serious offenses or whose records show ingrained delinquency behavior patterns.

The Military Services are responsible for the defense of the nation and should not be viewed as a source of rehabilitation for those who have not subscribed to the legal and moral standards of society at large. Moral standards of acceptability for service are designed to disqualify the following kinds of persons:

E1.2.7.1. Individuals under any form of judicial restraint (bond, probation, imprisonment, or parole).

E1.2.7.2. Those with significant criminal records. Section 504 of reference (a) states that, "no person . . . who has been convicted of a felony, may be enlisted in an Armed Force. However, the Secretary concerned may authorize exceptions in meritorious cases, for the enlistment of . . . persons convicted of felonies."

E1.2.7.2.1. Persons convicted of felonies may request a waiver to permit their enlistment. The waiver procedure is not automatic, and approval is based on each individual case. One of the considerations in determining whether a waiver will be granted is the individual's ability to adjust successfully to civilian life for a period of time following his or her release from judicial control.

E1.2.7.2.2. In processing waiver requests, the Military Services shall require information about the "who, what, when, where, and why" of the offense in question; and a number of letters of recommendation attesting to the applicant's character or suitability for enlistment. Such letters must be from responsible community leaders such as school officials, ministers, and law enforcement officials.

E1.2.7.3. Those who have been previously separated from the Military Services under conditions other than honorable or for the good of the Service. E1.2.7.4. Those who have exhibited antisocial behavior or other traits of character that would render them unfit to associate with military personnel.

E1.2.8. Provisions Related to Homosexual Conduct

E1.2.8.1. A person's sexual orientation is considered a personal and private matter, and is not a bar to service entry or continued service unless manifested by homosexual conduct in the manner described in subparagraph E1.2.8.2., below. Applicants for enlistment, appointment, or induction shall not be asked or required to reveal whether they are heterosexual, homosexual or bisexual. Applicants also will not be asked or required to reveal whether they have engaged in homosexual conduct, unless independent evidence is received indicating that an applicant engaged in such conduct or unless the applicant volunteers a statement that he or she is a homosexual or bisexual, or words to that effect.

E1.2.8.2. Homosexual conduct is grounds for barring entry into the Armed Forces, except as otherwise provided in this section. Homosexual conduct is a homosexual act, a statement by the applicant that demonstrates a propensity or intent to engage in homosexual acts, or a homosexual marriage or attempted marriage.

Propensity to engage in homosexual acts means more than an abstract preference or desire to engage in homosexual acts; it indicates a likelihood that a person engages in or will engage in homosexual acts.

E1.2.8.2.1. An applicant shall be rejected for entry into the Armed Forces if, in the course of the accession process, evidence is received demonstrating that the applicant engaged in, attempted to engage in, or solicited another to engage in a homosexual act or acts, unless there is a further determination that:

E1.2.8.2.1.1. Such acts are a departure from the applicant's usual and customary behavior;

E1.2.8.2.1.2. Such acts, under all the circumstances, are unlikely to recur;

E1.2.8.2.1.3. Such acts were not accomplished by use of force, coercion, or intimidation, and;

E1.2.8.2.1.4. The applicant does not have a propensity or intent to engage in homosexual acts. Such a determination will be made in the course of the normal accession process. A homosexual act means:

E1.2.8.2.1.4.1. Any bodily contact, actively undertaken or passively permitted, between members of the same sex for the purpose of satisfying sexual desires, and

E1.2.8.2.1.4.2. Any bodily contact that a reasonable person would understand to demonstrate a propensity or intent to engage in an act described in subparagraph E1.2.8.2.1.4.1., above.

E1.2.8.2.2. An applicant shall be rejected for entry if he or she makes a statement that he or she is a homosexual or bisexual, or words to that effect, unless there is a further determination that the applicant has demonstrated that he or she is not a person who engages in, attempts to engage in, has a propensity to engage in, or intends to engage in homosexual acts. Such a determination will be made in the course of the normal accession process.

E1.2.8.2.3. An applicant shall be rejected for entry if, in the course of the accession process, evidence is received demonstrating that an applicant has married or attempted to marry a person known to be of the same biological sex (as evidenced by the external anatomy of the persons involved).

E1.2.8.3. Applicants will be informed of separation policy (Section 654 of 10 U.S.C. (reference (a))). Failure to receive such information shall not constitute a defense in any administrative or disciplinary proceeding.

E1.2.8.4. Nothing in these procedures requires rejection for entry into the Armed Forces when the relevant Military Service Command authority determines:

E1.2.8.4.1. That an applicant or inductee made a statement, engaged in acts, or married or attempted to marry a person of the same sex for the purpose of avoiding military service; and

E1.2.8.4.2. Rejection of the applicant or inductee would not be in the best interest of the Armed Forces.

Source: Department of Defense Directive Number 1304.26, December 21, 1993, http://biotech.law.lsu.edu/blaw/dodd/corres/pdf/d130426wch1_122193/d130426p.pdf.

Notes

PREFACE

1. Department of Defense, *Annual Report on Sexual Assault in the Military, Fiscal Year 2012*, vol. 1 (Washington, DC: Department of Defense, Sexual Assault Prevention and Response, 2013), 2, 3, 12, 73, http://www.sapr.mil/index.php/annual-reports; Lolita C. Baldor, "Military Sexual Assaults by the Numbers," AP.org, May 16, 2013, http://bigstory.ap.org/article/military-sexual-assaults-numbers.

2. Military Justice Fact Sheets, "The Military Justice System (The Uniform Code of Military Justice and Manual for Courts-Martial)," Marine Corps, n.d., http://www.hqmc.marines.mil/Portals/135/MJFACTSHTS%5B1%5D.html.

3. Uniform Code of Military Justice, History, 2015, http://www.ucmj.us/history-of-the-ucm.

4. Uniform Code of Military Justice, History.

5. Department of Defense, *Annual Report on Sexual Assault in the Military, Fiscal Year 2012*, vol. 2 (Washington, DC: Department of Defense, Sexual Assault Prevention and Response, 2013), 2, http://www.sapr.mil/index.php/annual-reports.

6. Jeffrey J. Snow and Nathan Galbreath, *DoD Fiscal Year 2013 Annual Report on Sexual Assault in the Military*, Press Briefing, May 1, 2014, 12, http://www.sapr.mil/public/docs/press/FY13_DoD_SAPRO_Annual_Report-Press_Briefing.pdf.

7. "Men Sexually Assaulted in the Military Speak Out," *Baltimore Sun*, December 20, 2013, http://www.military.com/daily-news/2013/12/20/men-sexually-assaulted-in-the-military-speak-out.html.

8. Mark Thompson, "Obama to Military: Clean Up Your Act," *Time* 181, no. 22 (June 10, 2013), Database: Business Source Premier.

9. "Sexual Assault in the Military," Foreword, *Congressional Digest* 92, no. 8 (October 2013).

10. Rosemarie Skaine, "How Should Allegations of Sexual Assault in the U.S. Military Be Handled?" In *World at War: Understanding Conflict and Society* (Santa Barbara, CA: ABC-CLIO, 2014-web).

11. UCMJ Articles 120 and 125; 10 U.S.C. §§ 920, 925 (2012).

12. David Vergun, "New Law Brings Changes to Uniform Code of Military Justice," *Army News Service*, Department of Defense, January 8, 2014, http://www.defense.gov/news/newsarticle.aspx?id=121444.

CHAPTER 1

1. George Vukotich, "Military Sexual Assault Prevention and Response: The Bystander Intervention Training Approach," *Journal of Organizational Culture, Communications and Conflict* 17, no. 1 (2013): 20.

2. C. Wright Mills, *The Sociological Imagination* (New York: Oxford University Press, 1959), 5, 7; in Rosemarie Skaine, *Power and Gender: Issues in Sexual Dominance and Harassment* (Jefferson, NC: McFarland, 1996), 3.

3. Peter Berger, *Invitation to Sociology: A Humanistic Perspective* (Garden City, NY: Doubleday, 1963), 67, in Skaine, *Power and Gender*, 73.

4. RADM George W. Davis VI, USN, Naval Inspector General (NIG), *Report of Investigation, Department of the Navy/Tailhook Association Relationship, Personal Conduct Surrounding Tailhook 91 Symposium*, April 29, 1992, 1, 6–9, in Skaine, *Power and Gender*, 321.

5. CNN Staff, "Pentagon Says Women in All Combat Units by 2016," *CNN*, June 18, 2013, http://www.cnn.com/2013/06/18/politics/women-combat/.

6. U.S. Commission on Civil Rights, "Sexual Assault in the Military," *2013 Statutory Enforcement Report*, 2013, 8.

7. Margaret C. Harrell, Laura Werber Castaneda, Marisa Adelson, Sarah Gaillot, Charlotte Lynch, and Amanda Pomeroy, *A Compendium of Sexual Assault Research*, Santa Monica, CA: RAND Corp., 2009, iii, http://www.rand.org/content/dam/rand/pubs/technical_reports/2009/RAND_TR617.pdf.

8. Claire Gordon, "Sexual Assault Reports Jump 61 Percent at Top Colleges in Two Years," *America Tonight*, Aljazeera America, October 7, 2014, http://america.aljazeera.com/watch/shows/america-tonight/articles/2014/10/7/colleges-clery-sexualassault1.html.

9. Tyler Kingkade, "64 Colleges Are Now under Investigation for Their Handling of Sexual Assaults," *Huffington Post*, June 20, 2014, http://www.huffingtonpost.com/2014/06/30/colleges-under-investigation-sex-assault_n_5543694.html.

10. CAPT Lory Manning, USN (Ret.), telephone interview by Rosemarie Skaine, October 5, 2014.

11. Department of Defense, *Annual Report on Sexual Assault in the Military, Fiscal Year 2012*, vol. 1 (Washington, DC: Department of Defense, Sexual Assault Prevention and Response, 2013), 23, http://www.sapr.mil/index.php/annual-reports.

12. Department of Defense. *Annual Report on Sexual Assault in the Military, Fiscal Year 2013* (Washington, DC: Department of Defense), 3, http://www.sapr.mil/index.php/annual-reports.

13. Department of Defense, *Annual Report on Sexual Assault in the Military, Fiscal Year 2014* (Washington, DC: Department of Defense), 6–7, http://www.sapr.mil/index.php/annual-reports.

14. Andrew R. Morral and Kristie L. Gore, *Sexual Assault and Sexual Harassment in the U.S. Military: Top-Line Results from the RAND Military Workplace Study* (Santa Monica, CA: RAND Corporation, National Defense Research Institute, 2014), x, http://www.rand.org/.

15. Morral and Gore, 9–10, x.

16. Austin Wright and Tim Mak, "Sexual Assault Scandals a Pentagon Test—DoD's Top Spokesman Rebukes Air Force Chief," *Politico*, May 16, 2013, http://www.politico.com/morningdefense/0513/morningdefense10695.html.

17. MAJ Lillian Pfluke, U.S. Army (Ret.), telephone Interview by Rosemarie Skaine, November 8, 2014.

18. U.S. Commission on Civil Rights, Commission on Civil Rights," 9.

19. DoD 6495.01, "SAPR Program," Reissued January 23, 2012, 32 CFR Part 103Final Rule (RIN 0790-AI37), http://www.sapr.mil/index.php/law-and-dod-policies/directives-andinstructions, in Department of Defense, *Annual Report on Sexual Assault in the Military, Fiscal Year 2012*, vol. 1, 98, 99, 76, 77.

20. DoD, UCMJ, Article 120, Rape and Sexual Assault generally, http://www.loc.gov/rr/frd/Military_Law/pdf/MCM-2012.pdf (see page 352); Article 80, Attempts, http://www.jordanucmjlaw.com/Articles/Article-80-Attempts.aspx; Article 125, Sodomy, http://www.loc.gov/rr/frd/Military_Law/pdf/MCM-2012.pdf (see page 368) in Department of Defense. *Annual Report on Sexual Assault in the Military, Fiscal Year 2012*, vol. 1. 99, 79, 80.

21. Department of Justice, "What Is Sexual Assault?" Office on Violence against Women, n.d., http://www.justice.gov/ovw/sexual-assault.

22. "Sexual Assault Overview," Ask a Criminal Lawyer, FindLaw, 2013, http://criminal.findlaw.com/criminal-charges/sexual-assault-overview.html#sthash.JyoaGsG6.dpuf.

23. Manning, telephone interview.

24. Manning, telephone interview.

25. Army OneSource, "Family Advocacy Program," April 4, 2015, http://www.myarmyonesource.com/familyprogramsandservices/familyprograms/familyadvocacyprogram/default.aspx.

26. Kirsten Gillibrand, *Snapshot Review of Sexual Assault Report Files at the Four Largest U.S. Military Bases in 2013* (Washington, DC: Office of U.S. Senator, May 2015), 2, http://www.gillibrand.senate.gov/imo/media/doc/Gillibrand_Sexual%20Assault%20Report.pdf.

27. Richard Lardner, "Pentagon Accused of Withholding Information about Sex Crimes," AP, May 4, 2015, https://in.news.yahoo.com/apnewsbreak-pentagon-accused-withholding-sex-crimes-070448248—politics.html.

28. Gillibrand, *Snapshot Review of Sexual Assault Report*, 2–3.

29. Gillibrand, *Snapshot Review of Sexual Assault Report*, 3.

CHAPTER 2

1. Les Aspin, chairman, Defense Policy Panel, and Beverly B. Byron, chairman, Military Personnel and Compensation Subcommittee, Committee on Armed

Services, House of Representatives, *Women in at the Military: At the Tailhook Affair and at the Problem of Sexual Harassment Report*. Washington, DC: U.S. GPO. September 14, 1992, 16, 1–121, in Rosemarie Skaine, *Women at War: Gender Issues of Americans in Combat* (Jefferson, NC: McFarland, 1999), 66.

2. Col. W. Hays Parks, U.S. Marine Corps Reserve (Ret.), "Tailhook: What Happened, Why and What's to Be Learned," *Proceedings* (Annapolis, MD: U.S. Naval Institute, September 1994), 90–103, in Rosemarie Skaine, *Power and Gender: Issues in Sexual Dominance and Harassment* (Jefferson, NC: McFarland, 1996), 315–316.

3. Naval Investigative Service (NIS), *Report of Investigation (closed)*, Indecent Assault, Case Summary, April 15, 1992, 1, in Skaine, *Power and Gender*, 316.

4. Donald Mancuso, Assistant Inspector General for Investigations, DoD, Memorandum for Deputy Inspector General, DoN, May 8, 1992, 1, Attachment 2; Daniel J. Howard, to his memo to Sean O'Keefe, Acting Secretary of the Navy (SECNAV), October 16, 1992, in Skaine, *Power and Gender*, 316.

5. Kingsley R. Browne, "Military Sex Scandals from Tailhook to the Present: The Cure Can Be Worse Than the Disease," *Duke Journal of Gender Law & Policy* 14 (2007): 753–754, http://scholarship.law.duke.edu/cgi/viewcontent.cgi?article=1128&context=djglp.

6. DoDIG, *Tailhook 91 Part 2: Events at the 35th Annual Tailhook Symposium, February 1993*, F. 26, in Skaine, *Power and Gender*, 316–317.

7. DoDIG, *Tailhook 91 Part 2*, III, 1, in Skaine, *Power and Gender*, 316.

8. *United States Code Annotated*, Title 10, Armed Forces, SS 5001 to 8010, in Skaine, *Power and Gender*, 316.

9. RADM George W. Davis VI, USN, *Naval Inspector General (NIG) Report of Investigation, Department of the Navy/Tailhook Association Relationship. Personal Conduct Surrounding Tailhook 91 Symposium*, Case no. 920684, April 29, 1992, 4–6, Tab F; O'Keefe Memo, in Skaine, *Power and Gender*, 316.

10. Parks, "Tailhook: What Happened," 90–103, in Skaine, *Power and Gender*, 323.

11. *NIG Report*, 1, 6–10; RADM George W. Davis, VI, Memorandum for SECNAV, NIG Response to DoDIG Report on *Tailhook 91 Part 1*, October 19, 1992, Enc. (1) 2–4, *in* Sean O'Keefe, DoN, Office of the Secretary, cover Memorandum for the DoDIG, Tab F, October 22, 1992 (hereafter referred to as Davis, "NIG Response"), in Skaine, *Power and Gender*, 321–322.

12. CAPT J. Robert Lunney, JAGC, USNR (Ret.), Interview with RADM Duvall M. "Mac" Williams, Jr., JAGC, USN (Ret.), Immediate Past Commander, NIS Command, "A Question of Fairness," *NRA Naval Reserve Association News* 40, no. 2 (February. 1993): 8 (hereafter referred to as "Lunney interview, Williams"), in Skaine, *Power and Gender*, 322.

13. Derek J. Vander Schaaf, Deputy Inspector General, DoD, "Memorandum for Secretary of Defense, April 12, 1993," *Tailhook 91 Part 2*, in Skaine, *Power and Gender*, 322.

14. DoDIG, *Tailhook 91 Part 2*, II, 1, in Skaine, *Power and Gender*, 322.

15. RADM George W. Davis and RADM(L) D. M. Williams, Appended letters to the chain of command, April 30–May 26, 1992, in RADM(L) D. M. Williams Jr., "Supplemental Statement Concerning DoDIG Report of Investigation on *Tailhook*

91 - Part 1," in O'Keefe, Memorandum, Tab H, October 22, 1992, in Skaine, *Power and Gender*, 322.

16. Lunney interview, Williams, 8, in Skaine, *Power and Gender*, 322.
17. DoDIG, *Tailhook 91, Part 1*, 26, in Skaine, *Power and Gender*, 330.
18. NIS, "Report of Investigation (Supp)," My 13, 1992. Because the author has a FOIA copy of this report, the page number cannot be ascertained. RADM "Mac" Williams, JAGC, USN (Ret.), can be contacted through the USN, Washington, DC, in Skaine, *Power and Gender*, 330.
19. Miller, Tritt, Samples Findings 27, 64, 31–32, 72–74, in Skaine, *Power and Gender*, 330.
20. Miller, Tritt, Samples II, nn. 3, 10, in Skaine, *Power and Gender*, 330.
21. Miller, Tritt, Samples I, (8), 4, *Power and Gender*, 330.
22. Davis, "NIG Response," 5, nn. 7, 8, 9, in Skaine, *Power and Gender*, 330.
23. Lunney interview, Williams, 7–11.
24. Browne, "Military Sex Scandals," 753, 760.
25. Browne, "Military Sex Scandals," n. 71.
26. Derek J. Vander Schaaf, DoDIG, "Memorandum for Acting Secretary of the Navy," September 21, 1992, 1.
27. DoDIG, *Part 2*, I-1–VIII-8.
28. Andrew Mollison and Marcia Kunstel, *The Des Moines Register*, June 27, 1992, 1A, in Skaine, *Power and Gender*, 51.
29. Robert J. Finan II, Assistant Director, Government Liaison and Public Affairs, Department of the Navy, Headquarters, Naval Criminal Investigative Service, letter, November 3, 1993, 1, in Skaine, *Power and Gender*, 46.
30. David Samples, Lieutenant, U.S. Navy, Petitioner, v. Captain W.T. Vest, U.S. Navy, Navy-Marine Trial, Judiciary, Tidewater Judicial Circuit, and the UNITED STATES, Respondents, Misc. No. 94-8022, United States Court of Military Appeals, Argued November 9, 1993, Decided January 11, 1994, Counsel, for petitioner: Lieutenant David P. Sheldon, JAGC USNR (argued); Lieutenant Alan D. Titus, JAGC, USNR (on brief). For Respondents: Lieutenant Commander David B. Auclair, JAGC, USN (argued); Colonel T.G. Hess, USMC and Commander S.A. Stallings, JAGC, USN (on brief). *Samples v. Vest*, No. 94-8022/NA, Opinion of the Court, WISS, Judge, 5; in Skaine, *Power and Gender*, 50.
31. Robert C. Jenks, Warrant Officer, Public Affairs Office, Marine Corps Combat Development Command, Quantico, Virginia, *U.S. Marine Corps Tailhook Proceedings, Release #12*, October 21, 1993, 2, in Skaine, *Power and Gender*, 327.
32. Steve Marshall, "Tailhook Victim Quitting Navy Coughlin Points to Continuing Abuse," *USA Today*, February 11, 1994, 2A, in Skaine, *Power and Gender*, 57.
33. Richard Lacayo, "Lost in the Fun House, A Navy Judge Blasts the Chief of Naval Operations as the Last Cases in the Tailhook Investigations Flame Out," *Time*, February 21, 1994, 45, in Skaine, *Power and Gender*, 57.
34. Admiral Frank B. Kelso, II, Department of the Navy, Office of the Chief of Naval Operations, "Statement of the Chief of Naval Operations," Washington, DC., February 15, 1994, in Skaine, *Power and Gender*, 51.
35. Senate, "Executive Session," *Congressional Record Proceedings and Debates of the 103d Congress, Second Session* 140 no. 43 Washington, April 19, 1994, S4459.82 in Skaine, *Power and Gender*, 51.

36. "Last Charges Are Dropped by Navy in Tailhook Probe," *Los Angeles Times*, February 12, 1994, http://articles.latimes.com/1994-02-12/news/mn-21900_1_navy-judge.

37. Bureau of Naval Personnel, Navy Personnel Research and Development Center (BUPERS PAO), *Navy Actions on Sexual Harassment*, August 31, 1993, 1–4; BUPERS PAO, *Examples of Navy Programs Currently Addressing Sexual Harassment*, March 27, 1993, 1.84, in Skaine, *Power and Gender*, 51.

38. Zero Tolerance Unclassified Message from CNO to NAVADMIN, 282024Z February 1992; Zero Tolerance Unclassified Message from CNO to NAVOP (all Navy Personnel), 16134ez February 1992; Zero Tolerance Unclassified Message from CNO to NAVOP (date unclear, unless February 1992), 85, in Skaine, *Power and Gender*, 52.

39. Navy News Release, "Navy Releases Information on the Recommendations of the Standing Committee on Military and Civilian Women in the Department of the Navy," n. 451–92, October 13, 1992, 86, in Skaine, *Power and Gender*, 52.

40. Department of the Navy, *Define Navy Actions on Sexual Harassment*, August 31, 1993, 1–4; BUPERS PAO, *Examples of Navy Programs Currently Addressing Sexual Harassment*, March 27, 1993, 1, in Skaine, *Power and Gender*, 52.

41. BUPERS PAO, "Toll-Free Telephone Number Sexual Harassment Advice, Counseling," San Diego, August 31, 1993, 1.88, in Skaine, *Power and Gender*, 52.

42. Department of the Navy, *Resolving Conflict: Following the Light of Personal Behavior*, NP-15620, n.d. 89, in Skaine, *Power and Gender*, 52.

43. Eric Schmitt, "Navy Prepares a Manual about Sexual Harassment," *New York Times*, April 10, 1994, sec. 1, 16.90 in Skaine, *Power and Gender*, 52.

44. BUPERS PAO, *Summary of Responses on Sexual Harassment 1992 Navy-wide Personnel Survey*, San Diego, April 13, 1993, 1.91, in Skaine, *Power and Gender*, 52.

45. Office of Assistant Secretary of Defense, "SECDEF Announces Action in Tailhook," October 4, 1993, and attached "Memorandum for the SECNAV," from Les Aspin, Secretary of Defense, October 4, 1993, 2, in Skaine, *Power and Gender*, 333.

46. J. Daniel Howard, Undersecretary of the Navy, Memo to Sean O'Keefe, Acting SECNAV, October 16, 1992, 1–2; Donald Mancuso, Assistant Inspector General for Investigations, Memorandum for Deputy Inspector General on the back of Tab C, in "Statement of RADM John E. Gordon, JAGC, USN, JAG of the Navy," in Response to the *DoDIG Report*; Davis, Memorandum, enc. (1), 7–9, 13–14; Williams, "Supplemental Statement," 6–12, enc. (2), in Skaine, *Power and Gender*, Ch. 9.

47. J. E. Gordon JAG, DoN, Memorandum to the SECNAV, October 9, 1992, 1, in Skaine, *Power and Gender*, Ch. 9.

48. Duvall M. "Mac" Williams, Jr., RADM(L) JAGC, USN (Ret.), Immediate Past Commander, Naval Investigative Service Command; RADM Williams can be contacted through the U.S. Navy, Washington, DC.; Interview, September 8, 1993.

49. Elaine Donnelly, "Constructing the Co-Ed Military," *Duke Journal of Gender Law & Policy* 14 (2007): 815, n. 29.

50. Hon. Sam Nunn. (D-GA), "Retirement of Rear Adm. John E. Gordon," *Congressional Record—Senate*, February 14, 1995, S2667.

51. J. Daniel Howard, Undersecretary of the Navy, Memo to Sean O'Keefe, Acting Secretary of the Navy, October 16, 1992, 1–2, Tab D, O'Keefe Memo (hereafter referred to as Howard, Memo).

52. DoDIG, *Tailhook 91. Part 1*, 6.

53. Howard, Memo, 2.

54. Williams interview, May 16, 1994.

55. DoDIG, *Tailhook 91 Part 2*, VI, 15–16.

56. DoDIG, *Tailhook 91 Part 2*, X, 1, in Skaine, *Power and Gender*, 323.

57. DoDIG, *Tailhook 91 Part 2*, I, 1, II, 1–2, in Skaine, *Power and Gender*, 323.

58. DoDIG, *Tailhook 91 Part 1*, 8; DoDIG, *Tailhook 91 Part 2*, IV-1–2, in Skaine, *Power and Gender* 323.

59. Gordon, RADM John E., "Ted," JAGC, USNR (Ret.), Letter to author, Enclosure, May 29, 1994 (hereafter referred to as Gordon Letter. Enc.), in Skaine, *Power and Gender* 323–324.

60. Robert J. Finan II, Assistant Director, Government Liaison and Public Affairs, DoN, Headquarters, NCIS, letter, November 3, 93, 1, in Skaine, *Power and Gender*, 325.

61. Navy Consolidated Disposition Authority (Navy CDA), Summary, Norfolk, VA, December 14, 1993, in Skaine, *Power and Gender* 325.

62. DoDIG, *Tailhook 91 Part 2*, X, 3.

63. "Hearing of the Senate Judiciary Committee on the Nomination of Clarence Thomas to the Supreme Court, Testimony of Clarence Thomas, October 11, 1991," Electronic Text Center, University of Virginia Library.

64. Williams interview, March 22, 1995; RADM John E. Gordon JAGC, USN (Ret.), telephone interview, March 23, 1995.

65. John Martin, "TV—Tonight Top-Shelf Movie on Scandal Showcases Impressive Cast," *Charleston Gazette*, May 22, 1995, sec. News, 3B.

66. Susan Yoachum, "The Navy, before and after Tailhook: An Incisive Look at the Lasting Effects of the Scandal: A Review of Jean Zimmerman," *Tailspin: Women at War in the Wake of Tailhook San Francisco Chronicle*, June 25, 1995, 3.

67. DoDIG, *Tailhook 91 Part 2*, X, 5.

68. DoDIG, *Tailhook 91 Part 2*, VI, 6.

69. DoDIG, *Tailhook 91 Part 2*, X, 4–5.

70. Peter Cary and Bruce B. Auster with Douglas Pasternak, Joseph L. Galloway, Mary Lord and Mike Tharp in San Diego, "What's Wrong with the Navy?" *U.S. News & World Report*, July 12, 1992, 22.

71. Secretary of the Navy, *SECNAV Instruction 5300.26B*. to All Ships and Stations, subject: "DON Policy on Sexual Harassment," January 6, 1993, 2–3.

72. "Tailhook Report Details Abuses at 91 Naval Aviators' Convention," *Defense & Armed Forces*, Editorial on File, April 16–30, 1993.

73. Office of Assistant Secretary of Defense (Public Affairs), Washington, DC., "Secretary of the Navy Releases Tailhook Decision," October 15, 1993, and attached "Sentiment by Secretary of the Navy John H. Dalton," 1.

74. DoDIG, *Tailhook 91 Part 2*, i.

75. DoDIG, *Tailhook 91 Part 2*, III, 1, Appendix B, 1–6, and Appendix C, 1–2.

76. DoDIG, *Tailhook 91 Part 2*, i.

77. Mills, C. Wright, *The Sociological Imagination* (New York: Oxford University Press, 1959), 5, 7.

78. Peter L. Berger, *Invitation to Sociology: A Humanistic Perspective* (Garden City, NY: Doubleday, 1963), 18.

79. Gordon interview, March 23, 1995.

80. Gordon letter, May 29, 1994.

81. Margaret C. Harrell, Laura Werber Castaneda, Marisa Adelson, Sarah Gaillot, Charlotte Lynch, and Amanda Pomeroy, *A Compendium of Sexual Assault Research* (Santa Monica, CA: RAND Corp., 2009), 2, http://www.rand.org/content/dam/rand/pubs/technical_reports/2009/RAND_TR617.pdf.

82. Wendy E. Brinson, "It Is All about Respect: The Army's Problem with Sexual Assault," Master of Military Studies Research Paper, United States Marine Corps Command and Staff College, Marine Corps University, April 23, 2012, 6.

83. Browne, "Military Sex Scandals," 771–722.

84. Brinson, "It Is All about Respect," 6.

85. Brinson, "It Is All about Respect," 9.

86. *Report on the United States Air Force Academy Sexual Assault Survey*, Department of Defense Inspector General, Project No. 2003C004, September 11, 2003:5, http://www.dodig.mil/foia/ERR/USAFASexualAssaultSurvey.pdf.

87. *Report of the Panel to Review Sexual Misconduct Allegations at the U.S. Air Force Academy. Senate and House Armed Services Committees and DoD*, "Executive Summary," Arlington, VA, September 22, 2003, 1, 2, http://www.dodig.mil/foia/ERR/USAFASexualAssaultSurvey.pdf.

88. *Report on the United States Air Force Academy Sexual Assault Survey*, 15.

89. Harrell et al., *Compendium of Sexual Assault Research*, ix–x, 4.

90. R. Browne, "Military Sex Scandals," 778.

91. Megan N. Schmid, "Comment: Combating a Different Enemy: Proposals to Change the Culture of Sexual Assault in the Military," *Villanova Law Review* no. 55 (2010): n. 34.

92. Schmid, "Combating a Different Enemy," 481–482.

93. Brinson, "It Is All about Respect," 7–8.

94. Browne, "Military Sex Scandals," 778.

95. "The List: Military Scandals," *Washington Times*, January 8, 2011, http://www.washingtontimes.com/news/2011/jan/8/list-military-scandals/; Browne, "Military Sex Scandals," 782–786.

96. Nancy Montgomery, "After 2 Decades of Sexual Assault in Military, No Real Change in Message," *Stars and Stripes*, July 7, 2013, http://www.stripes.com/news/after-2-decades-of-sexual-assault-in-military-no-real-change-in-message-1.229091\.

97. Lindsay Rosenthal and Lawrence Korb, "Twice Betrayed: Bringing Justice to the U.S. Military's Sexual Assault Problem," Center for American Progress, November 2013, 8, http://cdn.americanprogress.org/wp-content/uploads/2013/11/MilitarySexualAssaultsReport.pdf.

98. "2012 SAPRO Analysis," Fact Sheet, Office of Kirsten Gillibrand, 2009–2015, http://www.gillibrand.senate.gov/mjia/stats-from-sapro-report.

99. "Department of Defense Fact Sheet: Secretary Hagel Issues New Initiatives to Eliminate Sexual Assault, Updates Prevention Strategy and Releases 2013

Annual Report on Sexual Assault in the Military," Office of the Secretary of Defense, Sexual Assault Prevention and Response Office, 3, http://www.sapr.mil/public/docs/reports/FY13_DoD_SAPRO_Annual_Report_Fact_Sheet.pdf.

100. Erin Solaro, "Women in the Military, Abuse of," in *Abuse: An Encyclopedia of Causes, Consequences, and Treatments*, ed. Rosemarie Skaine (Santa Barbara, CA: Greenwood, 2015), 310.

101. Women in Military Service for America Memorial Foundation, "Women Enter the Military Academies," History, Archive, n.d., http://www.womensmemorial.org/H&C/History/milacad.html.

102. MAJ Lillian Pfluke, U.S. Army (Ret.), telephone interview by Rosemarie Skaine, November 8, 2014.

CHAPTER 3

1. Uniform Code of Military Justice, History, 2015, http://www.ucmj.us/history-of-the-ucm.

2. CAPT Lory Manning, USN (Ret.), Telephone interview by Rosemarie Skaine, October 5, 2014.

3. U.S. Army War College, "Chain of Command," *The Battle Book IV: A Guide for Spouses in Leadership Roles*, 2009: Ch. 2, http://www.carlisle.army.mil/usawc/mfp/battlebook/pdf/Chapter%202.pdf.

4. Department of Defense, *Annual Report on Sexual Assault in the Military, Fiscal Year 2012*. vol. 1: 1 (Washington, DC: Department of Defense. Sexual Assault Prevention and Response, 2013), http://www.sapr.mil/index.php/annual-reports.

5. GAO, *Military Personnel: Prior GAO Work on DOD's Actions to Prevent and Respond to Sexual Assault in the Military*, GAO-12-571R: March 30, 2012: 10, http://www.gao.gov/assets/590/589780.pdf.

6. GAO, *Military* Personnel.

7. DoD SAPR, "DoD and Services' Policies," n.d., http://www.sapr.mil/index.php/dod-policy/dod-and-service-policy.

8. DoDD 6495.01, January 23, 2012: 2–3, http://www.sapr.mil/public/docs/instructions/DoDI_649501_20130430.pdf.

9. GAO, *Military Personnel*, 10.

10. DoDD 6495.01, 3.

11. DoDD 6495.01, 3.

12. GAO, *Military Personnel*, 17–18.

13. GAO, *Military Personnel*, 17–18.

14. Air Force Policy Directive 36-60, "Sexual Assault Prevention and Response (SAPR) Program," 1, March 28, 2008, http://www.sapr.mil/public/docs/policy/afpd36-60.pdf.

15. Army Command Policy, Sexual Assault Policy, Army Regulation 600-20, 8-2a, November 6, 2014, http://www.apd.army.mil/pdffiles/r600_20.pdf.

16. Marine Corps Order 1752.B, "Sexual Assault Prevention and Response (SAPR) Program," 1, Situation, March 1, 2013, http://www.marines.mil/Portals/59/Publications/MCO%201752.5B.pdf.

17. OPNAV INSTRUCTION 1752.1B, "Sexual Assault Victim Intervention (SAVI) Program," 6, Policy, December 29, 2006, http://www.sapr.mil/public/docs/directives/sexual-assault-victim-intervention-savi-program.pdf.

18. Coast Guard, "Sexual Assault Prevention and Response Program (SAPRP)," COMDINST 1754 10C, December 20, 2007, 1, http://www.sapr.mil/public/docs/policy/ci_1754_10c.pdf.

19. Molly O'Toole,. "Military Sexual Assault Epidemic Continues to Claim Victims as Defense Department Fails Females," *Huffington Post*, posted: October 6, 2012, updated: May 20, 2013, http://www.huffingtonpost.com/2012/10/06/military-sexual-assault-defense-department_n_1834196.html.

20. Manning, telephone interview.

21. UCMJ Arts, 120 & 125; 10 U.S.C. §§ 920, 925 (2012).

22. DoDD 6495.01, "SAPR Program," Reissued January 23, 2012, 32 CFR Part 103Final Rule (RIN 0790-AI37), http://www.sapr.mil/index.php/law-and-dod-policies/directives-andinstructions, in Department of Defense, *Annual Report 2012*, vol. 1, 98, 99, n. 76, 77.

23. *National Defense Authorization Act for FY 2014, Report 113-44, Senate, Committee on Armed Services,* 113th Cong. 1st sess. June 30, 2013. Title V Military Personnel Policy, Subtitle E Sexual Assault Prevention and Response and Military Justice Matters, Parts I, II, III: 111–115, http://www.dtic.mil/dtic/tr/fulltext/u2/a592402.pdf.

24. David Vergun, "New Law Brings Changes to Uniform Code of Military Justice," *Army News Service*, Department of Defense, January 8, 2014, http://www.defense.gov/news/newsarticle.aspx?id=121444.

25. "2014 Amendments to the Manual for Courts-Martial, United States," Executive Order 13669 of June 13, 2014, Presidential Documents, *Federal Register* 79, no. 117: June 18, 2014, 34999, http://www.caaflog.com/wp-content/uploads/EO-13669-2014-Amendments-to-the-MCM.pdf.

26. Vergun, "New Law Brings Changes."

27. Vergun, "New Law Brings Changes."

28. *AP*, "Navy Charges 3 Football Players," *ESPN College Football*, June 20, 2013, http://espn.go.com/college-football/story/_/id/9405033/navy-charges-three-football-players-sexual-assault-case.

29. Vergun, "New Law Brings Changes."

30. Vergun, "New Law Brings Changes."

31. Manning, telephone interview.

32. Article 120 Rape and Sexual Assault Generally, a. (a) Rape, UCMJ, June 28, 2012, http://www.sapr.mil/public/docs/ucmj/UCMJ_Article120_Rape_Sexual_Assault.pdf.

33. Article 120 Rape and Sexual Assault Generally, a. (c), (d) Aggravated Sexual Contact; Abusive Sexual Contact, UCMJ, June 28, 2012, http://www.sapr.mil/public/docs/ucmj/UCMJ_Article120_Rape_Sexual_Assault.pdf.

34. Article 120 Rape and Sexual Assault Generally, a. (g), (1) (2) Sexual Act; Sexual Contact, UCMJ, June 28, 2012, http://www.sapr.mil/public/docs/ucmj/UCMJ_Article120_Rape_Sexual_Assault.pdf.

35. Article 120 Rape and Sexual Assault Generally, a. (g), (3) (4) Bodily Harm; Grievous Bodily Harm, UCMJ, June 28, 2012, http://www.sapr.mil/public/docs/ucmj/UCMJ_Article120_Rape_Sexual_Assault.pdf.

36. 36 Article 120 Rape and Sexual Assault Generally, a. (g), (5) (6) Force; Unlawful Force, UCMJ, June 28, 2012, http://www.sapr.mil/public/docs/ucmj/UCMJ_Article120_Rape_Sexual_Assault.pdf.

37. Article 120 Rape and Sexual Assault Generally, a. (g), (7) Threatening or placing that other person in fear, *UCMJ*, June 28, 2012, http://www.sapr.mil/public/docs/ucmj/UCMJ_Article120_Rape_Sexual_Assault.pdf.

38. *Manual for Courts-Martial United States* (2012 Edition), "51. Article 125—Sodomy," a. Text of statute (a) (b), IV-84; b. Elements (2) (3) (4), IV-84, http://www.loc.gov/rr/frd/Military_Law/pdf/MCM-2012.pdf.

39. *Manual for Courts-Martial United States* (2012 Edition), "Article 80—Attempts," a. Text of statute a) (b) (c), IV-4, http://www.loc.gov/rr/frd/Military_Law/pdf/MCM-2012.pdf.

40. Kristina Wong, "Pentagon Issues Report on Sexual Harassment," *The Hill*, May 15, 2014, http://thehill.com/policy/defense/206273-pentagon-issues-report-on-sexual-harrassment; Nick Simeone, "DOD Releases Figures on Sexual Harassment in Military," *American Forces Press Service*, Department of Defense, May 15, 2014, http://www.defense.gov/news/newsarticle.aspx?id=122270.

41. Department of Defense, *Annual Report 2012*, vol. 1 (2013), 99.

42. Rosemarie Skaine, *Power and Gender: Issues in Sexual Dominance and Harassment* (Jefferson, NC: McFarland, 1996), 13.

43. Department of Defense, *Annual Report on Sexual Harassment and Violence at the Military Service Academies Academic Program Year 2012–2013* (December 2013), 18, http://www.sapr.mil/public/docs/reports/final_apy_12-13_msa_report.pdf.

44. U.S. Department of Army, "Prevention of Sexual Harassment," Army Regulation 600-20, *Army Command Policy*, Ch. 7, September 20, 2012, http://www.apd.army.mil/pdffiles/r600_20.pdf

45. U.S. Department of Army, "Prevention of Sexual Harassment," Ch. 7.

46. Andrew R. Morral and Kristie L. Gore, *Sexual Assault and Sexual Harassment in the U.S. Military: Top-Line Results from the RAND Military Workplace Study* (Santa Monica, CA: RAND Corporation, National Defense Research Institute, 2014), 13–15, http://www.rand.org/.

47. U.S. Department of Army, "Prevention of Sexual Harassment," Ch. 7.

CHAPTER 4

1. RADM D. M. "Mac." Williams Jr., USN (Ret.), former NIS Commander, telephone interview by Rosemarie Skaine, October 17, 2014.

2. Paul J. Rice, "Court Martial Jurisdiction—The Service Connection Standard in Confusion," *Journal of Criminal Law and Criminology* 61, no. 3, Article 2 (1971): 339, http://scholarlycommons.law.northwestern.edu/cgi/viewcontent.cgi?article=5668&context=jclc.

3. Rice, "Court Martial Jurisdiction," 339.

4. *O'Callahan v. Parker*, s395 US 258, Supreme Court 1969, https://scholar.google.com/scholar_case?case=15968363962625244153&q=o%27callahan+v.+parker,+395+u.s.+258+(1969):&hl=en&as_sdt=1000006&as_vis=1.

5. *O'Callahan v. Parker.*

6. *Reid v. Covert*, 354 U.S. 1 (1957); *Reid v. Covert*, 354 U.S. 1 (1956), http://www.oyez.org/cases/1950-1959/1955/1955_701_2.

7. *Reid v. Covert*, 354 U.S. 1 (1957); *Reid v. Covert*, 354 U.S. 1 (1956).

8. *Reid v. Covert*, 354 U.S. 1 (1957); *Reid v. Covert*, 354 U.S. 1 (1956).

9. Family Advocacy Program, Army OneSource, U.S. Army, 2015, http://www.myarmyonesource.com/familyprogramsandservices/familyprograms/familyadvocacyprogram/default.aspx

10. Family Advocacy Program.

11. Family Advocacy Program.

12. Family Advocacy Program.

13. U.S. Navy, "Restricted/Unrestricted Options," Family Advocacy Program, 2015, http://www.cnic.navy.mil/ffr/family_readiness/fleet_and_family_support_program/family_advocacy/restricted_unrestricted_options.html.

14. R. Chuck Mason, "Military Justice: Courts-Martial, an Overview," Congressional Research Service, August 12, 2013, 2, https://www.fas.org/sgp/crs/natsec/R41739.pdf.

15. Mason, "Military Justice," 2.

16. Mason, "Military Justice," 6.

17. Mason, "Military Justice," 6.

18. Mason, "Military Justice," 7.

19. David Vergun, "New Law Brings Changes to Uniform Code of Military Justice," *Army News Service*, Department of Defense, January 8, 2014, http://www.defense.gov/news/newsarticle.aspx?id=121444.

20. Joe Doty and Jeff Fenlason, "The Military's Sexual Assault Problem and Solutions," *Army*, January 2014, 20, http://www.ausa.org/publications/armymagazine/archive/2014/Documents/01January/FC_DotyFenlason_January2014.pdf.

21. Rosemarie Skaine, "How Should Allegations of Sexual Assault in the U.S. Military Be Handled? " In *World at War: Understanding Conflict and Society*, ABC-CLIO, 2014-web.

22. Williams Jr., telephone interview.

23. Maj. Steven J. Smart, USAF, "Setting the Record Straight: The Military Justice System and Sexual Assault," Commentaries, Air Force Judge Advocate, July 27, 2012, http://www.afjag.af.mil/sexualassaultprosecution/index.asp.

24. Smart, "Setting the Record Straight."

25. Smart, "Setting the Record Straight."

26. Smart, "Setting the Record Straight."

27. MAJ Lillian Pfluke, U.S. Army (Ret.), telephone interview by Rosemarie Skaine, November 8, 2014.

28. Pfluke, telephone interview.

29. CAPT Lory Manning, USN (Ret.), telephone interview by Rosemarie Skaine, October 5, 2014.

30. Manning, telephone interview.

31. Manning, telephone interview.

32. Manning, telephone interview.

33. "Military versus Civilian Court Authority," Military Law Basics, Lawyers.com, 2015, http://military-law.lawyers.com/military-law-basics/military-versus-civilian-court-authority.html.

34. Williams Jr., telephone interview.

35. *O'Callahan v. Parker*, 395 U.S. 258 (1969): New Limitation on Court-Martial Jurisdiction, *Journal of Criminal Law, Criminology and Police Science* 61, no. 2 (1970): 195, http://scholarlycommons.law.northwestern.edu/cgi/viewcontent.cgi?article=5653&context=jclc.

36. U.S. Supreme Court, *Feres v. United States*, 340 U.S. 135 (1950), http://supreme.justia.com/cases/federal/us/340/135/case.html.

37. Austin Wright and Tim Mak, "Sexual Assault Scandals a Pentagon Test—DoD's Top Spokesman Rebukes Air Force Chief . . .," Politico, Morning Defense, May 16, 2013, http://www.politico.com/morningdefense/0513/morningdefense10695.html.

38. RADM D. M. "Mac" Williams Jr., USN (Ret.), former NIS Commander, e-mail to Rosemarie Skaine, November 18, 2014.

39. Nancy Montgomery, "Case Dismissed against Aviano IG Convicted of Sexual Assault," *Stars and Stripes*, February 27, 2013, http://www.stripes.com/news/air-force/case-dismissed-against-aviano-ig-convicted-of-sexual-assault-1.209797.

40. Craig Whitlock, "Air Force General to Retire after Criticism for Handling of Sexual-Assault Cases," *Washington Post*, January 8, 2014, http://www.washingtonpost.com/world/national-security/air-force-general-criticized-for-handling-of-sexual-assault-cases-to-retire/2014/01/08/9942df96-787d-11e3-b1c5-739e63e9c9a7_story.html.

41. Craig Whitlock, "Air Force General Defends Overturning Sexual-Assault Conviction," *Washington Post*, April 10, 2013, http://www.washingtonpost.com/world/national-security/air-force-general-defends-overturning-sexual-assault-conviction/2013/04/10/42f8162c-a215-11e2-ac00-8ef7caef5e00_story.html.

42. Williams Jr.

43. Charles "Cully" Stimson, "Military Sexual Assault Reform: Real Change Takes Time," Heritage Foundation, March 6, 2014, http://www.heritage.org/research/reports/2014/03/military-sexual-assault-reform-real-change-takes-time.

44. Vergun, "New Law Brings Changes."

CHAPTER 5

1. CAPT Lory Manning, USN (Ret.), telephone interview by Rosemarie Skaine, October 5, 2014.

2. Matthew Cox, "Air Force Tests Standards to Open Combat Jobs to Women," Military.com, April 22, 2015, http://www.military.com/daily-news/2015/04/22/air-force-tests-standards-to-open-combat-jobs-to-women.html.

3. Cox, "Air Force Tests Standards."

4. "Amazing Women in War and Peace," http://userpages.aug.com/captbarb/femvets.html; "Women Were There," http://userpages.aug.com/captbarb/femvets2.html.

5. Rosemarie Skaine, "Background and History," in *Women in Combat: A Reference Handbook* (Santa Barbara, CA: ABC-CLIO, 2011), 25, 28, http://ebooks.abc-clio.com/reader.aspx?isbn=9781598844603&id=A2913C-329.

6. Rosemarie Skaine, "Female Participation in Combat," in *World at War: Understanding Conflict and Society* (Santa Barbara, CA: ABC-CLIO, 2013)-, accessed January 21, 2015, http://worldatwar2.abc-clio.com/.

7. Skaine, "Female Participation in Combat."

8. Amaani Lyle, "Women in Service Review Rollout Due in 2016," DoD News, U.S. Department of Defense, January 12, 2015, http://www.defense.gov/news/newsarticle.aspx?id=123952.

9. C. Kay Larson, *Til I Come Marching Home: A Brief History of American Women in World War II* (Pasadena, MD: The Minerva Center, 1995), xiii, in *Women at War: Gender Issues of Americans in Combat*, Rosemarie Skaine (Jefferson, NC: McFarland, 1999), Ebook, 64.

10. Rosemarie Skaine, *Women at War: Gender Issues of Americans in Combat* (Jefferson, NC: McFarland, 1999), Ebook, 64.

11. Skaine, *Women at War,* 64.

12. Skaine, "Female Participation in Combat."

13. Skaine, *Women at War,* 64.

14. Testimony on Sexual Assaults in the Military: Hearing before the Subcommittee on Personnel of the Committee on Armed Services, U.S. Senate, 113 Congress, 11 (March 13, 2013) (testimony of Ms. Brigette McCoy, former Specialist, U.S. Army).

15. Hearing (March 13, 2013), 19 (testimony of Mr. Brian K. Lewis, former Petty Officer Third Class, U.S. Navy, Advocacy Board Member, Protect Our Defenders).

16. Hearing (March 13, 2013), 162–164 (prepared statement, Aviano Air Base Sexual Assault Victim).

17. Jesse Ellison, "The Military's Secret Shame," *Newsweek*, April 3, 2011, http://www.newsweek.com/militarys-secret-shame-66459.

18. Molly O'Toole, "Military Sexual Assault Epidemic Continues to Claim Victims as Defense Department Fails Females," *Huffington Post*, Posted: October 6, 2012, Updated: May 20, 2013, http://www.huffingtonpost.com/2012/10/06/military-sexual-assault-defense-department_n_1834196.html.

19. Department of Defense, *Annual Report on Sexual Assault in the Military, Fiscal Year 2012*, vol. 1. (Washington, DC: Department of Defense, Sexual Assault Prevention and Response, 2013), 61, 86, http://www.sapr.mil/index.php/annual-reports.

20. Lolita C. Baldor, AP, "Sexual Assault Circumstances Differ for Military Men, Women," *ABC News*, May 1, 2015, http://abcnews.go.com/Health/wireStory/sexual-assault-circumstances-differ-military-men-women-30743977.

21. Elizabeth Robbins, "Alcohol Abuse Is Fueling Military Sexual Assault," *Washington Post*, June 13, 2013, http://www.washingtonpost.com/opinions/alcohol-abuse-is-fueling-military-sexual-assault/2013/06/13/da2f5ada-d37c-11e2-a73e-826d299ff459_story.html.

22. Kirsten Gillibrand, *Snapshot Review of Sexual Assault Report Files at the Four Largest U.S. Military Bases in 2013*, Office of U.S. Senator, Case File 1: Wright-Patterson Air Force Base, May 2015: 13, http://www.gillibrand.senate.gov/imo/media/doc/Gillibrand_Sexual%20Assault%20Report.pdf.

23. Hearing (March 13, 2013): 11 (testimony of Ms. Brigette McCoy, former Specialist, U.S. Army).

24. Mark Thompson, "TSgt Raped at Sather Air Base Iraq," *My Duty to Speak, Blog at WordPress.com*, September 13, 2013, http://mydutytospeak.com/.

25. Mary F. Calvert, "Photos: Women Who Risked Everything to Expose Sexual Assault in the Military," September 8, 2014, http://www.motherjones.com/politics/2014/09/sexual-violence-american-military-photos.

26. Calvert, "Photos: Women Who Risked Everything."

27. Calvert, "Photos: Women Who Risked Everything."

28. Calvert, "Photos: Women Who Risked Everything."

29. Rosemarie Skaine, "Female Participation in Combat"; "Carter Names New Sexual Assault Prevention Office Director," DoD News, Defense Media Activity, Department of Defense, May 22, 2015, http://www.defense.gov/news/newsarticle.aspx?id=128876.

30. U.S. Army, "Today's Women Soldiers," Women in the U.S. Army, http://www.army.mil/women/today.html.

31. U.S. Navy, "Women in Naval Service," Navy Personnel Command, June 2014, http://www.public.navy.mil/BUPERS-NPC/ORGANIZATION/BUPERS/WOMENSPOLICY/Pages/NavyWomenFactsStatistics.aspx.

32. Defense Manpower Research, "Demographics of Active Duty U.S. Military," April 12, 2015, http://www.statisticbrain.com/demographics-of-active-duty-u-s-military/.

33. U.S. Air Force, "Service Demographics Offer Snapshot of Force," January 25, 2008, http://www.af.mil/News/ArticleDisplay/tabid/223/Article/124527/service-demographics-offer-snapshot-of-force.aspx.

34. Department of Defense, *Annual Report Fiscal Year 2012*, vol. 1, 19, 25, 26.

35. Department of Defense, *Annual Report on Sexual Assault in the Military, Fiscal Year 2014* (Washington, DC: Department of Defense), 8–9, http://www.sapr.mil/index.php/annual-reports.

36. Jennifer Hlad, "Retaliation Still a Major Issue for Troops Who Report Sexual Assault, Study Finds," *Stars and Stripes*, December 5, 2014, http://www.stripes.com/news/retaliation-still-a-major-issue-for-troops-who-report-sexual-assault-study-finds-1.317544.

37. Manning, telephone interview.

38. Manning, telephone interview.

39. Department of Defense, *Annual Report Fiscal Year 2012*, vol. 1, 27.

40. Jessica A., Turchik and Susan M. Wilson, "Sexual Assault in the U.S. Military: A Review of the Literature and Recommendations for the Future," *Aggression and Violent Behavior*, 15 (2010), 269, doi:10.1016/j.avb.2010.01.005.

41. Rosemarie Skaine, "How Should Allegations of Sexual Assault in the U.S. Military Be Handled?" In *World at War: Understanding Conflict and Society*, ABC-CLIO, 2014 web.

42. *Relationships Between Military Sexual Assault, Post- Traumatic Stress Disorder and Suicide, and Department of Defense and Department of Veterans Affairs Medical Treatment and Management of Victims of Sexual Trauma. Hearing before Personnel Subcommittee of the Senate Armed Services Committee*, "Gillibrand Opening Statement at Senate Subcommittee Hearing Examining Impact of Military Sexual Assault, Links to PTSD and Suicides," 113th Cong., 2nd sess., February 26, 2014, http://www.gillibrand.senate.gov/newsroom/press/release/gillibrand-opening-statement-at

-senate-subcommittee-hearing-examining-impact-of-military-sexual-assault-links-to-ptsd-and-suicides.

43. Steven Nelson, "California 'Yes Means Yes' Law Worries Skeptics," *U.S. News and World Report*, September 29, 2014, http://www.usnews.com/news/articles/2014/09/29/california-yes-means-yes-law-worries-skeptics.

44. Cindy Struckman-Johnson, David Struckman-Johnson, and Peter B. Anderson, "Tactics of Sexual Coercion: When Men and Women Won't Take No for an Answer," *Journal of Sex Research* 40, no. 1 (2003): 76–86. DOI:10.1080/00224490309552168; in Livia Gershon, "When Women Sexually Assault Men: How Gendered Cultural Scripts Help Conceal and Laugh Away a Legitimate Problem," *Pacific Standard*, October 9, 2014, http://www.psmag.com/politics-and-law/women-sexually-assault-men-92099.

CHAPTER 6

1. Testimony on Sexual Assaults in the Military: Hearing before the Subcommittee on Personnel of the Committee on Armed Services, U.S. Senate, 113th Cong. 22 (March 13, 2013) (testimony of Brian K. Lewis, former Petty Officer Third Class, U.S. Navy Advocacy Board Member, Protect Our Defenders), http://www.gpo.gov/fdsys/pkg/CHRG-113shrg88340/pdf/CHRG-113shrg88340.pdf.

2. "Lesbians and Gay Men in the U.S. Military: Historical Background," http://psychology.ucdavis.edu/faculty_sites/rainbow/html/military_history.html.

3. "American soldier Pictures & Images," photobucket.com, http://photobucket.com/images/american%20soldier.

4. Hayes Brown, "More Men Than Women Were Victims of Sexual Assault in Military, Report Finds," May 1, 2014, http://thinkprogress.org/world/2014/05/01/3433055/dod-men-mst/.

5. Jennifer Hlad, "Military Grapples with Stigma of Men Reporting Sexual Assault," *Stars and Stripes*, December 9, 2014, http://www.stripes.com/news/military-grapples-with-stigma-of-men-reporting-sexual-assault-1.318203.

6. Brown, "More Men Than Women Were Victims."

7. Megan N. Schmid, "Comment: Combating a Different Enemy: Proposals to Change the Culture of Sexual Assault in the Military," *Villanova Law Review* no. 55 (2010): 504, 505.

8. Missy Ryan, "Instances of Sexual Assault among Troops Decrease, Report Suggests; Details on Male Victims Were Also Revealed; Officials Vowed to Fight Retaliation for Those Reporting Abuse," Blogs, *Washington Post*, May 1, 2015.

9. "Sexual Trauma among Men in the Military," Recovery Ranch.com, 2015, http://www.recoveryranch.com/articles/trauma-and-ptsd-articles/sexual-trauma-among-men-in-the-military/.

10. Terri J. Rau, Lex L. Merrill, Stephanie K. McWhorter, Valerie A. Stander, Cynthia J. Thomsen, Christopher W. Dyslin, Julie L Crouch, Mandy M. Rabenhorst, and Joel S. Milner, "Evaluation of a Sexual Assault Education/Prevention Program for Male U.S. Navy Personnel," *Military Medicine* 175, no. 6 (2010):429, http://www.dtic.mil/dtic/tr/fulltext/u2/a523463.pdf.

11. Christopher J. Goewert and Andrew R. Norton, "Sexual Assault: Four Commonly Held Beliefs," *The Reporter* 40, no. 2(2013): 27, http://www.afjag.af.mil/shared/media/document/AFD-131017-010.pdf.

12. Jesse Ellison, "The Military's Secret Shame," *Newsweek*, April 3, 2011, http://www.newsweek.com/militarys-secret-shame-66459.

13. "Retired Marine Reveals Secret Suffering of Male Military Rape Victims," *The Daily Beast*, February 27, 2014, http://www.thedailybeast.com/articles/2014/02/27/retired-marine-reveals-secret-suffering-of-male-military-rape-victims.html.

14. Nathaniel Penn, "Son, Men Don't Get Raped," GQ, Conde Nast, 2014, http://www.gq.com/long-form/male-military-rape.

15. Penn, "Son, Men Don't Get Raped."

16. Ellison, "The Military's Secret Shame."

17. James Dao, "In Debate over Military Sexual Assault, Men Are Overlooked Victims," *New York Times*, http://www.nytimes.com/2013/06/24/us/in-debate-over-military-sexual-assault-men-are-overlooked-victims.html?pagewanted=all&_r=0.

18. "Men Sexually Assaulted in the Military Speak Out," *Baltimore Sun*, December 20, 2013, http://www.military.com/daily-news/2013/12/20/men-sexually-assaulted-in-the-military-speak-out.html.

19. "Men Sexually Assaulted in the Military Speak Out."

20. Department of Defense, *Annual Report on Sexual Assault in the Military, Fiscal Year 2012*, vol. 1 (Washington, DC: Department of Defense, Sexual Assault Prevention and Response, 2013), 18, http://www.sapr.mil/index.php/annual-reports.

21. Hlad, "Military Grapples with Stigma."

22. Department of Defense, *Annual Report Fiscal Year 2012*, vol. 1, 26.

23. CAPT Lory Manning, USN (Ret.), telephone interview by Rosemarie Skaine, October 5, 2014.

24. Manning, telephone interview.

25. AP, "Male Military Sex Assault Victims Slow to Complain," Time.com, December 9, 2014, Database: Business Source Elite.

26. DoD, Report to the President of the United States on Sexual Assault Prevention and Response, 2014, 32, 101–102, http://www.sapr.mil/public/docs/reports/FY14_POTUS/FY14_DoD_Report_to_POTUS_Full_Report.pdf.

27. DoD, Report to the President, 102–103.

28. GAO, "Personnel: Actions Needed to Address Sexual Assaults of Male Servicemembers," GAO-15-284, March 19, 2015, Highlights, http://www.gao.gov/products/GAO-15-284.

29. GAO, "Personnel."

30. AP, "Male Military Sex Assault Victims Slow to Complain."

31. "Justice Denied," CD, http://www.justicedeniedmovie.com/.

32. SWAN Service Women's Action Network, "Military Sexual Violence: Rape, Sexual Assault and Sexual Harassment," n.d., http://servicewomen.org/military-sexual-violence/.

33. "Men Sexually Assaulted in the Military Speak Out."

34. Center for Deployment Psychology, "Military Sexual Assault," Uniformed Services University of the Health Sciences, Bethesda, MD, n.d. http://www.deploymentpsych.org/disorders/sexual-assault-main.

35. Afterdeployment.org, *JUST THE FACTS: Military Sexual Trauma*, "Men as Survivors of Sexual Trauma," 2010, http://afterdeployment.dcoe.mil/sites/default/files/pdfs/client-handouts/mst-sexual-assault-harassment.pdf.

36. Afterdeployment.org.

37. Jessica A., Turchik and Susan M. Wilson, "Sexual Assault in the U.S. Military: A Review of the Literature and Recommendations for the Future," *Aggression and Violent Behavior*, 15 (2010): 269, doi:10.1016/j.avb.2010.01.005.

CHAPTER 7

1. "Defense Force Management: DOD's Policy on Homosexuality," U.S. Government Accountability Office (GAO), June 12, 1992, http://archive.gao.gov/d33t10/146980.pdf 2.

2. "Transgender" is the preferred term instead of "transgendered." See Katy Steinmetz, "Why It's Best to Avoid the Word 'Transgendered,'" *Time*, December 15, 2014, http://time.com/3630965/transgender-transgendered/.

3. Keren Lehavot and Tracy L. Simpson, "Incorporating Lesbian and Bisexual Women into Women Veterans' Health Priorities," *Journal of General Internal Medicine* 28 no. 2 (Suppl 2:S609, 2013), DOI: 10.1007/s11606-012-2291-2. © Society of General Internal Medicine.

4. Robert Crown Law Library, "Don't Ask Don't Tell Don't Pursue," Digital Law Project, Stanford Law School, September 7, 1999, #2 in Rosemarie Skaine, *Women in Combat: A Reference Handbook* (Santa Barbara, CA: ABC-CLIO, 2011), 33, http://ebooks.abc-clio.com/reader.aspx?isbn=9781598844603.

5. The terms "homosexual" and "homosexuality" are used to reflect their historical meanings. The terms "gay," "lesbian," "bisexual," and "transgender" are otherwise used. See GLAAD Media Reference Guide—Terms To Avoid," http://www.glaad.org/reference/offensive.

6. Directive Number 1304.26, Department of Defense, December 21, 1993, http://biotech.law.lsu.edu/blaw/dodd/corres/pdf/d130426wch1_122193/d130426p.pdf.

7. Gary J. Gates, "Lesbian, Gay, and Bisexual Men and Women in the US Military: Updated Estimates," The Williams Institute, May 2010, http://williamsinstitute.law.ucla.edu/wp-content/uploads/Gates-GLBmilitaryUpdate-May-20101.pdf.

8. Gates, "Lesbian, Gay, and Bisexual Men and Women in the US Military."

9. David F. Burrelli and Charles Dale, "Homosexuals and U.S. Military Policy: Current Issues," *CRS Report for Congress*. Congressional Research Service, February 10, 2005: 9, http://sldn.3cdn.net/4e028c78119835e283_i4m6vg3ra.pdf.

10. Derek J. Burks, "Lesbian, Gay, and Bisexual Victimization in the Military: An Unintended Consequence of 'Don't Ask, Don't Tell'?" *American Psychologist* 66, no. 7 (October 2011): 604, DOI: 10.1037/a0024609.

11. Servicemembers Legal Defense Network, "Women in Uniform Disproportionately Affected by 'Don't Ask, Don't Tell' Law," Newsroom, June 23, 2008,

www.sldn.org, in Rosemarie Skaine, *Women in Combat: A Reference Handbook* (Santa Barbara, CA: ABC-CLIO, 2011), 39, http://ebooks.abc-clio.com/reader.aspx?isbn=9781598844603.

12. Rowan Scarborough, "Victims of Sex Assaults in Military Are Mostly Men: Women Are More Likely to Speak Up," *Washington Times*, May 20, 2013, http://www.washingtontimes.com/news/2013/may/20/victims-of-sex-assaults-in-military-are-mostly-sil/#ixzz3Qi451p45.

13. Burks, "Lesbian, Gay, and Bisexual Victimization in the Military," 604.

14. Jessica A., Turchik and Susan M. Wilson, "Sexual Assault in the U.S. Military: A Review of the Literature and Recommendations for the Future," *Aggression and Violent Behavior*, 15 (2010), 269, doi:10.1016/j.avb.2010.01.005.

15. CAPT Lory Manning, USN (Ret.), telephone interview by Rosemarie Skaine, October 5, 2014.

16. "Pentagon Hunting Serial Predators in Attempt to Stop Military Sexual-Assault Epidemic," *RT*, February 26, 2014, http://rt.com/usa/military-sexual-assault-predator-756/.

17. "Pentagon Hunting."

18. Service Women's Action Network, "After Repeal: LGBT Service Members and Veterans: The Facts," n. 5., http://servicewomen.org/wp-content/uploads/2011/10/LGBT-Fact-Sheet-091411.pdf.

19. Chad, U.S. Army, "Years of Abuse," *My Duty to Speak*, Blog at WordPress.com. November 17, 2014, http://mydutytospeak.com/.

20. Jordan Larson. "Allowing Transgender People to Serve in the US Military Is 'Inevitable,'" *Vice News*, August 29, 2014, https://news.vice.com/article/allowing-transgender-people-to-serve-in-the-us-military-is-inevitable.

21. Felicia Schwartz and Byron Tau," Military May Allow Openly Transgender Personnel," *Wall Street Journal*, February 23, 2015, http://www.wsj.com/articles/u-s-military-may-allow-openly-transgender-personnel-1424739209.

22. Service Women's Action Network, "After Repeal," nn. 18, 19.

23. DoD Instruction 6130.03. "Medical Standards for Appointment, Enlistment, or Induction in the Military Services," April 28, 2010, http://www.dtic.mil/whs/directives/corres/pdf/613003p.pdf; in Service Women's Action Network, "After Repeal," n. 14.

24. David Crary (AP), "Panel Urges End to U.S. Ban on Transgender Troops," *Air Force Times*, March 13, 2014, http://www.airforcetimes.com/article/20140313/CAREERS/303130023/.

25. American Military Partner Association and the Transgender American Veterans Association, *How the Department of Defense Transgender Ban Harms Our Military Families*, A Report, March 30, 2015, http://militarypartners.org/transgender-report/.

26. Carolyn Martin, "Transgender Individuals," in *Abuse: An Encyclopedia of Causes, Consequences, and Treatments*, ed. Rosemarie Skaine (Santa Barbara, CA: Greenwood, 2015), 297.

27. Human Rights Campaign: Working for Lesbian, Gay, Bisexual and Transgender Equal Rights, "Don't Ask, Don't Tell Repeal Act of 2010," September 20, 2011, http://www.hrc.org/resources/entry/dont-ask-dont-tell-repeal-act-of-2010.

28. Heather Wilder and Jami Wilder, "In the Wake of Don't Ask Don't Tell: Suicide Prevention and Outreach for LGB Service Members," *Military Psychology* no. 24 (2012), 639, DOI: 10.1080/08995605.2012.737725.

29. Peter Sprigg, "Homosexual Assault in the Military," *Insight*, Family Research Council, Washington DC., May 2010, http://www.frc.org/insight/homosexual-assault-in-the-military.

30. "Gays in Military Is 'Social Engineering,' Responsible for Sexual Assault Spike: FRC's Jerry Boykin," *HuffPost Gay Voices*, Updated: June 4, 2013, http://www.huffingtonpost.com/2013/06/04/military-gays-jerry-boykin-_n_3380626.html.

31. Lila Shapiro, "Don't Ask Don't Tell Study Shows No Negative Effects on Military One Year after Repeal," *HuffPost Gay Voices*. Updated: September 10, 2012, http://www.huffingtonpost.com/2012/09/10/dont-ask-dont-tell-study_n_1868892.html.

32. Flag and General Officers for the Military, "Supporting the 1993 Law that Protects Morale and Readiness," n.d., http://www.flagandgeneralofficersforthemilitary.com/.

33. Kaye Dyer, ed., *Gays in Uniform: The Pentagon's Secret Reports* (Boston: Alyson Publications, 1990), in Nathaniel Frank, "Does the Empirical Research Say about the Impact of Openly Gay Service on the Military? A Research Memo," Palm Center, March 3, 2010, http://www.palmcenter.org/files/WhatDoesEmpiricalResearchSayAboutOpenlyGayService.pdf.

34. GAO, *Homosexuals in the Military*; Rand, *Sexual Orientation*; GAO, "Defense Force Management" in Frank, 1, 2 n. 1, 5, 6, 7.

35. Pamela Wolf, "Federal Legislation Targets Sexual Assault in Military, Transgender/Gender Nonconforming Discrimination," *Wolters Kluwer*, 2015, http://www.employmentlawdaily.com/index.php/news/federal-legislation-targets-sexual-assault-in-military-transgendergender-nonconforming-discrimination/.

36. Tom Philpott, "Gay, Lesbian Spouses to Gain Full Military Benefits," *Stars and Stripes*, June 27, 2013, http://www.stripes.com/news/us/gay-lesbian-spouses-to-gain-full-military-benefits-1.227956.

37. Philpott, "Gay, Lesbian Spouses."

38. DOD Instruction (DoDI) 6130.03. 2011:1 in Endia T. Mendez, "Transgenders in the U.S. Military: Policies, Problems, and Prospects," Master's Thesis, Monterey, CA: Naval Postgraduate School, March 2014: 26, http://www.dtic.mil/dtic/tr/fulltext/u2/a607720.pdf.

39. DoDI 6130.03. 2011:1 in Mendez, "Transgenders in the U.S. Military," 30.

40. Sandhya Somashekhar, "In Move Hailed by Advocates, Army Adjusts Process for Dismissing Transgender Soldiers," *Washington Post*, March 6, 2015, http://www.washingtonpost.com/news/post-nation/wp/2015/03/06/in-move-hailed-by-advocates-army-adjusts-process-for-dismissing-transgender-soldiers/.

41. Tom Vanden Brook, "Military Approves Hormone Therapy for Chelsea Manning," February 13, 2015, http://www.usatoday.com/story/news/nation/2015/02/12/chelsea-manning-hormone-therapy/23311813/.

42. American Military Partner Association and the Transgender American Veterans Association.

43. Jeremy Johnson, "Challenges: Returning to Life in Uniform as a DADT Discharged Vet," Blog Entry, Palm Center, May 8, 2012, http://www.palmcenter.org/blog/challenges_returning_life_uniform_dadt_discharged_vet.

44. Barack Obama, "Presidential Proclamation—LGBT Pride Month, 2015," White House, May 29, 2015, www.whitehouse.gov/the-press-office/2015/05/29/presidential-proclamation-lgbt-pride-month-2015.

CHAPTER 8

1. Wendy E. Brinson, "It Is All about Respect: The Army's Problem with Sexual Assault," Master of Military Studies Research Paper, United States Marine Corps Command and Staff College, Marine Corps University, April 23, 2012, v. (Statement appears in original: "DISCLAIMER THE OPINIONS AND CONCLUSIONS EXPRESSED HEREIN ARE THOSE OF THE INDIVIDUAL STUDENT AUTHOR AND DO NOT NECESSARILY REPRESENT THE VIEWS OF EITHER THE MARINE CORPS COMMAND AND STAFF COLLEGE OR ANY OTHER GOVERNMENTAL AGENCY."), i.

2. Women in Military Service for America Memorial Foundation, "Women Enter the Military Academies," History, Archive, n.d.

3. MAJ Lillian Pfluke, U.S. Army (Ret.), telephone interview by Rosemarie Skaine, November 8, 2014.

4. Pfluke, telephone interview.

5. Col W. Hays Parks, U.S. Marine Corps Reserve (Ret.), "Tailhook What Happened, Why and What's to be Learned," *Proceedings*, Annapolis, MD: U.S. Naval Institute, September 1994, 90–103, in Rosemarie Skaine, *Power and Gender: Issues in Sexual Dominance and Harassment* (Jefferson, NC: McFarland, 1996), 315–316.

6. Center for Deployment Psychology, "Military Sexual Assault," Uniformed Services University of the Health Sciences, Bethesda, MD, n.d.

7. CAPT Lory Manning, USN (Ret.), telephone interview by Rosemarie Skaine, October 5, 2014.

8. Manning, telephone interview.

9. Manning, telephone interview.

10. Manning, telephone interview.

11. Manning, telephone interview.

12. Manning, telephone interview.

13. Coreen Farris, Terry L. Schell, and Terri Tanielian, *Physical and Psychological Health Following Military Sexual Assault: Recommendations for Care, Research, and Policy* (Santa Monica, CA: RAND, 2013), 6.4.

14. Farris et al., *Physical and Psychological Health*, 6.

15. Farris et al., *Physical and Psychological Health*, 6.

16. Farris et al., *Physical and Psychological Health*, 6.

17. Tom Vanden Brook and David M. Jackson, "Obama Says Sexual Assault Crisis Hurts National Security," *USA TODAY*, May 16, 2013, http://www.usatoday.com/story/news/politics/2013/05/16/obama-hagel-military-sexual-assaults/2165763/.

18. Robyn A. Diehl, "Sexual Assault in the Military: Ethical Dilemma or National Security Issue?" Master of Arts in Liberal Studies Thesis, Washington, DC: Georgetown University, October 25, 2012, 92, https://repository.library.georgetown.edu/handle/10822/557559.

19. DoD, "Washington: Carter: Sexual Assault Undermines Military's Values," Plus Media Solutions Private Limited, April 6, 2015.

20. "Zero Tolerance," Cambridge Dictionaries Online, n.d., http://dictionary.cambridge.org/us/dictionary/british/zero-tolerance.

21. "Zero Tolerance," The Free Dictionary, http://legal-dictionary.thefreedictionary.com/Zero+Tolerance.

22. Lawrence Downes, "How the Military Talks About Sexual Assault," Taking Note, *New York Times*, May 26, 2013, http://takingnote.blogs.nytimes.com/2013/05/26/how-the-military-talks-about-sexual-assault/?_r=1.

23. Eric Schmitt, "Wall of Silence Impedes Inquiry into a Rowdy Navy Convention," *New York Times*, June 14, 1992, http://www.nytimes.com/1992/06/14/us/wall-of-silence-impedes-inquiry-into-a-rowdy-navy-convention.html?pagewanted=all&src=pm.

24. Downes, "How the Military Talks About Sexual Assault."

25. Downes, "How the Military Talks About Sexual Assault."

26. Editorial Board, "The Military's 'Zero Tolerance' Policy on Sexual Misconduct Isn't Working," *Washington Post*, July 4, 2012, http://www.washingtonpost.com/opinions/the-militarys-zero-tolerance-policy-on-sexual-misconduct-isnt-working/2012/07/04/gJQANSa6NW_story.html.

27. Cambridge Dictionaries Online.

28. The Free Dictionary.

29. Bruce Schneier, "'Zero Tolerance' Really Means Zero Discretion," *MPR News*, November 3, 2009, http://www.mprnews.org/story/2009/11/03/schneier.

30. Schneier, "'Zero Tolerance' Really Means Zero Discretion."

31. Jennifer Hlad, "Restriction of 'Good Soldier' Defense at Center of Senate Bill," *Stars and Stripes*, March 11, 2014, http://www.stripes.com/news/us/restriction-of-good-soldier-defense-at-center-of-senate-bill-1.272243.

32. RADM Duvall M. "Mac" Williams, telephone interview by Rosemarie Skaine, October 17, 2014.

33. Williams, telephone interview.

34. Department of Defense Annual Report on Sexual Assault in the Military Fiscal Year 2014, Sexual Assault Prevention and Response, May 2015: 19, http://sapr.mil/public/docs/reports/FY14_Annual/FY14_DoD_SAPRO_Annual_Report_on_Sexual_Assault.pdf.

35. Lawrence Korb and Dennis Laich, "Korb and Laich: Sex Assault and the Chain of Command," *Military Times*, November 19, 2013, http://www.militarytimes.com/article/20131119/NEWS01/311190015/Korb-Laich-Sex-assault-chain-command.

36. Kirsten Gillibrand, "Should Decisions Regarding the Chain of Command in the Military Be Removed?" *Congressional Digest* (September 2013), http://www.CongressionalDigest.com.

37. Sexual Assault Prevention and Response, Together We Can Prevent Sexual Assault, Commander's Guide, Department of the Navy Sexual Assault Prevention

and Response Office (DON SAPRO), http://www.secnav.navy.mil/sapro/Publications/DON%20SAPRO%20Commanders%20Guide.pdf.

38. Department of Defense, *Annual Report on Sexual Assault in the Military, Fiscal Year 2012*, vol. 1 (Washington, DC: Department of Defense, Sexual Assault Prevention and Response, 2013), 2, 3, 12, 73, http://www.sapr.mil/index.php/annual-reports; Lolita C. Baldor, "Military Sexual Assaults by the Numbers," AP.org. May 16, 2013, http://bigstory.ap.org/article/military-sexual-assaults-numbers.

39. Jim Garamone, "DoD Efforts to Combat Sexual Assault Begin Paying Off," DoD News, Defense Media Activity, Department of Defense, May 1, 2015, http://www.defense.gov/news/newsarticle.aspx?id=128717.

40. Department of Defense, *Annual Report Fiscal Year 2012*, vol. 1: 2, 3, 12, 73 (Washington DC); Baldor, "Military Sexual Assaults by the Numbers."

41. Williams, telephone interview.

42. Pfluke, telephone interview.

43. Pfluke, telephone interview.

44. Laura Bassett, "Obama Gives Military 1 Year to Fix Sexual Assault Problem," *Huffington Post*, December 20, 2013, http://www.huffingtonpost.com/2013/12/20/obama-military-sexual-assault_n_4480888.html.

45. 45 Manning, telephone interview.

46. Manning, telephone interview.

47. Bassett, "Obama Gives Military 1 Year."

48. Gillibrand, "Should Decisions Regarding the Chain of Command in the Military Be Removed?"

49. Rosemarie Skaine, "How Should Allegations of Sexual Assault in the U.S. Military Be Handled?" in *World at War: Understanding Conflict and Society* (Santa Barbara, CA: ABC-CLIO, 2014).

50. Skaine, "How Should Allegations of Sexual Assault in the U.S. Military Be Handled?"

CHAPTER 9

1. Department of Defense, "Secretary Hagel Releases Progress Report to the President on Sexual Assault in the Military, Announces Four New Directives to Strengthen Department Response," Release No: NR-603-14, December 4, 2014, http://www.defense.gov/Releases/Release.aspx?ReleaseID=17063.

2. Douglas C. Lovelace Jr., Foreword, Robert L. Caslen Jr., Cindy R. Jebb, Daniel Gade, and Hope C. Landsem, "Getting to the Left of Sharp: Lessons Learned from West Point's Efforts to Combat Sexual Harassment and Assault," Carlisle, PA: Strategic Studies Institute, United States Army War College, January 2015, v, http://www.strategicstudiesinstitute.army.mil/pubs/display.cfm?pubID=1244.

3. Department of Defense, *Annual Report on Sexual Assault in the Military, Fiscal Year 2012*, vol. 1 (Washington, DC: Department of Defense, Sexual Assault Prevention and Response, 2013), 2, 3, 12, 73, http://www.sapr.mil/index.php/annual-reports; Lolita C. Baldor, "Military Sexual Assaults by the Numbers," AP.org, May 16, 2013, http://bigstory.ap.org/article/military-sexual-assaults-numbers.

4. Kirsten Gillibrand, "Should Decisions Regarding the Chain of Command in the Military Be Removed?" *Congressional Digest* (September 2013), http://www.CongressionalDigest.com.

5. Jennifer Hlad, "Restriction of 'Good Soldier' Defense at Center of Senate Bill," *Stars and Stripes*, March 11, 2014, http://www.stripes.com/news/us/restriction-of-good-soldier-defense-at-center-of-senate-bill-1.272243.

6. Laura Bassett, "Obama Gives Military 1 Year to Fix Sexual Assault Problem," *Huffington Post*, December 20, 2013, http://www.huffingtonpost.com/2013/12/20/obama-military-sexual-assault_n_4480888.html.

7. American Forces Press Service, "Obama Directs Review of Sexual Assault Prevention Progress," DoD News, U.S. Department of Defense, December 20, 2013, http://www.defense.gov/news/newsarticle.aspx?id=121378.

8. Department of Defense, *Annual Report on Sexual Assault in the Military Fiscal Year 2014*, Sexual Assault Prevention and Response, May 2015, http://sapr.mil/public/docs/reports/FY14_Annual/FY14_DoD_SAPRO_Annual_Report_on_Sexual_Assault.pdf.

9. *The 2014 RAND Military Workplace Study*, Rand Corporation, 2015, http://www.rand.org/nsrd/projects/rmws.html.

10. "Initial Results from Major Survey of U.S. Military Sexual Assault, Harassment," RAND Corporation, December 4, 2014, http://www.rand.org/news/press/2014/12/04.html.

11. "Complete Results from Major Survey of U.S. Military Sexual Assault, Harassment Released," RAND Corporation, May 1, 2015, http://www.rand.org/news/press/2015/05/01.html.

12. "Complete Results," RAND.

13. MAJ Lillian Pfluke, U.S. Army (Ret.), telephone interview by Rosemarie Skaine, November 8, 2014.

14. Caslen et al., "Getting to the Left of Sharp," v.

15. Nita Lowey, "Lowey Amendment to Help Prevent Sexual Assault at Military Academies Included in Bipartisan Defense Bill," U.S. House of Representatives, June 14, 2013, http://www.lowey.house.gov/press-releases/lowey-amendment-to-help-prevent-sexual-assault-at-military-academies-included-in-bipartisan-defense-bill/.

16. Pfluke, telephone interview.

17. Pfluke, telephone interview.

18. Caslen et al., "Getting to the Left of Sharp," 3.

19. Caslen et al., "Getting to the Left of Sharp," ix.

20. CAPT Lory Manning, USN (Ret.), telephone interview by Rosemarie Skaine, October 5, 2014.

21. Government Accountability Office (GAO), *Military Personnel: DoD Needs to Take Further Actions to Prevent Sexual Assault during Initial Military Training*, Report to Congressional Committees, September 2014: 42, 44, http://www.gao.gov.

22. George Vukotich, "Military Sexual Assault Prevention and Response: The Bystander Intervention Training Approach," *Journal of Organizational Culture, Communications and Conflict* 17, no. 1 (2013):24.

23. Department of Defense, *Report of the Defense Task Force on Sexual Harassment and Violence at the Military Service Academies*, June 2005: ES-1.

24. RADM D. M. "Mac" Williams Jr. USN (Ret.), former NIS Commander, telephone interview by Rosemarie Skaine, October 17, 2014.

25. Coreen Farris and Kimberly A. Hepner, "Targeting Alcohol Misuse: A Promising Strategy for Reducing Military Sexual Assaults?" RAND Corporation, National Defense Research Institute, 2014: 2, 6.

26. Farris and Hepner, "Targeting Alcohol Misuse," 2.

27. Williams, telephone interview.

28. Williams, telephone interview.

29. Williams, telephone interview.

30. Williams, telephone interview.

31. *See also* Dan Lamothe, "Army General, Accused of Sexual Assault by Senior Adviser, Retired Quietly with Demotion," *Washington Post*, October 1, 2014, http://www.washingtonpost.com/news/checkpoint/wp/2014/10/01/army-general-accused-of-sexual-assault-by-senior-adviser-retired-quietly-with-demotion/.

32. Williams, telephone interview.

33. Williams, telephone interview.

34. "Remarks by the President at 'It's on Us' Campaign Rollout," Office of the Press Secretary, The White House, September 19, 2014, https://www.whitehouse.gov/the-press-office/2014/09/19/remarks-president-its-us-campaign-rollout.

35. "Remarks by the President."

36. Manning, telephone interview.

37. Manning, telephone interview.

38. Manning, telephone interview.

39. Department of Defense, *Annual Report on Sexual Assault in the Military Fiscal Year 2014.*

40. Department of Defense, *Annual Report on Sexual Assault in the Military Fiscal Year 2014.*

41. Department of Defense, *Annual Report on Sexual Assault in the Military Fiscal Year 2014.*

Bibliography

ARTICLES AND BOOK CHAPTERS

"2012 SAPRO Analysis." Fact Sheet. Office of Kirsten Gillibrand. 2009–2015. http://www.gillibrand.senate.gov/mjia/stats-from-sapro-report.

"2014 Amendments to the Manual for Courts-Martial, United States." Executive Order 13669 of June 13, 2014. Presidential Documents. *Federal Register* 79, no. 117 (June 18, 2014): 34999. http://www.caaflog.com/wp-content/uploads/EO-13669-2014-Amendments-to-the-MCM.pdf.

Amazing Women in War and Peace. http://userpages.aug.com/captbarb/femvets.html.

American Forces Press Service. "Obama Directs Review of Sexual Assault Prevention Progress." *DoD News*. U.S. Department of Defense. December 20, 2013. http://www.defense.gov/news/newsarticle.aspx?id=121378.

"American Soldier Pictures & Images." photobucket.com. http://photobucket.com/images/american%20soldier.

AP. "Male Military Sex Assault Victims Slow to Complain." Time.com. December 9, 2014. Database: Business Source Elite.

AP. "Navy Charges 3 Football Players." *ESPN College Football*. June 20, 2013. http://espn.go.com/college-football/story/_/id/9405033/navy-charges-three-football-players-sexual-assault-case.

Army OneSource. "Family Advocacy Program." April 4, 2015. http://www.myarmyonesource.com/familyprogramsandservices/familyprograms/familyadvocacyprogram/default.aspx.

Associated Press. Baldor, Lolita C. "Military Sexual Assaults by the Numbers." *AP.org*. May 16, 2013. http://bigstory.ap.org/article/military-sexual-assaults-numbers.

Associated Press. Baldor, Lolita C. "Reports of Sexual Assault in the Military Increase." *Huffington Post*. December 3, 2014. http://www.huffingtonpost.com/2014/12/03/military-sex-assaults_n_6265492.html.

Baldor, Lolita C. "Sexual Assault Circumstances Differ for Military Men, Women." *ABC News*. May 1, 2015. http://abcnews.go.com/Health/wireStory/sexual-assault-circumstances-differ-military-men-women-30743977.

Bassett, Laura. "Obama Gives Military 1 Year to Fix Sexual Assault Problem." *Huffington Post*. December 20, 2013. http://www.huffingtonpost.com/2013/12/20/obama-military-sexual-assault_n_4480888.html.

"A Broken Military Justice System." *New York Daily News*. Editorial. March 17, 2014. http://www.nytimes.com/2014/03/18/opinion/a-broken-military-justice-system.html?_r=2.

Brown, Hayes. "More Men than Women Were Victims of Sexual Assault in Military, Report Finds." May 1, 2014. http://thinkprogress.org/world/2014/05/01/3433055/dod-men-mst/.

Browne, Kingsley R. "Military Sex Scandals from Tailhook to the Present: The Cure Can Be Worse Than the Disease." *Duke Journal of Gender Law & Policy* 14 (2007): 749. http://scholarship.law.duke.edu/cgi/viewcontent.cgi?article=1128&context=djglp.

Bumiller, Elisabeth. "Obama Ends 'Don't Ask, Don't Tell' Policy." *New York Times*. July 22, 2011. http://www.nytimes.com/2011/07/23/us/23military.html?_r=0.

Bureau of Naval Personnel. Navy Personnel Research and Development Center (BUPERS PAO). *Examples of Navy Programs Currently Addressing Sexual Harassment*. March 27, 1993, 1.

Bureau of Naval Personnel. Navy Personnel Research and Development Center (BUPERS PAO). *Navy Actions on Sexual Harassment*. August 31, 1993, 1–4.

Bureau of Naval Personnel. Navy Personnel Research and Development Center (BUPERS PAO). *Summary of Responses on Sexual Harassment 1992 Navy-wide Personnel Survey*. San Diego. April 13, 1993, 1.

Bureau of Naval Personnel. Navy Personnel Research and Development Center (BUPERS PAO). *Toll-Free Telephone Number Sexual Harassment Advice, Counseling*. San Diego. August 31, 1993, 1.

Burks, Derek J. "Lesbian, Gay, and Bisexual Victimization in the Military: An Unintended Consequence of 'Don't Ask, Don't Tell'?" *American Psychologist* 66, no. 7 (October 2011): 604–613. DOI: 10.1037/a0024609.

Burrelli, David F., and Charles Dale. "Homosexuals and U.S. Military Policy: Current Issues." *CRS Report for Congress*. Congressional Research Service. February 10, 2005, 9. http://sldn.3cdn.net/4e028c78119835e283_i4m6vg3ra.pdf.

Calvert, Mary F. "Photos: Women Who Risked Everything to Expose Sexual Assault in the Military." September 8, 2014. http://www.motherjones.com/politics/2014/09/sexual-violence-american-military-photos.

"Carter Names New Sexual Assault Prevention Office Director." *DoD News*, Defense Media Activity. Department of Defense. May 22, 2015. http://www.defense.gov/news/newsarticle.aspx?id=128876.

Cary, Peter, and Bruce B. Auster with Douglas Pasternak, Joseph L. Galloway, Mary Lord, and Mike Tharp in San Diego, "What's Wrong with the Navy?" *U.S. News & World Report*, July 12, 1992, 22.

Caslen, Jr., Robert L., Cindy R. Jebb, Daniel Gade, and Hope C. Landsem. "Getting to the Left of Sharp: Lessons Learned from West Point's Efforts to Combat Sexual Harassment and Assault." Carlisle, PA: Strategic Studies Institute. United States Army War College. January 2015: 1–26. http://www.strategicstudies institute.army.mil/pubs/display.cfm?pubID=1244.

Chad, United States Army. "Years of Abuse." *My Duty to Speak. Blog at WordPress.com*. November 17, 2014. http://mydutytospeak.com/.

CNN Staff. "Pentagon Says Women in All Combat Units By 2016." *CNN*. June 18, 2013. http://www.cnn.com/2013/06/18/politics/women-combat/.

"Complete Results from Major Survey of U.S. Military Sexual Assault, Harassment Released." RAND Corporation. May 1, 2015. http://www.rand.org/news/press/2015/05/01.html.

"Courts-Martial Explained." Military.com. 2015. http://www.military.com/benefits/military-legal-matters/courts-martial-explained.html.

Cox, Matthew. "Air Force Tests Standards to Open Combat Jobs to Women." Military.com. April 22, 2015. http://www.military.com/daily-news/2015/04/22/air-force-tests-standards-to-open-combat-jobs-to-women.html.

Crary, David. (*AP*). "Panel Urges End to U.S. Ban on Transgender Troops." *Air Force Times*. March 13, 2014. http://www.airforcetimes.com/article/20140313/CAREERS/303130023/.

Crown, Robert, Law Library. "Don't Ask Don't Tell Don't Pursue." Digital Law Project. Stanford Law School. September 7, 1999.

Dao, James. "In Debate Over Military Sexual Assault, Men Are Overlooked Victims." *New York Times*. June 24, 2013. http://www.nytimes.com/2013/06/24/us/in-debate-over-military-sexual-assault-men-are-overlooked-victims.html?pagewanted=all&_r=0.

Defense Manpower Research. "Demographics of Active Duty U.S. Military." April 12, 2015. http://www.statisticbrain.com/demographics-of-active-duty-u-s-military/.

"Definition of Sexual Harassment," "Glossary of Terms," and "Range of Behaviors Which Constitute Sexual Harassment." SECNAVINST 5300.26B. Washington, DC: Department of Navy. January 6, 1993.

Department of Defense. "Directive Number 1304.26: Qualification Standards for Enlistment, Appointment, and Induction." December 21, 1993. http://biotech.law.lsu.edu/blaw/dodd/corres/pdf/d130426wch1_122193/d130426p.pdf.

Department of Defense. "Fact Sheet: Secretary Hagel Issues New Initiatives to Eliminate Sexual Assault, Updates Prevention Strategy and Releases 2013 Annual Report on Sexual Assault in the Military." Office of the Secretary of Defense. Sexual Assault Prevention and Response Office. http://www.sapr.mil/public/docs/reports/FY13_DoD_SAPRO_Annual_Report_Fact_Sheet.pdf.

Department of Defense. Office of Assistant Secretary of Defense. "SECDEF Announces Action in Tailhook," October 4, 1993, and attached "Memorandum for the SECNAV," from Les Aspin, Secretary of Defense. October 4, 1993, 2.

Department of Defense. "Secretary Hagel Releases Progress Report to the President on Sexual Assault in the Military, Announces Four New Directives to Strengthen Department Response." Release No: NR-603-14. December 4, 2014.

Department of Defense. "Washington: Carter: Sexual Assault Undermines Military's Values." Plus Media Solutions Private Limited. April 6, 2015.

Department of Justice. "What Is Sexual Assault?" Office on Violence against Women. n.d. http://www.justice.gov/ovw/sexual-assault.

Department of the Navy. *Define Navy Actions on Sexual Harassment*, August 31, 1993, 1–4.

Department of the Navy. *Resolving Conflict: Following the Light of Personal Behavior*, NP-15620, n.d.

DoD Instruction 6130.03. "Medical Standards for Appointment, Enlistment, or Induction in the Military Services." April 28, 2010. http://www.dtic.mil/whs/directives/corres/pdf/613003p.pdf.

DoD Instruction 6130.03. "Washington: Carter: Sexual Assault Undermines Military's Values." Plus Media Solutions Private Limited. April 6, 2015.

Donnelly, Elaine. "Constructing the Co-Ed Military." *Duke Journal of Gender Law & Policy* 14 (2007): 815.

Doty, Joe, and Jeff Fenlason. "The Military's Sexual Assault Problem and Solutions." *Army*. January 2014, 19–20. http://www.ausa.org/publications/armymagazine/archive/2014/Documents/01January/FC_DotyFenlason_January2014.pdf.

Downes, Lawrence. "How the Military Talks About Sexual Assault. Taking Note." *New York Times*. May 26, 2013. http://takingnote.blogs.nytimes.com/2013/05/26/how-the-military-talks-about-sexual-assault/?_r=1.

Editorial Board. "The Military's 'Zero Tolerance' Policy on Sexual Misconduct Isn't Working." *Washington Post*. July 4, 2012. http://www.washingtonpost.com/opinions/the-militarys-zero-tolerance-policy-on-sexual-misco

Editorial Board. "Protecting Our Service Members against Sexual Assault." *Washington Post*. May 7, 2015. http://www.washingtonpost.com/opinions/protecting-our-service-members/2015/05/07/0b4481d2-f346-11e4-84a6-6d7c67c50db0_story.html.

Ellison, Jesse. "Male Rape in the Military Being Confronted." *Newsweek*. April 3, 2011. http://www.thedailybeast.com/articles/2011/04/03/male-rape-in-the-military-being-confronted.html.

Ellison, Jesse. "The Military's Secret Shame." *Newsweek*. April 3, 2011. http://www.newsweek.com/militarys-secret-shame-66459.

Finan II, Robert J. Assistant Director, Government Liaison and Public Affairs. Department of the Navy, Headquarters. Naval Criminal Investigative Service, Letter. November 3, 1993, 1.

Flag and General Officers for the Military. "Supporting the 1993 Law that Protects Morale and Readiness." n.d. http://www.flagandgeneralofficersforthemilitary.com/.

Frank, Nathaniel. "Does the Empirical Research Say about the Impact of Openly Gay Service on the Military? A Research Memo." Palm Center. March 3, 2010. http://www.palmcenter.org/files/WhatDoesEmpiricalResearchSayAboutOpenlyGayService.pdf.

Garamone, Jim. "DoD Efforts to Combat Sexual Assault Begin Paying Off." *DoD News*, Defense Media Activity, Department of Defense. May 1, 2015. http://www.defense.gov/news/newsarticle.aspx?id=128717.

Gates, Gary J. "Lesbian, Gay, and Bisexual Men and Women in the U.S. Military: Updated Estimates." The Williams Institute. May 2010. http://williamsinstitute.law.ucla.edu/wp-content/uploads/Gates-GLBmilitaryUpdate-May-20101.pdf.

"Gays in Military Is 'Social Engineering,' Responsible for Sexual Assault Spike: FRC's Jerry Boykin." *HuffPost Gay Voices*. Updated: June 4, 2013. http://www.huffingtonpost.com/2013/06/04/military-gays-jerry-boykin-_n_3380626.html.

Gershon, Livia. "When Women Sexually Assault Men: How Gendered Cultural Scripts Help Conceal and Laugh Away a Legitimate Problem." *Pacific Standard*. October 9, 2014. http://www.psmag.com/politics-and-law/women-sexually-assault-men-92099.

Gilberd, Kathleen. "Military Law and the New NDAA." *Military Law Task Force*. National Lawyers Guild. March 12, 2014. http://nlgmltf.org/military-law/2014/military-law-and-the-new-ndaa/.

Gillibrand, Kirsten. "Allied Force Commanders Testified That the MJIA Will Not Disrupt 'Good Order and Discipline'." The Office of Kirsten Gillibrand. 2015. http://www.gillibrand.senate.gov/mjia/allies-testimony.

Gillibrand, Kirsten. "Editorials & OpEds in Support of the Military Justice Improvement Act." The Office of Kirsten Gillibrand. 2015. http://www.gillibrand.senate.gov/mjia/editorials.

Gillibrand, Kirsten. "Should Decisions Regarding the Chain of Command in the Military Be Removed?" *Congressional Digest*. September 2013. http://www.CongressionalDigest.com.

GLAAD. Media Reference Guide. "Terms to Avoid." glaad. http://www.glaad.org/reference/offensive.

Gordon, Claire. "Sexual Assault Reports Jump 61 Percent at Top Colleges in Two Years." America Tonight. *Aljazeera America*. October 7, 2014. http://america.aljazeera.com/watch/shows/america-tonight/articles/2014/10/7/colleges-clery-sexualassault1.html.

GQ. Conde Nast. "Son, Men Don't Get Raped." 2014. http://www.gq.com/long-form/male-military-rape.

Hlad, Jennifer. "Does Military Culture Foster Sex Abuse?" *Stars and Stripes*. May 24, 2013. http://www.usafawebguy.com/files/Falcon%20Clips%2020130524.pdf.

Hlad, Jennifer. "Hagel: Military Has in Many Ways Failed on Sexual Assault." *Stars and Stripes*. May 17, 2013. http://www.stripes.com/news/us/hagel-military-has-in-many-ways-failed-on-sexual-assault-1.221358.

Hlad, Jennifer. "Military Grapples with Stigma of Men Reporting Sexual Assault." *Stars and Stripes*. December 9, 2014. http://www.stripes.com/news/military-grapples-with-stigma-of-men-reporting-sexual-assault-1.318203.

Hlad, Jennifer. "Restriction of 'Good Soldier' Defense at Center of Senate Bill." *Stars and Stripes*. March 11, 2014. http://www.stripes.com/news/us/restriction-of-good-soldier-defense-at-center-of-senate-bill-1.272243.

Hlad, Jennifer. "Retaliation Still a Major Issue for Troops Who Report Sexual Assault, Study Finds." *Stars and Stripes*. December 5, 2014. http://www.stripes.com/news/retaliation-still-a-major-issue-for-troops-who-report-sexual-assault-study-finds-1.317544.

"Initial Results from Major Survey of U.S. Military Sexual Assault, Harassment." RAND Corporation. December 4, 2014. http://www.rand.org/news/press/2014/12/04.html.

Jenks, Robert C., Warrant Officer, Public Affairs Office, Marine Corps Combat Development Command, Quantico, Virginia. *U.S. Marine Corps Tailhook Proceedings, Release #12*. October 21, 1993.

Johnson, Jeremy. "Challenges: Returning to Life in Uniform as a DADT Discharged Vet." Blog Entry. Palm Center. May 8, 2012. http://www.palmcenter.org/blog/challenges_returning_life_uniform_dadt_discharged_vet.

Kelso, II, Admiral Frank B. Department of the Navy. Office of the Chief of Naval Operations. "Statement of the Chief of Naval Operations." Washington, DC. February 15, 1994.

Kingkade, Tyler. "64 Colleges Are Now Under Investigation for Their Handling of Sexual Assaults." *Huffington Post*. June 20, 2014. http://www.huffingtonpost.com/2014/06/30/colleges-under-investigation-sex-assault_n_5543694.html.

Korb, Lawrence, and Dennis Laich. "Korb and Laich: Sex Assault and the Chain of Command." *Military Times*. November 19, 2013. http://www.militarytimes.com/article/20131119/NEWS01/311190015/Korb-Laich-Sex-assault-chain-command.

Lacayo, Richard. "Lost in the Fun House: A Navy Judge Blasts the Chief of Naval Operations as the Last Cases in the Tailhook Investigations Flame Out." *Time*. February 21, 1994, 45.

Lamothe, Dan. "Army General, Accused of Sexual Assault by Senior Adviser, Retired Quietly with Demotion." *Washington Post*. October 1, 2014. http://www.washingtonpost.com/news/checkpoint/wp/2014/10/01/army-general-accused-of-sexual-assault-by-senior-adviser-retired-quietly-with-demotion/.

Lardner, Richard. "Pentagon Accused of Withholding Information about Sex Crimes." *AP*. May 4, 2015. https://in.news.yahoo.com/apnewsbreak-pentagon-accused-withholding-sex-crimes-070448248—politics.html.

Larson, Jordan. "Allowing Transgender People to Serve in the U.S. Military Is 'Inevitable.' " *Vice News*. August 29, 2014. https://news.vice.com/article/allowing-transgender-people-to-serve-in-the-us-military-is-inevitable.

"Last Charges Are Dropped by Navy in Tailhook Probe." *Los Angeles Times*. February 12, 1994. http://articles.latimes.com/1994-02-12/news/mn-21900_1_navy-judge.

Lehavot, Karen, and Tracy L. Simpson. "Incorporating Lesbian and Bisexual Women into Women Veterans' Health Priorities." *Journal of General Internal Medicine* 28, no. Suppl 2 (2012): S609–S614. DOI: 10.1007/s11606-012-2291-2.

"Lesbians and Gay Men in the U.S. Military: Historical Background." 2015. http://psychology.ucdavis.edu/faculty_sites/rainbow/html/military_history.html.

Lisak, David, Lori Gardinier, Sarah C. Nicksa, and Ashley M. Cote. "False Allegations of Sexual Assault: An Analysis of Ten Years of Reported Cases." *Violence against Women* 16, no. 12 (2010): 1318–1334. http://www.icdv.idaho.gov/conference/handouts/False-Allegations.pdf. DOI: 10.1177/1077801210387747.

"The List: Military Scandals." *Washington Times*. January 8, 2011. http://www.washingtontimes.com/news/2011/jan/8/list-military-scandals/.

Lowey, Nita. "Lowey Amendment to Help Prevent Sexual Assault at Military Academies Included in Bipartisan Defense Bill." U.S. House of Representatives. June 14, 2013. http://www.lowey.house.gov/press-releases/lowey-amendment-to-help-prevent-sexual-assault-at-military-academies-included-in-bipartisan-defense-bill/.

Lyle, Amaani. "Women in Service Review Rollout Due in 2016." *DoD News*. U.S. Department of Defense. January 12, 2015. http://www.defense.gov/news/newsarticle.aspx?id=123952.

Marshall, Steve. "Tailhook Victim Quitting Navy Coughlin Points to Continuing Abuse." *USA Today*. February 11, 1994, 2A.

Martin, Carolyn. "Transgender Individuals." In Rosemarie Skaine (ed). *Abuse: An Encyclopedia of Causes, Consequences, and Treatments*. Santa Barbara, CA: Greenwood. 2015, 295–297.

Martin, John. "TV–Tonight Top-Shelf Movie on Scandal Showcases Impressive Cast." *Charleston Gazette*. May 22, 1995, sec. News, 3B.

McCaskill, U.S. Senator Claire (D-MO). "Curbing Sexual Assault in the U.S. Military." *Ccombating Sexual Violence*. http://www.mccaskill.senate.gov/violence.

"Men Sexually Assaulted in the Military Speak Out." *Baltimore Sun*. December 20, 2013. http://www.military.com/daily-news/2013/12/20/men-sexually-assaulted-in-the-military-speak-out.html.

"Military versus Civilian Court Authority." Military Law Basics. Lawyers.com. 2015. http://military-law.lawyers.com/military-law-basics/military-versus-civilian-court-authority.html.

Mollison, Andrew and Marcia Kunstel. *The Des Moines Register*. June 27, 1992, 1A.

Montgomery, Nancy. "After 2 Decades of Sexual Assault in Military, No Real Change in Message." *Stars and Stripes*. July 7, 2013. http://www.stripes.com/news/after-2-decades-of-sexual-assault-in-military-no-real-change-in-message-1.229091\.

Montgomery, Nancy. "Case Dismissed against Aviano IG Convicted of Sexual Assault." *Stars and Stripes*. February 27, 2013. http://www.stripes.com/news/air-force/case-dismissed-against-aviano-ig-convicted-of-sexual-assault-1.209797.

Mulhall, Erin. "Women Warriors Supporting She 'Who Has Borne the Battle.'" Iraq and Afghanistan Veterans of America. *Issue Report*. October 2009. http://media.iava.org.

Navy News Release. "Navy Releases Information on the Recommendations of the Standing Committee on Military and Civilian Women in the Department of the Navy." 451–92, October 13, 1992.

Nelson, Steven. "California 'Yes Means Yes' Law Worries Skeptics." *U.S. News and World Report*. September 29, 2014. http://www.usnews.com/news/articles/2014/09/29/california-yes-means-yes-law-worries-skeptics.

Nunn, Sam. "Statement." 141 *Congressional Record*, S2667 (1995).

Obama, Barack. "Presidential Proclamation—LGBT Pride Month, 2015." White House. May 29, 2015. www.whitehouse.gov/the-press-office/2015/05/29/presidential-proclamation-lgbt-pride-month-2015.

Obama, Barack. "Remarks by President Obama and President Park of South Korea in a Joint Press Conference." The White House. Press release. May 7, 2013. http://www.whitehouse.gov/the-press-office/2013/05/07/remarks-president-obama-and-president-park-south-korea-joint-press-confe.

"Obama to Military: Clean Up Your Act." *Time* 181, no. 22 (June 10, 2013): Database: Business Source Premier.

O'Toole, Molly. "Military Sexual Assault Epidemic Continues to Claim Victims As Defense Department Fails Females." *Huffington Post*. Posted: October 6, 2012. Updated: May 20, 2013. http://www.huffingtonpost.com/2012/10/06/military-sexual-assault-defense-department_n_1834196.html.

Parks, W. Hays. "Tailhook What Happened, Why and What's to Be Learned." *Proceedings*. Annapolis, MD: U.S. Naval Institute. September 1994. 90–103.

"Pentagon Hunting Serial Predators in Attempt to Stop Military Sexual-Assault Epidemic." *RT*. February 26, 2014. http://rt.com/usa/military-sexual-assault-predator-756/.

Philpott, Tom. "Gay, Lesbian Spouses to Gain Full Military Benefits." *Stars and Stripes*. June 27, 2013. http://www.stripes.com/news/us/gay-lesbian-spouses-to-gain-full-military-benefits-1.227956.

"President Proclaims June as LGBT Pride Month." *DoD News*, Defense Media Activity. Department of Defense. May 29, 2015. http://www.defense.gov/news/newsarticle.aspx?id=128938.

"Prosecuting Rapes in the Ranks: Our View." *USA Today*. Editorial. December 2, 2013. http://www.usatoday.com/story/opinion/2013/12/02/military-sexual-assault-prosecution-editorials-debates/3817387/.

Purchia, Brian. "New Evidence: Emails from Aviano Sexual Assault Scandal Shows Bias and Blind Loyalty from Military Brass; Case Is Poster Child for an Independent and Impartial Justice System." The Invisible War. Not Invisible.org. September 3, 2013. http://www.notinvisible.org/tags/not_invisible.

Rau, Terri J., Lex L. Merrill, Stephanie K. McWhorter, Valerie A. Stander, Cynthia J. Thomsen, Christopher W. Dyslin, Julie L. Crouch, Mandy M. Rabenhorst, and Joel S. Milner. "Evaluation of a Sexual Assault Education/Prevention Program for Male U.S. Navy Personnel." *Military Medicine* 175, no. 6 (2010): 429. http://www.dtic.mil/dtic/tr/fulltext/u2/a523463.pdf.

"Remarks by the President at 'It's On Us' Campaign Rollout." Office of the Press Secretary. The White House. September 19, 2014. https://www.whitehouse.gov/the-press-office/2014/09/19/remarks-president-its-us-campaign-rollout.

Rice, Paul J. "Court Martial Jurisdiction—The Service Connection Standard in Confusion." *Journal of Criminal Law and Criminology* 61, no. 3. Article 2. (1971): 339. http://scholarlycommons.law.northwestern.edu/cgi/viewcontent.cgi?article=5668&context=jclc.

Robbins, Elizabeth. "Alcohol Abuse Is Fueling Military Sexual Assault." *Washington Post*. June 13, 2013. http://www.washingtonpost.com/opinions/alcohol-abuse-is-fueling-military-sexual-assault/2013/06/13/da2f5ada-d37c-11e2-a73e-826d299ff459_story.html.

Ryan, Missy. Instances of Sexual Assault among Troops Decrease, Report Suggests; Details on Male Victims Were Also Revealed; Officials Vowed to Fight Retaliation for Those Reporting Abuse." Blogs. *Washington Post*. May 1, 2015.

Scarborough, Rowan. "Victims of Sex Assaults in Military Are Mostly Men: Women Are More Likely to Speak Up." *Washington Times*. May 20, 2013. http://www.washingtontimes.com/news/2013/may/20/victims-of-sex-assaults-in-military-are-mostly-sil/#ixzz3Qi451p45.

Schmid, Megan N. "Comment: Combating a Different Enemy: Proposals to Change the Culture of Sexual Assault in the Military." *Villanova Law Review* 55 (2010): 475–507.

Schmitt, Eric. "Navy Prepares a Manual about Sexual Harassment." *New York Times*. April 10, 1994, sec. 1, 16.

Schmitt, Eric. "Wall of Silence Impedes Inquiry into a Rowdy Navy Convention." *New York Times*. June 14, 1992. http://www.nytimes.com/1992/06/14/us/wall-of-silence-impedes-inquiry-into-a-rowdy-navy-convention.html?pagewanted=all&src=pm.

Schneier, Bruce. " 'Zero Tolerance' Really Means Zero Discretion." *MPRNews*. November 3, 2009. http://www.mprnews.org/story/2009/11/03/schneier.

Schwartz, Felicia, and Byron Tau. "Military May Allow Openly Transgender Personnel." *Wall Street Journal*. February 23, 2015. http://www.wsj.com/articles/u-s-military-may-allow-openly-transgender-personnel-1424739209.

Secretary of the Navy. SECNAV Instruction 5300.26B. to All Ships and Stations, subject: "DON Policy on Sexual Harassment." January 6, 1993, 2–3.

Senate. "Executive Session." *Congressional Record Proceedings and Debates of the 103d Congress. Second Session* 140, no 43. Washington. April 19, 1994, S4459.82.

Service Womens Action Network. "After Repeal: LGBT Service Members and Veterans: The Facts." http://servicewomen.org/wp-content/uploads/2011/10/LGBT-Fact-Sheet-091411.pdf.

"Sexual Assault in the Military." Foreword. *Congressional Digest* 92, no. 8 (October 2013): 1–1.

"Sexual Assault Overview." Ask a Criminal Lawyer. FindLaw. 2013. http://criminal.findlaw.com/criminal-charges/sexual-assault-overview.html#sthash.JyoaGsG6.dpuf.

Shane III, Leo. "Senate Blocks Change to Military Sex Assault Cases." *Navy Times*. March 6, 2014. http://www.navytimes.com/article/20140306/NEWS05/303060024/Senate-blocks-change-military-sex-assault-cases.

Shapiro, Lila. "Don't Ask Don't Tell Study Shows No Negative Effects on Military One Year after Repeal." *HuffPost Gay Voices*. Updated: September 10, 2012. http://www.huffingtonpost.com/2012/09/10/dont-ask-dont-tell-study_n_1868892.html.

Simeone, Nick. "DoD Releases Figures on Sexual Harassment in Military." *American Forces Press Service*. Department of Defense. May 15, 2014. http://www.defense.gov/news/newsarticle.aspx?id=122270.

Skaine, Rosemarie. "Female Participation in Combat." In *World at War: Understanding Conflict and Society*. ABC-CLIO, 2013. Accessed January 21, 2015. http://worldatwar2.abc-clio.com/.

Skaine, Rosemarie. "How Should Allegations of Sexual Assault in the U.S. Military Be Handled?" In *World at War: Understanding Conflict and Society.* ABC-CLIO, 2014-web.

Smart, Steven J., Maj. USAF. "Setting the Record Straight: The Military Justice System and Sexual Assault." Commentaries. Air Force Judge Advocate. July 27, 2012. http://www.afjag.af.mil/sexualassaultprosecution/index.asp.

Solaro, Erin. "Women in the Military, Abuse of." In Rosemarie Skaine (ed.). *Abuse: An Encyclopedia of Causes, Consequences, and Treatments.* Santa Barbara, CA: Greenwood, 2015, 310.

Somashekhar, Sandhya, "In Move Hailed by Advocates, Army Adjusts Process for Dismissing Transgender Soldiers." *Washington Post.* March 6, 2015. http://www.washingtonpost.com/news/post-nation/wp/2015/03/06/in-move-hailed-by-advocates-army-adjusts-process-for-dismissing-transgender-soldiers/.

Sprigg, Peter. "Homosexual Assault in the Military." *Insight.* Family Research Council. Washington, DC. May 2010. http://www.frc.org/insight/homosexual-assault-in-the-military.

Steinmetz, Katy. "Why It's Best to Avoid the Word 'Transgendered.' " *Time.* December 15, 2014. http://time.com/3630965/transgender-transgender/.

Stimson, Charles. "Cully." "Military Sexual Assault Reform: Real Change Takes Time." Heritage Foundation. March 6, 2014. http://www.heritage.org/research/reports/2014/03/military-sexual-assault-reform-real-change-takes-time.

Struckman-Johnson, Cindy, David Struckman-Johnsonb, and Peter B. Andersonc. "Tactics of Sexual Coercion: When Men and Women Won't Take No for an Answer." *Journal of Sex Research* 40, no. 1 (2003): 76–86. DOI:10.1080/00224490309552168.

"Tailhook Report Details Abuses at 91 Naval Aviators' Convention." *Defense & Armed Forces.* Editorial on File. April 16–30, 1331.

Thompson, Mark. "The 'Good Soldier' Defense Is Mortally Wounded." *Time.* March 11, 2014. http://time.com/19942/the-good-soldier-defense-is-mortally-wounded/.

Thompson, Mark. "Obama to Military: Clean Up Your Act." *Time* 181, no. 22 (June 10, 2013): Database: Business Source Premier.

Thompson, Mark. "TSgt Raped at Sather Air Base Iraq." My Duty to Speak. Blog at WordPress.com. September 13, 2013. http://mydutytospeak.com/.

Turchik, Jessica A., Claire L. Hebenstreit, and Stephanie S. Judson. "An Examination of the Gender Inclusiveness of Current Theories of Sexual Violence in Adulthood: Recognizing Male Victims, Female Perpetrators, and Same-Sex Violence." *Trauma, Violence, and Abuse* (2015): 1–16. DOI: 10.1177/1524838014566721.

Turchik, Jessica A., and Susan M. Wilson. "Sexual Assault in the U.S. Military: A Review of the Literature and Recommendations for the Future." *Aggression and Violent Behavior* 15 (2010): 267–277. doi:10.1016/j.avb.2010.01.005.

Uniform Code of Military Justice, 1949. http://www.loc.gov/rr/frd/Military_Law/pdf/morgan.pdf.

United States Code Annotated. Title 10. Armed Forces. SS 5001 to 8010.

U.S. Navy. "Restricted/Unrestricted Options." Family Advocacy Program. 2015. http://www.cnic.navy.mil/ffr/family_readiness/fleet_and_family_support_program/family_advocacy/restricted_unrestricted_options.html.

Vanden Brook, Tom. "Military Approves Hormone Therapy for Chelsea Manning." February 13, 2015. http://www.usatoday.com/story/news/nation/2015/02/12/chelsea-manning-hormone-therapy/23311813/.

Vanden Brook, Tom and David M. Jackson. "Obama Says Sexual Assault Crisis Hurts National Security." *USA Today*. May 16, 2013. http://www.usatoday.com/story/news/politics/2013/05/16/obama-hagel-military-sexual-assaults/2165763/.

Vergun, David. "New Law Brings Changes to Uniform Code of Military Justice." *Army News Service*. Department of Defense. January 8, 2014. http://www.defense.gov/news/newsarticle.aspx?id=121444.

Vukotich, George. "Military Sexual Assault Prevention and Response: The Bystander Intervention Training Approach." *Journal of Organizational Culture, Communications and Conflict* 17, no. 1 (2013): 20.

Ward, Stephanie Francis. "Schools Start to Rethink Zero Tolerance Policies." *ABA Journal* 100 no. 8 (August 2014): 55–61. http://www.abajournal.com/magazine/article/schools_start_to_rethink_zero_tolerance_policies/.

Whitlock, Craig. "Air Force General Defends Overturning Sexual-Assault Conviction." *Washington Post*. April 10, 2013. http://www.washingtonpost.com/world/national-security/air-force-general-defends-overturning-sexual-assault-conviction/2013/04/10/42f8162c-a215-11e2-ac00-8ef7caef5e00_story.html.

Whitlock, Craig. "Air Force General to Retire After Criticism for Handling of Sexual-Assault Case." *Washington Post*. January 8, 2014. http://www.washingtonpost.com/world/national-security/air-force-general-criticized-for-handling-of-sexual-assault-cases-to-retire/2014/01/08/9942df96-787d-11e3-b1c5-739e63e9c9a7_story.html.

Wilder, Heather, and Jami Wilder. "In the Wake of Don't Ask Don't Tell: Suicide Prevention and Outreach for LGB Service Members." *Military Psychology* 24 (2012): 624–642. DOI: 10.1080/08995605.2012.737725.

Wolf, Pamela. "Federal Legislation Targets Sexual Assault in Military, Transgender/Gender Nonconforming Discrimination." *Wolters Kluwer*. 2015. http://www.employmentlawdaily.com/index.php/news/federal-legislation-targets-sexual-assault-in-military-transgendergender-nonconforming-discrimination/.

Wong, Kristina. "Pentagon Issues Report on Sexual Harassment." *The Hill*. May 15, 2014. http://thehill.com/policy/defense/206273-pentagon-issues-report-on-sexual-harrassment.

Wright, Austin, and Tim Mak. "Sexual Assault Scandals a Pentagon Test—DoD's Top Spokesman Rebukes Air Force Chief." *Politico*. May 16, 2013. http://www.politico.com/morningdefense/0513/morningdefense10695.html.

Yoachum, Susan. "The Navy, Before and After Tailhook: An Incisive Look at the Lasting Effects of the Scandal: A Review of Jean Zimmerman. *Tailspin: Women at War in the Wake of Tailhook*. NY, Doubleday, 1995." *San Francisco Chronicle*. June 25, 1995, 3.

Zero Tolerance Unclassified Message from CNO to NAVADMIN, 282024Z February 1992; Zero Tolerance Unclassified Message from CNO to NAVOP (all Navy Personnel), 16134ez February 1992; Zero Tolerance Unclassified Message from CNO to NAVOP (date unclear, unless February 1992).

Zornick, George. "New Study Demands Zero-Tolerance for Military Sexual Assault." *The Nation*. March 26, 2013. http://www.thenation.com/blog/173522/new-study-demands-zero-tolerance-military-sexual-assault#.

BOOKS

Berger, Peter. *Invitation to Sociology: A Humanistic Perspective*. Garden City, NY: Doubleday. 1963.

Dyer, Kaye, ed. *Gays in Uniform: The Pentagon's Secret Reports*. Boston: Alyson Publications. 1990.

Mills, C. Wright. *The Sociological Imagination*. New York: Oxford University Press. 1959.

Skaine, Rosemarie. *Power and Gender: Issues in Sexual Dominance and Harassment*. Jefferson, NC: McFarland. 1996.

Skaine, Rosemarie. *Women at War: Gender Issues of Americans in Combat*. Jefferson, NC: McFarland. 1999.

Skaine, Rosemarie. *Women in Combat: A Reference Handbook*. Santa Barbara, CA: ABC-CLIO. 2011. http://ebooks.abc-clio.com/reader.aspx?isbn=9781598844603.

U.S. Army War College. "Chain of Command." *The Battle Book IV: A Guide for Spouses in Leadership Roles*. 2009: Ch. 2. http://www.carlisle.army.mil/usawc/mfp/battlebook/pdf/Chapter%202.pdf.

Women Were There. http://userpages.aug.com/captbarb/femvets2.html.

COURT CASES

Cioca v. Rumsfeld, No. 12–1065 (U.S. 4th Circuit, July 23, 2013). http://www.caaflog.com/wp-content/uploads/Cioca-v.-Rumsfeld.pdf.

Feres v. United States, 340 U.S. 135 (1950). http://supreme.justia.com/cases/federal/us/340/135/case.html.

O'Callahan v. Parker, 395 U.S. 258 (1969): New Limitation on Court-Martial Jurisdiction. *Journal of Criminal Law, Criminology and Police Science* 61, no. 2 (1970): 195. http://scholarlycommons.law.northwestern.edu/cgi/viewcontent.cgi?article=5653&context=jclc.

Reid v. Covert, 354 U.S. 1 (1957); *Reid v. Covert*, 354 U.S. 1 (1956). http://www.oyez.org/cases/1950-1959/1955/1955_701_2.

David Samples, Lieutenant, U.S. Navy, Petitioner, v. Captain William T. Vest, U.S. Navy, Navy-Marine Trial, Judiciary, Tidewater Judicial Circuit, and the United States, Respondents, Misc. No. 94-8022, United States Court of Military Appeals, argued November 9, 1993, decided January 11, 1994. Counsel, for petitioner: Lieutenant David P. Sheldon, JAGC USNR (argued); Lieutenant Alan D. Titus, JAGC, USNR (on brief). For respondents: Lieutenant Commander David B. Auclair, JAGC, USN (argued); Colonel T.G. Hess, USMC and Commander S.A. Stallings, JAGC, USN (on brief). *Samples v. Vest*, No. 94-8022/NA, Opinion of the Court. WISS, Judge, 5.

United States v. Thomas R. Miller, CDR, USN; United States v. Gregory E. Tritt, CDR, USN, and *United States v. Samples, LT, USN*. "Essential Findings and Ruling on Defense Motion to Dismiss." William T. Vest, Jr. CAPT, JAGC, USN, Circuit Military Judge, General Court-Martial, United States Navy, Tidewater Judicial Circuit, Norfolk, VA, February 7, 1994, 112.

INTERVIEWS

Cushman, Marilla, LTC, USA (Ret.). Interview by Rosemarie Skaine. Tape recording. September 23, 2009. Women in Military Service for America Memorial Foundation, Inc., Arlington, VA.

Gordon, RADM John E., JAGC, USN (RET). Former Judge Advocate General of the Navy. Interview by Rosemarie Skaine. Telephone. March 23, 1995. Admiral Gordon Can Be Contacted through the United States Navy, Washington, DC.

Lunney, JAGC, USNR (RET), CAPT. J. Robert. "Interview with RADM Duvall M. "Mac" Williams, Jr., JAGC, USN (RET), Immediate Past Commander, NIS Command. 'A Question of Fairness.' " *NRA Naval Reserve Association News* 40, no. 2 (February 1993).

Manning, Lory. CAPT, USN (Ret.). Interview by Rosemarie Skaine. Telephone. October 5, 2014.

Pfluke, Lillian. MAJ, U.S. Army (Ret.). Interview by Rosemarie Skaine. Telephone. November 8, 2014.

Vaught, Wilma L BGen, USAF (Ret.). Interview by Rosemarie Skaine. Tape recording. September 23, 2009. Women in Military Service for America Memorial Foundation, Inc., Arlington, VA.

Williams, Jr., D.M. "Mac." RADM USN (Ret.). Former NIS Commander. Interview by Rosemarie Skaine. Telephone. October 17, 2014.

Williams, Jr., D.M. Immediate Past Commander, Naval Investigative Service Command. Interviews by Rosemarie Skaine. Telephone. September 8, 1993, May 16, 1994, and March 22, 1995. RADM Williams Can Be Contacted through the United States Navy, Washington, DC.

REPORTS

Air Force Policy Directive 36-60. "Sexual Assault Prevention and Response (SAPR) Program." March 28, 2008. http://www.sapr.mil/public/docs/policy/afpd36-60.pdf.

American Military Partner Association and the Transgender American Veterans Association. *How the Department of Defense Transgender Ban Harms Our Military Families*. A report. March 30, 2015. http://militarypartners.org/transgender-report/.

Army Command Policy. "Sexual Assault Policy." Army Regulation 600-20. 8-2a. November 6, 2014. http://www.apd.army.mil/pdffiles/r600_20.pdf.

Aspin, Les, Chairman, Defense Policy Panel and Beverly B. Byron, Chairman, Military Personnel and Compensation Subcommittee. Committee on Armed

Services. House of Representatives. *Women in the Military: At the Tailhook Affair and at the Problem of Sexual Harassment Report*. Washington, DC: U.S. G. P. O. September 14, 1992.

Coast Guard. "Sexual Assault Prevention and Response Program (SAPRP)." COMDINST 1754 10C. December 20, 2007. http://www.sapr.mil/public/docs/policy/ci_1754_10c.pdf.

Davis VI, RADM George W. USN. *Naval Inspector General (NIG), Report of Investigation. Department of the Navy/Tailhook Association Relationship, Personal Conduct Surrounding Tailhook 91 Symposium*. Case no. 920684. April 29, 1992, 4–6. Tab F, O'Keefe Memo.

"Defense Force Management: DOD's Policy on Homosexuality." U.S. Government Accountability Office (GAO). June 12, 1992. http://archive.gao.gov/d33t10/146980.pdf.

Department of Defense. Office of Inspector General (DODIG). Assistant Inspector General for Investigations: Assistant Inspector General for Departmental Inquiries. *Tailhook 91, Part 1: Review of the Navy Investigations*. September 1992.

Department of Defense. Office of Inspector General (DODIG). Assistant Inspector General for Investigations: Assistant Inspector General for Departmental Inquiries. *Tailhook 91 Part 2: Events at the 35th Annual Tailhook Symposium*. February 1993.

Department of Defense. Office of Inspector General (DODIG). *Report of the Defense Task Force on Sexual Harassment and Violence at the Military Service Academies*. June 2005.

Department of Defense. *Annual Report on Sexual Assault in the Military, Fiscal Year 2012*. vols.1, 2. Washington, DC: Department of Defense. Sexual Assault Prevention and Response. 2013. http://www.sapr.mil/index.php/annual-reports.

Department of Defense. *Annual Report on Sexual Harassment and Violence at the Military Service Academies Academic Program Year 2012–2013*. December 2013. http://www.sapr.mil/public/docs/reports/final_apy_12-13_msa_report.pdf.

Department of Defense. *Annual Report on Sexual Assault in the Military, Fiscal Year 2013*. Washington, DC: Department of Defense. http://www.sapr.mil/index.php/annual-reports.

Department of Defense. *Annual Report on Sexual Assault in the Military, Fiscal Year 2014*. Washington, DC: Department of Defense, 6–7. http://www.sapr.mil/index.php/annual-reports.

Department of Defense. "DoD Policy." Sexual Assault Prevention and Response (SAPRO). (n.d.). http://www.sapr.mil/index.php/dod-policy.

Department of Defense. *Report of the Defense Task Force on Sexual Harassment and Violence*. June 2005. http://www.sapr.mil/public/docs/research/high_gpo_rrc_tx.pdf/.

Department of Defense. *Report to the President of the United States on Sexual Assault Prevention and Response*. 2014. http://www.sapr.mil/public/docs/reports/FY14_POTUS/FY14_DoD_Report_to_POTUS_Full_Report.pdf.

Department of Defense. SAPR. "DoD and Services' Policies." n.d. http://www.sapr.mil/index.php/dod-policy/dod-and-service-policy.

DODD 6495.01. January 23, 2012, 2–3. http://www.sapr.mil/public/docs/instructions/DoDI_649501_20130430.pdf.

Farris, Coreen, and Kimberly A. Hepner. "Targeting Alcohol Misuse: A Promising Strategy for Reducing Military Sexual Assaults?" RAND Corporation, National Defense Research Institute. 2014.

Farris, Coreen, Terry L. Schell, and Terri Tanielian. *Physical and Psychological Health Following Military Sexual Assault: Recommendations for Care, Research, and Policy.* RAND. 2013.

Gillibrand, Kirsten. *Snapshot Review of Sexual Assault Report Files at the Four Largest U.S. Military Bases in 2013.* Office of U.S. Senator. May 2015. http://www.gillibrand.senate.gov/imo/media/doc/Gillibrand_Sexual%20Assault%20Report.pdf.

Goewert, Christopher J., and Andrew R. Norton. "Sexual Assault: Four Commonly Held Beliefs." *The Reporter* 40, no. 2 (2013): 24–31.

Government Accountability Office (GAO). *Homosexuals in the Military: Policies and Practices of Foreign Countries.* June 25, 1993. http://archive.gao.gov/t2pbat5/149440.pdf.

Government Accountability Office (GAO). *Military Personnel: DoD Needs to Take Further Actions to Prevent Sexual Assault during Initial Military Training.* Report to Congressional Committees. September 2014, 46. http://www.gao.gov.

Government Accountability Office (GAO). *Military Personnel: Prior GAO Work on DOD's Actions to Prevent and Respond to Sexual Assault in the Military.* GAO-12-571R: March 30, 2012. http://www.gao.gov/assets/590/589780.pdf.

Government Accountability Office (GAO). "Personnel: Actions Needed to Address Sexual Assaults of Male Servicemembers." GAO-15-284. March 19, 2015. Highlights. http://www.gao.gov/products/GAO-15-284.

Harrell, Margaret C., Laura Werber Castaneda, Marisa Adelson, Sarah Gaillot, Charlotte Lynch, and Amanda Pomeroy. *A Compendium of Sexual Assault Research.* RAND Corp. 2009. http://www.rand.org/content/dam/rand/pubs/technical_reports/2009/RAND_TR617.pdf..

"Hearing of the Senate Judiciary Committee on the Nomination of Clarence Thomas to the Supreme Court, Testimony of Clarence Thomas. October 11, 1991." Electronic Text Center. University of Virginia Library.

Mancuso, Donald. Assistant Inspector General for Investigations. DOD. Memorandum for Deputy Inspector General. DON, May 8, 1992, 1, Attachment 2, Daniel J. Howard, to his memo to Sean O'Keefe, Acting Secretary of the Navy (SECNAV), October 16, 1992.

Manual for Courts-Martial United States (2012 Edition). http://www.loc.gov/rr/frd/Military_Law/pdf/MCM-2012.pdf.

Marine Corps Order 1752.B. "Sexual Assault Prevention and Response (SAPR) Program." March 1, 2013. http://www.marines.mil/Portals/59/Publications/MCO%201752.5B.pdf.

Morral, Andrew R., and Kristie L. Gore. *Sexual Assault and Sexual Harassment in the U.S. Military: Top-Line Results from the RAND Military Workplace Study.* RAND Corporation, National Defense Research Institute. 2014. http://www.rand.org/.

National Defense Authorization Act for FY 2014. Report 113-44. Senate. Committee on Armed Services. 113th Cong. 1st sess. June 30, 2013. http://www.dtic.mil/dtic/tr/fulltext/u2/a592402.pdf.

Naval Investigative Service (NIS). *Report of Investigation (closed)*. Indecent Assault, Case Summary. April 15, 1992. http://www.rand.org/content/dam/rand/pubs/occasional_papers/OP300/OP382/RAND_OP382.pdf.

Navy Consolidated Disposition Authority (Navy CDA). Summary. Norfolk, VA, December 14, 1993.

O'Keefe, Sean. Department of the Navy, Office of the Secretary. "Response to Report of Investigation: Tailhook 91 – Part I, Review of the Navy Investigations," Memorandum for the Deputy Inspector General, Department of Defense, October 22, 1992, 1–5; Attachments, "Statement by Acting Secretary of the Navy, Hon. Sean O'Keefe." News Release, Office of Assistant Secretary of Defense Public Affairs, Washington, DC, September 24, 1992, 1–5; Frank B. Kelso, II, ADM, U.S. Navy, Chief of Naval Operations. "Memorandum for the General Counsel of the Navy, Tab B, October 1, 1992, 1; C. E. Mundy, Jr., Commandant of the Marine Corps. "Memorandum for the General Counsel of the Navy." Tab C, September 30, 1992, 1; J. Daniel Howard, The Under Secretary of the Navy, letter to Hon. Sean O'Keefe, Acting Secretary of the Navy, October 16, 1992. "Comments," Tab D, 1–6; Barbara Spyridon Pope, Manpower and Reserve Affairs. "Memorandum for the General Counsel," Tab E, October 1, 1992, 1; George W. Davis, VI, Rear ADM, U.S. Navy. "Memorandum for Secretary of the Navy," Tab F, October 19, 1992, 1; "Office of the Naval Inspector General Response to DODIG Report on Tailhook '91 Part 1." 1–21; J. E. Gordon, Office of the Judge Advocate General, Department of the Navy. "Memorandum for the Secretary of the Navy," Tab G, October 9, 1992, 3, with "Statement of RADM John E. Gordon, JAGC, USN, Judge Advocate General of the Navy, in Response to the *DOD IG Report on the Navy's Investigation of Tailhook '91*," October 9, 1992, 1–25; D.M. Williams, Jr., "Memorandum for the Acting Secretary of the Navy," Tab H, October 9, 1992, 1, with "Supplemental Statement of RADM (L) D.M. Williams, Jr., Concerning *Department of Defense Inspector General Report of Investigation on Tailhook '91 – Part 1*," 1–15.

Opnav Instruction 1752.1B. "Sexual Assault Victim Intervention (SAVI) Program." December 29, 2006. http://www.sapr.mil/public/docs/directives/sexual-assault-victim-intervention-savi-program.pdf.

Rand National Defense Research Institute. *Sexual Orientation and U.S. Military Personnel Policy: Options and Assessments*. Santa Monica, CA: Rand Corporation. 1993. http://www.rand.org/pubs/monograph_reports/MR323/index.html.

Relationships between Military Sexual Assault, Post- Traumatic Stress Disorder and Suicide, and Department of Defense and Department of Veterans Affairs Medical Treatment and Management of Victims of Sexual Trauma: Hearing before Personnel Subcommittee of the Senate Armed Services Committee. H., 113th Cong. 2nd sess. February 26, 2014.

Report of the Defense Task Force on Sexual Assault in the Military Services: Hearing before the Military Personnel Subcommittee, Committee on Armed Services. H., 111th Cong. 2nd sess. February 3, 2010.

Report of the Panel to Review Sexual Misconduct Allegations at the U.S. Air Force Academy. Senate and House Armed Services Committees and DoD. Arlington, VA. September 22, 2003. http://www.dodig.mil/foia/ERR/USAFASexualAssault Survey.pdf.

Report on the United States Air Force Academy Sexual Assault Survey. Department of Defense Inspector General. Project No. 2003C004. September 11, 2003. http://www.dodig.mil/foia/ERR/USAFASexualAssaultSurvey.pdf.

Rosenthal, Lindsay, and Lawrence Korb. *Twice Betrayed Bringing Justice to the U.S. Military's Sexual Assault Problem*. Center for American Progress. November 2013, 1–41. http://cdn.americanprogress.org/wp-content/uploads/2013/11/MilitarySexualAssaultsReport.pdf.

Snow, Jeffrey J., and Nathan Galbreath. *DoD Fiscal Year 2013 Annual Report on Sexual Assault in the Military*. Press Briefing. May 1, 2014, 1–13. http://www.sapr.mil/public/docs/press/FY13_DoD_SAPRO_Annual_Report-Press_Briefing.pdf.

Testimony on Sexual Assaults in the Military: Hearing before the Subcommittee on Personnel of the Committee on Armed Services, United States Senate. 113th Cong. 20–23 (March 13, 2013).

Testimony on Sexual Assaults in the Military: Hearing before the Subcommittee on Personnel of the Committee on Armed Services, United States Senate. (prepared Statement of Aviano Air Base Sexual Assault Victim. 162–164).

Testimony on Sexual Assaults in the Military: Hearing before the Subcommittee on Personnel of the Committee on Armed Services, United States Senate. (testimony of Lewis, Mr. Brian K., former Petty Officer Third Class, U.S. Navy, Advocacy Board Member, Protect Our Defenders. 18–43). http://www.gpo.gov/fdsys/pkg/CHRG-113shrg88340/pdf/CHRG-113shrg88340.pdf.

Testimony on Sexual Assaults in the Military: Hearing before the Subcommittee on Personnel of the Committee on Armed Services, United States Senate. (testimony of McCoy, Ms. Brigette, former Specialist, U.S. Army. 11–14).

UCMJ Arts. 120 & 125; 10 U.S.C. §§ 920, 925 (2012).

U.S. Commission on Civil Rights. "Sexual Assault in the Military." *2013 Statutory Enforcement Report*. 2013. http://www.usccr.gov/pubs/09242013_Statutory_Enforcement_Report_Sexual_Assault_in_the_Military.pdf.

U.S. Department of Army. Army Regulation 600–20. *Army Command Policy*. September 20, 2012. http://www.apd.army.mil/pdffiles/r600_20.pdf.

THESES

Brinson, Wendy E. "It Is all about Respect: The Army's Problem with Sexual Assault." Master of Military Studies Research Paper. United States Marine Corps Command and Staff College, Marine Corps University. April 23, 2012. (Statement appears in original: "DISCLAIMER THE OPINIONS AND CONCLUSIONS EXPRESSED HEREIN ARE THOSE OF THE INDIVIDUAL STUDENT AUTHOR AND DO NOT NECESSARILY REPRESENT THE VIEWS OF EITHER THE MARINE CORPS COMMAND AND STAFF COLLEGE OR ANY OTHER GOVERNMENTAL AGENCY."), i.

Diehl, Robyn A. "Sexual Assault in the Military: Ethical Dilemma or National Security Issue?" Master of Arts in Liberal Studies Thesis. Washington, DC: Georgetown University. October 25, 2012: 92. https://repository.library.georgetown.edu/handle/10822/557559.

Mendez, Endia T. "Transgenders in the U.S. Military: Policies, Problems, and Prospects." Master's Thesis. Monterey, CA: Naval Postgraduate School. March 2014. http://www.dtic.mil/dtic/tr/fulltext/u2/a607720.pdf.

WEBSITES

Afterdeployment.org, *Just the Facts: Military Sexual Trauma.* "Men as Survivors of Sexual Trauma." 2010. http://afterdeployment.dcoe.mil/sites/default/files/pdfs/client-handouts/mst-sexual-assault-harassment.pdf.

Center for Deployment Psychology. "Military Sexual Assault." Uniformed Services University of the Health Sciences. Bethesda, MD. n.d. http://www.deploymentpsych.org/disorders/sexual-assault-main.

"Effects of Military Sexual Trauma." Make the Connection. 2014. http://maketheconnection.net/conditions/military-sexual-trauma?gclid=CJK36dOY6r4CFVQiMgoddg0AfQ.

Human Rights Campaign: Working for Lesbian, Gay, Bisexual and Transgender Equal Rights. "Don't Ask, Don't Tell Repeal Act of 2010." September 20, 2011. http://www.hrc.org/resources/entry/dont-ask-dont-tell-repeal-act-of-2010.

"Military versus Civilian Court Authority." Military Law Basics. Lawyers.com, 2015. http://military-law.lawyers.com/military-law-basics/military-versus-civilian-court-authority.html.

"Sexual Assault Prevention and Response: Together We Can Prevent Sexual Assaults. Commander's Guide." Department of the Navy Sexual Assault Prevention and Response Office (DON SAPRO). http://www.secnav.navy.mil/sapro/Publications/DON%20SAPRO%20Commanders%20Guide.pdf.

SWAN Service Women's Action Network. "Military Sexual Violence: Rape, Sexual Assault and Sexual Harassment." n.d. http://servicewomen.org/military-sexual-violence/.

U.S. Air Force. "Service Demographics Offer Snapshot of Force." January 25, 2008. http://www.af.mil/News/ArticleDisplay/tabid/223/Article/124527/service-demographics-offer-snapshot-of-force.aspx.

U.S. Army. "Today's Women Soldiers." Women in the U.S. Army. http://www.army.mil/women/today.html.

U.S. Navy. "Women in Naval Service." Navy Personnel Command. June 2014. http://www.public.navy.mil/BUPERS-NPC/ORGANIZATION/BUPERS/WOMENSPOLICY/Pages/NavyWomenFactsStatistics.aspx.

VIDEOS

Iowa Public Television. "The Invisible War." Video. (#1416). March 30, 2014. http://www.iptv.org/series.cfm/8117/independent_lens/ep:1416.

9 Points Productions. "Justice Denied." CD. http://www.justicedeniedmovie.com/.

Women in Military Service for America Memorial Foundation. "Women Enter the Military Academies." History. Archive. n.d. http://www.womensmemorial.org/H&C/History/milacad.html.

Index

About the Author

Rosemarie Skaine, M.A., Sociology, is an author who lives in Cedar Falls, Iowa. She has published 14 books: *Abuse: An Encyclopedia of Causes, Consequences, and Treatment* (ABC-CLIO/Greenwood, 2014); *Suicide Warfare: Culture, the Military, and the Individual as a Weapon* (ABC-CLIO/Praeger Security International, 2013); *Women in Combat: A Reference Handbook*, Contemporary World Issues Series (ABC-CLIO, 2011); *Women of Afghanistan in the Post-Taliban Era* (McFarland, 2008); *Women Political Leaders in Africa* (McFarland, 2008); *Female Suicide Bombers* (McFarland, 2006); *Female Genital Mutilation: Legal, Cultural and Medical Issues* (McFarland, 2005); *The Cuban Family: Custom and Change in an Era of Hardship* (McFarland, 2004); *Paternity and American Law* (McFarland, 2003); *The Women of Afghanistan under the Taliban* (McFarland, 2002); *Women College Basketball Coaches* (McFarland, 2001); *A Man of the Twentieth Century: Recollections of Warren V. Keller, A Nebraskan as told to Rosemarie Keller Skaine and James C. Skaine* (Author's Castle Publishing, 1999); *Women at War: Gender Issues of Americans in Combat* (McFarland, 1999); and *Power and Gender: Issues in Sexual Dominance and Harassment* (McFarland, 1996).

Relevant published articles include: "Neither Afghan nor Islam," Symposium on September 11, 2001: Terrorism, Islam and the West, *Ethnicities* (London: Sage Publications Ltd., Volume 02, Issue 02, June 2002), 142–144; "Soviet-Afghan War (1979–1989)," Stanley Sandler (ed.), *Ground Warfare: An International Encyclopedia* (Santa Barbara, CA: ABC-CLIO, 2002), 826; and "Properly Trained Servicewomen Can Overcome Physical Shortcomings," James Haley (ed.), *Women in the Military* (San Diego, CA: Greenhaven Press, 2004).

Skaine's special awards include: Keynote speech, "Suicide Warfare and Violence against Women," interactive dialogue panel, "Dying to Kill: The Allure of Female Suicide Bombers," United Nations Commission on the Status of Women 57: Elimination and Prevention of all Forms of Violence against Women and Girls, March 8, 2013, United Nations Plaza, NY; Grand Island Senior High School Hall of Honor inductee (2009); The Gustavus Myers Center Award for the Study of Human Rights in North America (1997) for her outstanding work on intolerance in North America in her book, *Power and Gender: Issues in Sexual Dominance and Harassment*, McFarland (1996). Since 2006, Skaine has been included in Marquis *Who's Who in the World*, *Who's Who in America*, and *Who's Who of American Women*.